All About Administering NIS+
Second Edition

Rick Ramsey

SunSoft
A Sun Microsystems, Inc. Business

The publisher offers discounts on this book when ordered in bulk quantities. For more information, contact: Corporate Sales Department, Prentice Hall PTR, 1 Lake Street, Upper Saddle River, NJ 07458, Phone: 201-236-7152, Fax: 201-236-7141.

Editorial/production supervision: *Camille Trentacoste*
Manufacturing manager: *Alexis Heydt*
Acquisitions editor: *Phyllis Eve Bregman*

10 9

ISBN 0-13-309576-2

SunSoft Press
A Prentice Hall Title

Contents

Contents

Preface

Not long after I began working with Solaris®, I learned about a great command called name. I needed to call someone, but had forgotten his phone number. "What's Mateo's extension?" I asked my officemate. "Use name," he said without turning around. Embarrassed because I could not understand an answer that sounded so easy to understand, I just sat there and stared at my computer, half-hoping it would offer to help.

```
% Pssst, what he means is, . . .
```

I wasn't about to ask him what he meant; he acted as if everyone, including my own grandmother, would have understood. So I did nothing and wondered whether I really needed to call Mateo. But my officemate wouldn't be denied. He stood up, came over, and shouldered me away from my keyboard. Then he typed:

```
% name mateo
```

"Hit Return and watch the lights go blink-blink" he said, and walked out of the office. Cursing his entire lineage, I smacked the Return key. Lo and behold, look what appeared on my screen:

```
% name mateo
LAMBIER, MATE0 (MATHEW)   elvis@graceland   B-15   ext 57612
```

I didn't know it then, but that was my first encounter with a network information service. Of course the name command is not a network information service. It is a network application that gets its information from a network information service. Nevertheless, it demonstrates how much network information services affect the working habits of not just network administrators, but workstation users.

In addition to time-saving conveniences like the name command, network information services make possible remote logins, shared filesystems, shared programs, easy access to the Internet, and a wide variety of other network services. All this in addition to their central purpose: to make the administration of medium to large networks not only manageable, but possible.

The subject of this book is not network information services in general, but a new network information service developed by SunSoft™. It is part of the Open Network Computing Plus (ONC+™) suite of products, and is called NIS+, which is the acronym for Network Information Service Plus. The ONC+ suite of products is available on Solaris 2.x, whether based on Intel® or SPARC® machines. These products can also be ported easily to other operating systems that support ONC RPC or ONC+ transport-independent RPC (TI-RPC). At the publication date of this book ONC, the predecessor of ONC+, was installed on over 3.1 million nodes worldwide.

Audience

This book is written primarily for system and network administrators, although MIS managers can use it to determine whether NIS+ offers what they need and exactly what is involved in setting up NIS+ and administering it.

Although this book takes some pains to introduce concepts relevant to NIS+, it makes no attempt to explain networking fundamentals or to describe the administration tools offered by the Solaris environment. If you administer networks, you already know how they work (we hope), and you have already picked out your favorite tools.

Scope and Organization

The first network information services developed for the UNIX® world were DNS (Domain Naming Service), which helped the Internet become viable as a nationwide computer network, and NIS (the Network Information Service), which expanded the role of network information services from an "address book" to a database of network information. Because of this heritage, the book begins by comparing NIS+ to DNS and

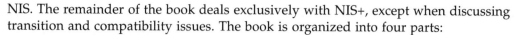

NIS. The remainder of the book deals exclusively with NIS+, except when discussing transition and compatibility issues. The book is organized into four parts:

- Understanding NIS+
- Planning for NIS+
- Setting Up NIS+
- Administering NIS+

Part 1—Understanding NIS+

The first part of the book focuses on the structure of NIS+. NIS+ is a powerful and flexible system; to set it up and take advantage of all its capabilities, you must understand what it has to offer and how it is put together. Part 1 has five chapters.

Chapter 1   *Understanding Network Information Services*

This chapter describes the purpose of network information services, explaining the advantages they offer and why they have become popular. It also provides a high-level, comparative overview of DNS, NIS, and NIS+. In that overview, it introduces the principal features of NIS+, which are described in detail in the remainder of Part 1.

Chapter 2   *Understanding the NIS+ Namespace*

This chapter describes the structure of an NIS+ namespace and introduces its structural components: directories and domains. It describes NIS+ servers and clients, and how they provide and receive NIS+ service. It includes a description of the naming conventions used by NIS+.

Chapter 3   *Understanding NIS+ Tables*

This chapter describes what NIS+ tables are, how they are structured, and what it takes to set them up and populate them. It also describes the information in each table, and how it should be formatted when loaded into NIS+ via an input file.

Chapter 4   *Understanding NIS+ Security*

This chapter describes the security features of NIS+. It provides an overview of the entire security process, describes the structure of NIS+ groups, credentials, and access rights, and summarizes what is involved in setting them up.

Chapter 5   Understanding the Name Service Switch

This chapter describes the Name Service Switch, a facility that allows you to specify the type of service that provides each category of information to your workstation: NIS+, NIS, DNS, or local /etc files.

Part 2—Planning for NIS+

The second part of the book provides guidelines for two different approaches to NIS+: a transition from NIS to NIS+ or setting up NIS+ from scratch. Part 2 has seven chapters:

Chapter 6   Planning and Transition Guidelines

This chapter recommends planning decisions for both a standard NIS+ setup or a transition from NIS+. Specific guidelines for making those decisions are provided in the remaining chapters of Part 2.

Chapter 7   Building a Prototype NIS+ Namespace

This chapter provides step-by-step instructions for four tasks that can be used to build a prototype namespace, one that is not functional but helps you become familiar with the elementary setup procedures.

Chapter 8   Designing the NIS+ Namespace

This chapter provides namespace design guidelines, such as considering the hierarchical structure, identifying servers, and selecting a table structure.

Chapter 9   Selecting NIS+ Security Measures

This chapter provides security selection guidelines, such as taking into account the impact of security on users and administrators, and how to select credentials, form groups, and establish authorization schemes for groups, directories, and tables.

Chapter 10   Using NIS Compatibility Mode

This chapter provides compatibility mode guidelines, including a view of NIS compatibility from the NIS client side, suggested use of compatibility mode during the transition, and equivalences and support of NIS commands in NIS+.

All About Administering NIS+

Chapter 11   Satisfying Prerequisites to Transition

This chapter describes a wide range of miscellaneous prerequisites that must be satisfied before the NIS+ transition can actually begin.

Chapter 12   Implementing the Transition

This chapter provides step-by-step instructions for using the decisions made in the previous chapters to implement a four-phase transition from NIS to NIS+.

Part 3—Setting Up the NIS+ Service

This part of the book provides step-by-step instructions for setting up the components of an NIS+ namespace, from the root domain itself to individual clients. Because you can set up NIS+ in many different configurations, no one set of instructions would be adequate for everyone. Conversely, one set of instructions for every different configuration would make the book unwieldy.

Instead, the setup process has been divided into building blocks, each of which is described in its own chapter. You can "build" your namespace by putting together the building blocks that you need. For instance, to set up the root domain, follow the instructions in Chapter 15. When you need to set up a client in the root domain, go to Chapter 17. To set up a subdomain, follow the instructions in Chapter 19. Then, to set up clients for that subdomain, go back to Chapter 17. And so on.

You can also set up the NIS+ service with the NIS+ setup scripts, available in Solaris 2.3 and subsequent releases. The scripts provide less flexibility than NIS+ commands, but they are much simpler to use. Part 3 has eight chapters:

Chapter 13   Setup Guidelines

This chapter suggests two setup sequences, one using standard NIS+ commands, the other using the NIS+ scripts.

Chapter 14   Setting Up an NIS+ Namespace, Using the NIS+ Scripts

This chapter provides step-by-step instructions for setting up an NIS+ namespace using the NIS+ scripts.

Chapter 15   Setting Up the Root Domain

This chapter provides step-by-step instructions for setting up the root domain of your NIS+ namespace.

Chapter 16   Setting Up NIS+ Tables

This chapter provides step-by-step instructions for populating NIS+ tables with information from input files or NIS maps.

Chapter 17   Setting Up an NIS+ Client

This chapter provides step-by-step instructions for setting up an NIS+ client and includes three different initialization methods. These instructions apply to clients in both the root domain and subdomains, whether all-NIS+ or NIS-compatible.

Chapter 18   Setting Up NIS+ Servers

This chapter provides step-by-step instructions for setting up a generic NIS+ server. These servers can be used for any role except root master.

Chapter 19   Setting Up a Nonroot Domain

This chapter provides step-by-step instructions for creating and setting up a subdomain, whether normal or NIS-compatible, including designating its master and replica servers.

Chapter 20   Setting Up the Name Service Switch

This chapter provides step-by-step instructions for setting up the Name Service Switch to be used with NIS, NIS+, or DNS, as well as to provide backward compatibility with the +/- syntax.

Part 4—Administering the NIS+ Service

The fourth part of this book describes the NIS+ commands. It divides them into administration categories, such as "commands used to administer credentials" and "commands used to administer groups," and places each category in its own chapter.

When first learning to use these commands, you may need to read through the detailed instructions, but after you become familiar with them, you may prefer a quick reminder of their syntax. To accommodate this usage, the command descriptions in this part of the book begin with a summary of syntax and then go into the details.

Chapter 21   Administering NIS+ Groups

This chapter describes the syntax of group-related NIS+ commands and provides instructions for using them to administer NIS+ groups.

All About Administering NIS+

Chapter 22   Administering NIS+ Credentials

This chapter describes the syntax of credential-related NIS+ commands and provides instructions for using them to administer NIS+ credentials.

Chapter 23   Administering NIS+ Access Rights

This chapter describes the syntax of rights-related NIS+ commands and provides instructions for using them to administer NIS+ access rights.

Chapter 24   Administering NIS+ Directories

This chapter describes the syntax of directory-related NIS+ commands, as well as other general NIS+ commands, such as `rpc.nisd`, and provides instructions for using them to administer NIS+ directories.

Chapter 25   Administering NIS+ Tables

This chapter describes the syntax of table-related NIS+ commands and provides instructions for using them to administer NIS+ tables.

Part 5—Appendices

The last part of this book provides four appendices:

Appendix A   Information in NIS+ Tables

This appendix describes the information in each NIS+ table, including the format required for input.

Appendix B   Pre-Setup Worksheets

This appendix provides extra sample setup worksheets. You can use these worksheets to enter information about decisions made during your planning stages.

Appendix C   NIS+ Scripts Error Messages

This appendix describes the error messages you can receive from NIS+ when using the NIS+ scripts.

Appendix D NIS+ API

This appendix describes the NIS+ API functions, which you can use to access NIS+ directly from an application. It includes code samples.

Conventions Used in This Book

As with most books about Solaris, commands, directories, and filenames are written in `courier` font. *Italics* are used for emphasis and to identify variables. To give you an idea of what's inside, the first page of each chapter contains a table that lists the important sections of the chapter and the pages they begin on. In Part 1, the tables list the top-level *heads* of a chapter, like this:

The Purpose of Network Information Services	Page 1
Overview of DNS	Page 8
Overview of NIS	Page 12
Overview of NIS+	Page 15

In Part 3, the tables list the *tasks* described in a chapter, like this:

▼ How to Populate NIS+ Tables from Files	Page 234
▼ How to Populate NIS+ Tables from NIS Maps	Page 239

Not only in the table, but throughout the book, tasks are called out with an inverted triangle at the margin:

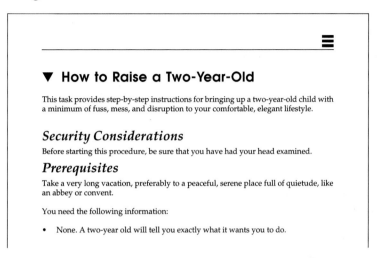

In Part 4, the tables list the commands described in the chapter, as well as the tasks described under each command, like this:

Acknowledgments

The SunSoft NIS+ engineering team put a great deal of time and effort into the NIS+ product. Without their hard work and cooperation, there would be no book. I would like to thank, in particular:

Helen Bradley, Vice President of Software Engineering, who supported the publication of this book, and Lou Delzompo, manager of the NIS+ team.

For their support of the second edition, Steve Bourne, Director of ONC technologies, and Craig Schamp, Lou's successor as manager of the NIS+ team.

Chuck McManis, who designed the heart of the product and spent countless hours explaining and re-explaining the intricacies of NIS+ to me.

Anil Gangolli, who is responsible for my understanding of the conceptual underpinnings of NIS+, especially the information on security. He also helped set up my laboratory environment so that I could test early versions of NIS+.

Vipin Samar, project leader of the NIS+ team, who took a personal interest in the book and provided me with details and information that I would have been unable to acquire on my own. Vipin was a great sounding board for design and presentation schemes, and did the final technical review of this book.

For their support of the second edition, Steve Bourne, Director of ONC technologies, and Craig Schamp, Lou's successor as manager of the NIS+ team.

Joe Dere tested this manual assiduously and made part of his lab available for me to run my own tests. The results of his real-world perspective and painstaking attention to detail are evident throughout the book.

Barry Holroyd clarified the notion of an NIS+ namespace. Rosanna Lee and Vikul Khosla reviewed the introductory chapters and provided valuable suggestions. Sanjay Dani and Thomas Maslen provided the information about the Name Service Switch and corrected the mistakes in my early drafts. William Malloy reviewed and corrected my drafts of the DNS material. Bob LeFave provided guidance and information about transitioning an organization from NIS to NIS+, and gave me a thorough review of the manual from the perspective of a real-world user.

Bill Edwards, Jeff Parker, Dave Miner, Paul Sawyer, and Randy Enger of the Admintool engineering team in the SunSoft Billerica office, also helped with quick answers to my questions.

For her help with the second edition, I would like to thank Jessica A. Bernhardt, SunSoft technical writer, who wrote Chapter 14, "Setting Up an NIS+ Namespace Using the NIS+ Scripts," Appendix C, "NIS+ Scripts Error Messages," and contributed to the chapters on NIS to NIS+ transition.

Kathy Slattery, Vipin Samar, and Bob Lefave also reviewed the NIS to NIS+ transition information, and Chuck McManis and Tom Fowler provided much of the source material.

I would also like to thank Vikul Khosla, SunSoft software engineer for information about, and code samples for, the NIS+ API appendix, and Chris Prael, SunSoft technical writer, for contributing information the NIS+ API appendix.

Most of the good ideas in this book come from the work done by a bicoastal team of SunSoft system and network administration writers managed by John Lazarus and led by Charla Mustard-Foote. The book's major structural elements are adapted from the design work done by Dave Damkoehler and Bruce Sesnovich, of the Sun Billerica office. The task-oriented approach came from discussions with Suzy Chapple, a SunSoft Information Products manager, and other writers in the group: Tom Amiro, Electra Coumou, and Janice Winsor. Janice was particularly helpful with design issues and with advice about what looks good on a page. Janice deserves special thanks for being a good workbuddy and putting up with my endless harangues about "good technical writing."

I would like to thank the management of SunSoft Information Products for their encouragement and support. Connie Howard, manager of DOE Documentation, for initially suggesting and encouraging my involvement with this project; Bridget Burke, SunSoft Information Products manager, for supporting this project and for providing the equipment; and, in particular, Suzy Chapple, manager of Networking Documentation, for her encouragement and appreciation. I would also like to thank Darell Sano, the illustrator at Sun Microsystems whose icons were used to create this book's beautiful cover. For his support of the second edition, I would like to thank Mike Rogers, Director of SunSoft Information Technology and Products.

Thanks are also due to Karin Ellison of SunSoft Press and Phyllis Eve Bregman of Prentice Hall for making this book possible. Without Karin's vision of SunSoft Press and her interest in this project, this book would have never been published. Phyllis's encouragement and direction made this experience rewarding; her tolerance and wry sense of humor made it a blast. Thanks also to Camille Trentacoste of Prentice Hall for the infinite patience and good humor of her production work, and to Mary Lou Nohr, an old friend and writing coach, for the satisfaction she got out of wearing her pencil down to a stub while copyediting this manuscript.

I would also like to thank Robin Greynolds and Al Cuenco for rescuing me and my workstations on numerous occasions. Al was particularly helpful with my home workstation. Having Al nearby is as reassuring as driving through the desert with a camel in your back seat.

Finally, I owe a warm and hearty Thank You to Laura, for not only supporting this project enthusiastically, but for putting up with unmowed lawns, unwashed cars, and unkilled spiders. She also had the clever idea to put the setup charts on the inside covers of the book. I would also like to thank my 2-year old daughter, Grace, for learning so quickly that crayons do not make OpenWindows prettier, they just make the screen messy. Of course, how could I not thank my dog, "The Chief," for sparing my hard drive that fateful Wednesday in August, when he ate his way through the rest of my office. Finally, I would like to thank my second daughter, Elizabeth, for sleeping through the night during my work on the second edition.

Part 1—Understanding NIS+

1 ***Understanding Network Information Services***
This chapter describes the purpose of network information services, explaining the advantages they offer and why they have become popular. It also provides an overview of DNS, NIS, and NIS+, including the NIS+ compatibility features.

2 ***Understanding the NIS+ Namespace***
This chapter introduces the NIS+ namespace components: directories, groups, tables, domains, servers, and clients. It explains what all these components (except groups and tables) are, how they are structured, and gives you a first look at what is involved in setting them up.

3 ***Understanding NIS+ Tables***
This chapter describes what NIS+ tables are, how they are structured, and what it takes to set them up and populate them. It also describes the information in each table, and how it should be formatted when loaded into NIS+ via an input file.

4 ***Understanding NIS+ Security***
This chapter describes the security features of NIS+, explaining how it works and describing credentials and access rights.

5 ***Understanding the Name Service Switch***
Describes the Name Service Switch, a facility that allows you to specify the type of service that provides each different category of information to your workstation: NIS+, NIS, DNS, or local /etc files.

Understanding Network Information Services 1

This chapter describes the purpose of network information services, points out their major features and benefits, and compares three of them: DNS, NIS, and NIS+. It has four sections:

The Purpose of Network Information Services

Network information services store information that users, workstations, and applications must have to communicate across the network. Without a network information service, each workstation would have to maintain its own copy of this information.

For example, take a simple network of three workstations, pine, elm, and oak:

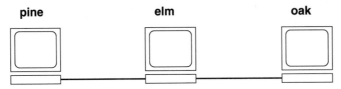

Before pine can send a message to either elm or oak, it must know their network addresses. For this reason, it keeps a file, /etc/hosts, that stores the network address of every workstation in the network, including itself.

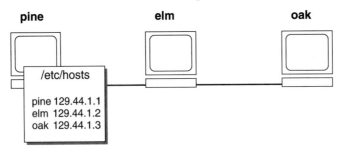

Likewise, in order for elm and oak to communicate with pine or with each other, they must keep similar files.

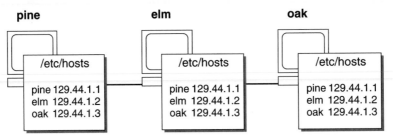

However, addresses are not the only network information that workstations need to store. They also need to store security information, mail information, information about their Ethernet interfaces, information about network services, and about groups of users allowed to use the network, about services offered on the network, and so on. As networks offer more services, the list grows. As a result, each workstation may need to keep an entire set of files similar to /etc/hosts.

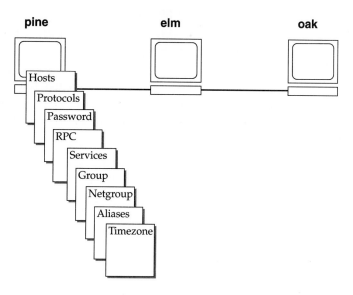

As this information changes, administrators must keep it current on every workstation in the network. In a small network this is simply tedious, but on a medium or large network, the job becomes not only time consuming, but unmanageable.

A network information service solves this problem. It stores network information on servers and provides it to any workstation that asks for it.

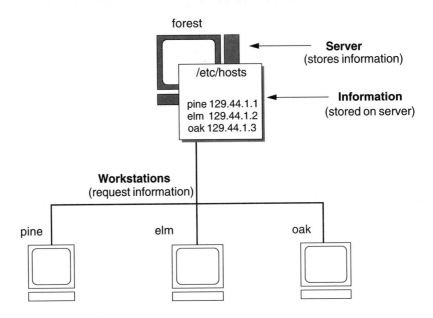

The workstations are known as *clients* of the server. Whenever information about the network changes, instead of updating each client's local file, an administrator updates only the information stored by the network information service. This practice reduces errors, inconsistencies among clients, and the sheer size of the task.

This arrangement, of a server providing centralized services to clients across a network, is known as *client-server computing*.

Although the chief purpose of a network information service is to centralize information, another purpose is to simplify network names. A network information service enables workstations to be identified by common names instead of by numerical addresses. (This is why these services are sometimes called "name services.") This makes communication simpler because users don't have to remember and try to enter cumbersome numerical addresses like 129.44.3.1. Instead, they can use descriptive names like Sales, Lab1, or Arnold.

For example, assume that a fictitious company called Wizard, Inc. has set up a network and connected it to the Internet. The Internet has assigned Wizard, Inc. the network number of 129.44.0.0. Wizard, Inc. has two divisions, Sales and Eng, so its network is divided into two subnets, one for each division. Each subnet, of course, has its own address.

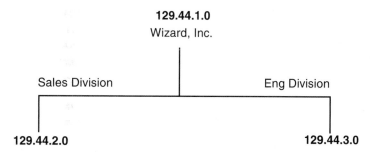

Each division could be identified by its network address, as shown above, but descriptive names made possible by network information services would clearly be preferable.

(As a convention, this book presents hardware connections with solid lines and network information service connections with less solid lines.)

So, instead of mail or other network communications being addressed to 129.44.1.0, they could be addressed simply to Wiz. Instead of being addressed to 129.44.2.0 or 129.44.3.0, they could be addressed to Sales.Wiz or Eng.Wiz.

Names are also more flexible than physical addresses. While physical networks tend to remain stable, the organizations that use them tend to change. A network information service can act as a buffer between an organization and its physical network, because a network information service is mapped to the physical network, not hard-wired to it. This principle is best demonstrated with an example.

Assume that the Wiz network is supported by three servers, S1, S2, and S3, and that two of those servers, S1 and S3, support clients.

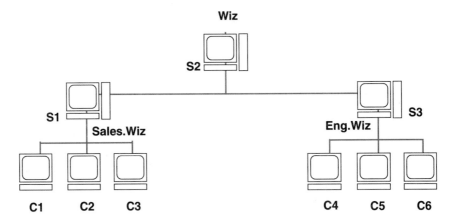

Clients C1, C2, and C3 obtain their network information from server S1. Clients C4, C5, and C6 obtain it from server S3. The resulting network is summarized in this table (a generalized representation of that network—actual network information maps do not look like this):

Network Address	Network Name	Server	Clients
129.44.1.0	Wiz	S1	
129.44.2.0	Sales.Wiz	S2	C1, C2, C3
129.44.3.0	Eng.Wiz	S3	C4, C5, C6

Now assume that Wizard, Inc. created a third division, Testing, which borrowed some resources from the other two divisions but did not create a third subnet. Unfortunately, the physical network would no longer parallel the corporate structure.

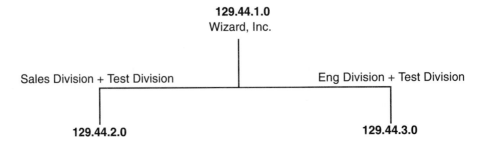

Traffic for the Test Division would not have its own subnet, but would instead be split between 129.44.2.0 and 129.44.3.0. However, with a network information service, the Test Division traffic could have its own dedicated "network."

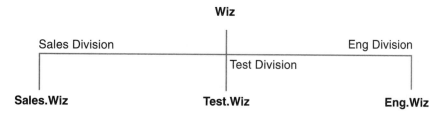

Thus, when an organization changed, its network information service would simply change its mapping.

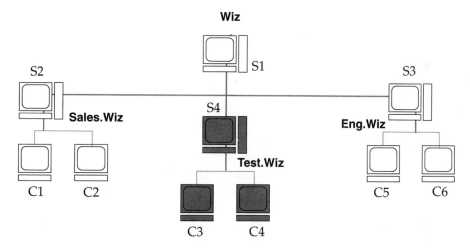

(As a convention in the illustrations used throughout this book, shading is used only to call attention to items—not to distinguish one type of item, such as a server, from another, such as a client.)

Now, clients C1 and C2 obtain their information from server S2; C3 and C4, from server S4; and C5 and C6, from server S3.

Subsequent changes in the Wizard Inc. organization would continue to be accommodated by changes to the "soft" network information structure without reorganizing the "hard" network structure.

Overview of DNS

DNS, the Domain Naming Service, is the network information service provided by the Internet for TCP/IP networks. It was developed so that workstations on the network could be identified with common names instead of Internet addresses.

The collection of networked workstations that use DNS are referred to as the DNS *namespace*. The DNS namespace can be divided into a hierarchy of *domains*. A DNS domain is simply a group of workstations. Each domain is supported by two or more *name servers*: a principal server and one or more secondary servers.

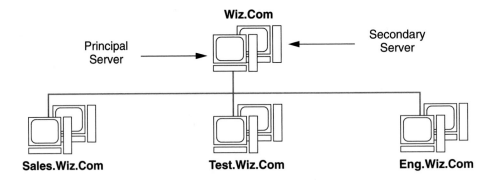

Both principal and secondary servers run the DNS software and store the names and addresses of the workstations in the domain. Principal servers store the original information, and secondary servers store copies.

DNS clients request service only from the servers that support their domain. If the domain's server does not have the information the client needs, it forwards the request to its parent server, which is the server in the next-higher domain in the hierarchy. If the request reaches the top-level server, the top-level server determines whether the domain is valid. If it is *not* valid, the server returns a "Not Found" message to the client. If the domain is valid, the server routes the request down to the server that supports that domain.

DNS and the Internet

DNS is the network information service used by the Internet. The Internet is a vast network that connects many smaller networks across the world. Organizations with networks of any size can join the Internet by applying for membership in two domain hierarchies: an organizational one and a geographical one.

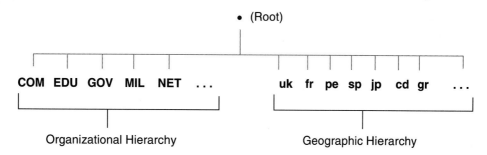

The organizational hierarchy divides its namespace into the top-level domains listed in Table 1-1.

Table 1-1   Internet Organizational Domains

Domain	Purpose
COM	Commercial organizations
EDU	Educational institutions
GOV	Government institutions
MIL	Military groups
NET	Major network support centers
ORG	Nonprofit organizations
INT	International organizations

The geographic hierarchy assigns each country in the world a two- or three-digit identifier and provides official names for the geographic regions within each country.

A site using DNS can use any top-level names it prefers, but if it wants to connect to the Internet, it cannot use any of the organizational or geographic names reserved by the Internet's top-level domains.

Networks that join the Internet append their Internet domain name to their own names. For example, if the Wiz domain from the previous example joined the Internet, it would be placed in the COM domain.

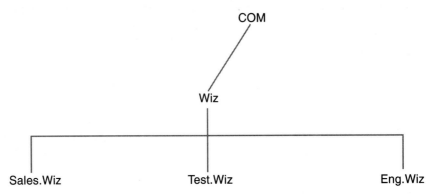

Thus, the full Internet names of the Wiz domains would be:

Wiz.COM
Sales.Wiz.COM
Test.Wiz.COM
Eng.Wiz.COM

Domain names are capitalized in this book simply as a convention; the DNS service does not require them to be capitalized. Workstation names precede their DNS domain names. They are *not* capitalized in this book (also by convention), to distinguish them from domain names. Here are some examples:

boss.Wiz.COM
neverhome.Sales.Wiz.COM
quota.Sales.Wiz.COM
lab.Test.Wiz.COM
worknights.Eng.Wiz.COM

The Internet regulates administration of its domains by granting each domain authority over the names of its workstations and expecting each domain to delegate authority to the levels below it. Thus, the COM domain has authority over the names of the workstations in its domain. It also authorizes the formation of the Wiz.COM domain and delegates authority over the names in that domain. The Wiz.COM domain, in turn, assigns names to the workstations in its domain and approves the formation of the Sales.Wiz.COM, Test.Wiz.COM, and Eng.Wiz.COM domains.

DNS Name Resolution and Mail Delivery

DNS provides two principal services: It translates hostnames to IP addresses (and also addresses to names) and it helps mail agents deliver mail along the Internet.

The process of translating names to addresses (and addresses to names) is called *name resolution*. To accomplish this translation, DNS stores the names and IP addresses of all the workstations in each domain in a set of maps, called *zone files*. One type of zone file stores IP addresses by name. When someone attempts a remote procedure such as `ftp` or `telnet`, the zone file provides the name of the remote workstation. DNS looks up the name in the zone file and converts (or *resolves*) it into its IP address. The IP address is sent along with the remote procedure, so the receiving workstation can know who sent the request. This process enables the receiving workstation to reply without having to also be a DNS client.

Another type of zone file stores workstation names by IP address. It converts IP addresses to workstation names, a process called *reverse resolution*. Reverse resolution is used primarily to verify the identity of the workstation that sent a message or to authorize remote operations on a local workstation (remote operations are usually authorized per IP addresses, which are more stable than workstation names).

To deliver mail across the Internet, DNS uses *mail exchange records*. Many organizations don't allow mail that comes across the Internet to be delivered directly to workstations within the organization. Instead, they use a central mailhost (or a set of mailhosts) to intercept incoming mail messages and route them to their recipients.

The purpose of a mail exchange record is to identify the mailhost that services each workstation. Therefore, a mail exchange record lists the DNS domain names of remote organizations and either the IP address or the name of its corresponding mailhost. For example:

DNS Domain	Mailhost
International.Com.	129.44.1.1
Sales.Wiz.Com.	SalesWizMailer
Eng.Wiz.Com.	EngWizMailer
Fab.Com.	FabMailer

When the mail agent receives a request to send mail to another domain, it parses the name of the recipient backwards and looks for a match in the table.   For example, if it receives a request to send mail to—

```
neverhome.Sales.Wiz.Com
```

—it first extracts the topmost label, Com. It examines the mail exchange record to see if there is an entry for Com. Since there is none, it continues parsing. It extracts the next label and looks for an entry for Wiz.Com; since there is none, it continues looking. The next entry it looks for is Sales.Wiz.Com. As you can see in the table above, the mailhost for that domain is SalesWizMailer. Because that is a workstation name, the mail agent asks DNS to resolve it. When DNS provides that mailhost's IP address, the mail agent sends the message.

If, instead of the mailhost name, the mail exchange record had specified an IP address, the mail agent would have sent the message directly to that address, since it would have needed no name resolution from DNS.

Overview of NIS

NIS was developed independently of DNS and had a slightly different focus. Whereas DNS focused on making communication simpler by using workstation names instead of addresses, NIS focused on making network administration more manageable by providing centralized control over a variety of network information. As a result, NIS stores information not only about workstation names and addresses, but also about users, the network itself, and network services. This collection of network *information* is referred to as the NIS *namespace*.

NIS uses a client-server arrangement similar to that of DNS. Replicated NIS servers provide services to NIS clients. The principal servers are called *master* servers, and, for reliability, they have backup, or *slave* servers. Both master and slave servers use the NIS information retrieval software and both store NIS maps.

NIS, like DNS, uses domains to arrange the workstations, users, and networks in its namespace. However, it does not use a domain hierarchy; an NIS namespace is flat. Thus, this physical network—

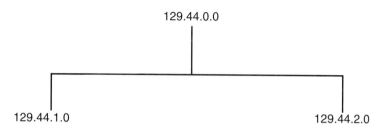

—would be arranged into one NIS domain:

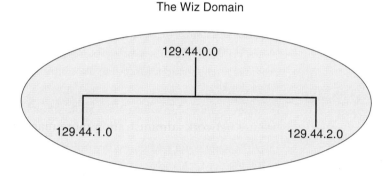

An NIS domain can't be connected directly to the Internet. However, organizations that want to use NIS and be connected to the Internet can combine NIS with DNS. They use NIS to manage all local information and DNS for hostname resolution. NIS provides special client routines for this purpose (DNS forwarding). When a client needs access to any type of information except IP addresses, the request goes to the client's NIS server. When a client needs name resolution, the request goes to the DNS server. From the DNS server, the client has access to the Internet in the usual way.

NIS Maps

Like DNS, NIS stores information in a set of maps. However, NIS maps were designed to replace UNIX® /etc files, as well as other configuration files, so they store much more than names and addresses. As a result, the NIS namespace has a large set of maps, as shown in Table 1-2.

NIS maps are essentially bicolumn tables. One column is the key and the other column is information about the key. NIS finds information for a client by searching through the keys. Thus, some information is stored in several maps because each map uses a different key. For example, the names and addresses of workstations are stored in two maps: `hosts.byname` and `hosts.byaddr`. When a server has a workstation's name and needs to find its address, it looks in the `hosts.byname` map. When it has the address and needs to find the name, it looks in the `hosts.byaddr` map.

Table 1-2   NIS Maps

NIS Map	Description
`bootparams`	Lists the names of the diskless clients and the location of the files they need during booting.
`ethers.byaddr`	Lists the Ethernet addresses of workstations and their corresponding names.
`ethers.byname`	Contains the names of workstations and their corresponding Ethernet addresses.
`group.bygid`	Provides membership information about groups, using the group ID as the key.
`group.byname`	Provides membership information about groups, using the group name as the key.
`hosts.byaddr`	Lists the names and addresses of workstations, using the address as the key.
`hosts.byname`	Lists the names and addresses of workstations, using the name as the key.
`mail.aliases`	Lists the mail aliases in the namespace and all the workstations that belong to them.
`mail.byaddr`	Lists the mail aliases in the namespace, but uses the address as the key.
`netgroup`	Contains netgroup information, using group name as the key.
`netgroup.byhost`	Contains information about the netgroups in the namespace, but with workstation names as the key.
`netgroup.byuser`	Contains netgroup information, but with user as the key.
`netid.byname`	Contains the secure RPC netname of workstations and users, along with their UIDs and GIDs.
`netmasks.byaddr`	Contains network masks used with IP subnetting, using address as the key.

Table 1-2   NIS Maps (Continued)

NIS Map	Description
networks.byaddr	Contains the names and addresses of the networks in the namespace, and their Internet addresses.
networks.byname	Contains the names and addresses of the networks in the namespace, using the names as the key.
passwd.byname	Contains password information, with username as the key.
passwd.byuid	Contains password information, with user ID as the key.
protocols.byname	Lists the network protocols used.
protocols.bynumber	Lists the network protocols used but uses their number as the key.
publickey.byname	Contains public and secret keys for secure RPC.
rpc.bynumber	Lists the known program name and number of RPCs.
services.byname	Lists the available Internet services.
ypservers	Lists the NIS servers in the namespace, along with their IP addresses.

Overview of NIS+

NIS+ was designed to replace NIS. NIS addresses the administration requirements of client-server computing networks prevalent in the 1980s. At that time, client-server networks did not usually have more than a few hundred clients and had only a few multipurpose servers. They were spread across only a few remote sites, and, since users were sophisticated and trusted, they did not require security.

However, client-server networks have grown tremendously since the mid-1980s. They now range from 100 to 10,000 multivendor clients supported by 10 to 100 specialized servers located in sites throughout the world, and they are connected to several "untrusted" public networks. In addition, the information they store changes much more rapidly than it did during the time of NIS. The size and complexity of these networks required new, autonomous administration practices. NIS+ was designed to address these requirements.

The NIS namespace, being flat, centralizes administration. Because networks in the 90s require scalability and decentralized administration, the NIS+ namespace was designed with hierarchical domains, like those of DNS.

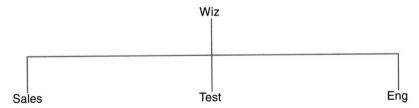

This design allows NIS+ to be used in a range of networks, from small to very large. It also allows the NIS+ service to adapt to the growth of an organization. For example, if a corporation divided itself into two divisions, its NIS+ namespace could be divided into two domains, which could be administered autonomously. Just as the Internet delegates administration of domains *downward*, NIS+ domains can be administered more or less independently of each other.

Although NIS+ uses a domain hierarchy similar to that of DNS, an NIS+ domain is much more than a DNS domain. A DNS domain stores only name and address information about its clients. An NIS+ domain, on the other hand, is a collection of *information* about the workstations, users, and network services in a part of an organization.

Although this division into domains makes administration more autonomous and growth easier to manage, it does not make information harder to access. Clients have the same access to information in other domains as they would have had under one umbrella domain. A domain can even be administered from within another domain.

The NIS+ client-server arrangement is similar to those of NIS and DNS in that each domain is supported by a set of servers. The principal server is called the *master* server, and the backup servers are called *replicas*. Both master and replica servers run NIS+ server software and both maintain copies of NIS+ tables. The principal server stores the original tables, and the backup servers store copies.

However, NIS+ uses an updating model that is completely different from the one used by NIS. Since at the time NIS was developed, the type of information it would store changed infrequently, NIS was developed with an update model that focused on stability. Its updates are handled manually and, in large organizations, can take more than a day to propagate to all the replicas. Part of the reason for this time lag is the need to remake and propagate an entire map every time any information in the map changes.

NIS+, however, accepts *incremental* updates to the replicas. Changes must still be made on the master server, but once made they are automatically propagated to the replica servers and immediately made available to the entire namespace. You don't have to "make" any maps or wait for propagation.

Details about NIS+ domain structure, servers, and clients are provided in Chapter 2.

An NIS+ domain can be connected to the Internet via its NIS+ clients, using the Name Service Switch, described below. The client, if it is also a DNS client, can set up its Switch configuration file to search for information in either DNS zone files or NIS maps—in addition to NIS+ tables.

NIS+ stores information in *tables* instead of maps or zone files. NIS+ provides 16 types of predefined, or *system*, tables.

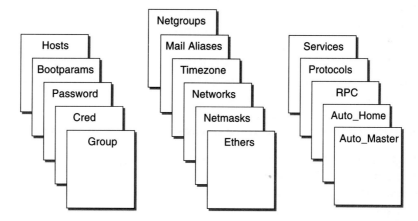

Each table stores a different type of information. For instance, the Hosts table stores information about workstation addresses, while the Password table stores information about users of the network.

NIS+ tables provide two major improvements over the maps used by NIS. First, an NIS+ table can be accessed by any column, not just the first column (sometimes referred to as the "key"). This plan eliminates the need for duplicate maps, such as the hosts.byname and hosts.byaddr maps used by NIS. Second, the information in NIS+ tables can be accessed and manipulated at three levels of granularity: the table level, the entry level, and the column level. NIS+ tables are described in Chapter 3. The information stored in them is described in Appendix A.

1

NIS+ Security

NIS+ protects the structure of the namespace, and the information it stores, by the complementary processes of *authorization* and *authentication*. First, every component in the namespace specifies the type of operation it will accept and from whom. This is authorization. Second, NIS+ attempts to *authenticate* every request for access to the namespace. Once it identifies the originator of the request, it can find out whether the component has authorized that particular operation for that particular individual. Based on its authentication and the component's authorization, NIS+ carries out or denies the request for access. A full description of this process is provided in Chapter 4.

NIS+ and the Name Service Switch

NIS+ works in conjunction with a separate facility called the *Name Service Switch*. The Name Service Switch, sometimes referred to as "the Switch," enables workstations based on Solaris 2.x to obtain their information from more than one network information service; specifically, from local or /etc files, from NIS maps, from DNS zone files, or from NIS+ tables. The Switch not only offers a choice of sources, but allows a workstation to specify different sources for different *types* of information. A complete description of the Switch is provided in Chapter 5.

NIS+ and Solaris 1.x

Although NIS+ is provided with the Solaris 2.3 package, it can be used by workstations running Solaris 1.x in two different ways:

- NIS compatibility mode
- Solaris 1.x Distribution package

NIS Compatibility Mode

NIS+ provides an *NIS compatibility mode*. The NIS compatibility mode enables an NIS+ server running Solaris 2.3 to answer requests from NIS clients while continuing to answer requests from NIS+ clients. NIS+ does this by providing two service interfaces. One responds to NIS+ client requests, while the other responds to NIS client requests.

This mode does not require any additional setup or changes to NIS clients. In fact, NIS clients are not even aware that the server that is responding isn't an NIS server—except for one difference: The NIS+ server running in NIS compatibility mode does not support the ypupdate and ypxfr protocols and thus cannot be used as a slave or master NIS server.

Note – In Solaris 2.3 and later releases, the NIS compatibility mode *supports* DNS forwarding. In Solaris 2.2, support for DNS forwarding is available as a *patch*. The DNS forwarding patch is *not* available in Solaris 2.0 and 2.1 releases.

Two more differences need to be pointed out. One is that instructions for setting up a server in NIS compatibility mode are slightly different from those used to set up a standard NIS+ server. For details, see Part 3. The other is that NIS compatibility mode has security implications for tables in the NIS+ namespace. Since the NIS client software does not have the capability to provide the credentials that NIS+ servers expect from NIS+ clients, all their requests end up classified as *unauthenticated*. Therefore, to allow NIS clients to access information in NIS+ tables, those tables must provide access rights to unauthenticated requests. This access is handled automatically by the utilities used to set up a server in NIS compatibility mode, as described in Part 3. However, to understand more about the authentication process, read Chapter 4.

Solaris 1.x Distribution

NIS+ provides a separate package called the *Solaris 1.x Distribution*, which enables workstations running Solaris 1.x to operate as NIS+ servers without having to upgrade to Solaris 2.x. The NIS+ Solaris 1.x Distribution consists of the NIS+ daemon, all the NIS+ commands, the NIS+ client libraries, and a README file. It is delivered in a tar file, NISPLUS.TAR, included in the Solaris 2.3 CD-ROM. To transfer the distribution from the CD-ROM to a Solaris 1.x-based workstation, first mount the CD-ROM, then transfer the NISPLUS.TAR file, using the tar command. If you have network access to the Solaris 1.x Distribution, you can use ftp or rcp. Instructions for installing it are provided in the README file.

NIS+ Administration Commands

NIS+ provides a full set of commands for administering a namespace. They are described throughout this book, but mostly in Part 4. Table 1-3 summarizes them.

Table 1-3   NIS+ Namespace Administration Commands

Command	Description	See
nisaddcred	Creates credentials for NIS+ principals and stores them in the Cred table.	page 306
nisaddent	Adds information from /etc files or NIS maps into NIS+ tables.	page 375
nis_cachemgr	Starts the NIS+ cache manager on an NIS+ client.	page 349

Table 1-3   NIS+ Namespace Administration Commands (Continued)

Command	Description	See
niscat	Displays the contents of NIS+ tables.	page 365
nischgrp	Changes the group owner of an NIS+ object.	page 334
nischmod	Changes an object's access rights.	page 329
nischown	Changes the owner of an NIS+ object.	page 333
nischttl	Changes an NIS+ object's time-to-live value.	page 355
nisdefaults	Lists an NIS+ object's default values: domain name, group name, workstation name, NIS+ principal name, access rights, directory search path, and time to live.	page 325
nisgrep	Searches for entries in an NIS+ table.	page 368
nisgrpadm	Creates or destroys an NIS+ group, or displays a list of its members. Also adds members to a group, removes them, or tests them for membership in the group.	page 296
nisinit	Initializes an NIS+ client or server.	page 347
nisln	Creates a symbolic link between two NIS+ objects.	page 372
nisls	Lists the contents of an NIS+ directory.	page 339
nismatch	Searches for entries in an NIS+ table.	page 368
nismkdir	Creates an NIS+ directory and specifies its master and replica servers.	page 341
nispasswd	Changes password information stored in the NIS+ Passwd table.	page 313
nisrm	Removes NIS+ objects (except directories) from the namespace.	page 344
nisrmdir	Removes NIS+ directories and replicas from the namespace.	page 344
nissetup	Creates org_dir and groups_dir directories and a complete set of (unpopulated) NIS+ tables for an NIS+ domain.	page 373
nisshowcache	Lists the contents of the NIS+ shared cache maintained by the NIS+ cache manager.	page 349
nistbladm	Creates or deletes NIS+ tables, and adds, modifies, or deletes entries in an NIS+ table.	page 358
nisupdkeys	Updates the public keys stored in an NIS+ object.	page 316

NIS+ API

The NIS+ Application Programmer's Interface (API) is a group of functions that can be called by an application to access and modify NIS+ objects. The NIS+ API has 54 functions that fall into nine categories:

- Object manipulation functions (`nis_names`)
- Table access functions (`nis_tables`)
- Local name functions (`nis_local_names`)
- Group manipulation functions (`nis_groups`)
- Application subroutine functions (`nis_subr`)
- Miscellaneous functions (`nis_misc`)
- Database access functions (`nis_db`)
- Error message display functions (`nis_error`)
- Transaction log functions (`nis_admin`)

The functions in each category are summarized in the Appendix D. The category names match the names by which they are grouped in the NIS+ manual pages.

What Next?

The remainder of this book shifts focus from network information services in general toward NIS+ in particular. DNS and NIS are no longer mentioned except when discussing how to use them with NIS+. Before attempting to set up NIS+, be sure you understand the information presented in the remaining chapters of Part 1:

- Chapter 2, "Understanding the NIS+ Namespace," describes NIS+ directories, domains, servers, clients, and the NIS compatibility mode.
- Chapter 3, "Understanding NIS+ Tables," describes NIS+ tables.
- Chapter 4, "Understanding NIS+ Security," describes the process of authentication and authorization.
- Chapter 5, "Understanding the Name Service Switch," describes the Switch.

Understanding the NIS+
Namespace

The NIS+ service conforms to the shape of the organization that installs it, wrapping itself around the bulges and corners of almost any network configuration. This design is implemented through the NIS+ *namespace*. This chapter describes the structure of the NIS+ namespace, the servers that support it, and the clients that use it. It has the following sections:

Structure of the NIS+ Namespace

The NIS+ namespace is the arrangement of information stored by NIS+. The namespace can be arranged in a variety of ways to suit the needs of an organization. For example, if an organization had three divisions, its NIS+ namespace would likely be divided into three parts, one for each division. Each part would store information about the users, workstations, and network services in its division, but the parts could easily communicate with each other. Such an arrangement would make information easier for the users to access and for the administrators to maintain.

Although the arrangement of an NIS+ namespace can vary from site to site, all sites use the same structural components: directories, tables, and groups. These components are called NIS+ *objects*. NIS+ objects can be arranged into a hierarchy that resembles a UNIX filesystem. For example, the illustration below shows, on the left, a namespace that consists of three directory objects, three group objects, and three table objects; on the right it shows a UNIX filesystem that consists of three directories and three files.

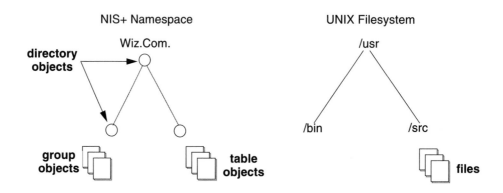

Although an NIS+ namespace resembles a UNIX filesystem, it has four important differences:

1. Although both use directories, the other objects in an NIS+ namespace are tables and groups, not files.
2. The NIS+ namespace is administered only through NIS+ administration commands (listed in Table 3-1 on page 45) or graphical user interfaces (GUIs) designed for that purpose; it cannot be administered with standard UNIX filesystem commands or GUIs.
3. The names of UNIX filesystem components are separated by slashes (`/usr/bin`), but the names of NIS+ namespace objects are separated by dots (Wiz.Com.).
4. The "root" of a UNIX filesystem is reached by stepping through directories from right to left (e.g., `/usr/src/file1`), while the root of the NIS+ namespace is reached by stepping from left to right (Sales.Wiz.Com).

Directories

Directory objects are the skeleton of the namespace. When arranged in a treelike structure, they divide the namespace into separate parts. You may find it helpful to visualize a directory hierarchy as an upside-down tree, with the root of the tree at the top and the leaves toward the bottom. The topmost directory in a namespace is the *root* directory. If a namespace is flat, it has only one directory, but that directory is nevertheless the root directory. The directory objects beneath the root directory are simply called "directories."

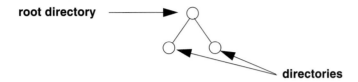

root directory ⟶

directories

A namespace can have several levels of directories.

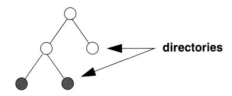

directories

When identifying the relation of one directory to another, the directory beneath is called the *child* directory, and the directory above is called the *parent* directory.

Whereas UNIX directories are designed to hold UNIX files, NIS+ directories are designed to hold NIS+ objects: other directories, tables, and groups. Any NIS+ directory that stores NIS+ groups is named `groups_dir`. Any directory that stores NIS+ system tables is named `org_dir`.

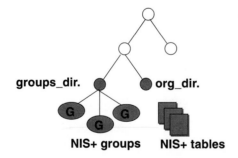

groups_dir.   **org_dir.**

NIS+ groups   **NIS+ tables**

Technically, you can arrange directories, tables, and groups into any structure that you like. However, NIS+ directories, tables, and groups in a namespace are normally arranged in configurations called *domains*. Domains are designed to support separate portions of the namespace. For instance, one domain may support the Sales Division of a company, while another may support the Engineering Division.

Domains

An NIS+ domain consists of a directory object, its `org_dir` directory, its `groups_dir` directory, and a set of NIS+ tables.

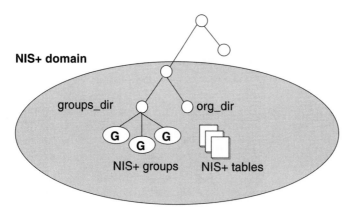

NIS+ domains are not tangible components of the namespace. They are simply a convenient way to refer to sections of the namespace that are used to support real-world organizations. Take the Wizard Corporation from Chapter 1 as an example. At one point it had a Sales division and an Engineering division. To support those divisions, its NIS+ namespace would most likely be arranged into three major directory groups, with a structure that looked like this:

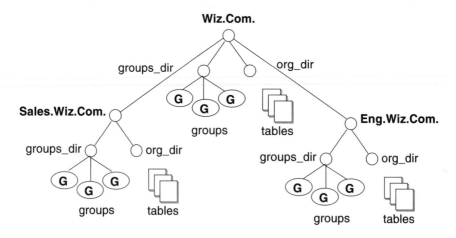

Instead of referring to such a structure as three directories, six subdirectories, and several additional objects, it is more convenient to refer to it as three domains.

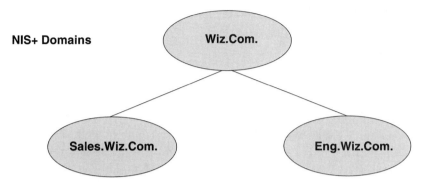

Part 2 of this manual provides step-by-step instructions for setting up two types of domains. Chapter 15, "Setting Up the Root Domain," describes how to set up a root domain. Chapter 19, "Setting Up a Nonroot Domain," describes how to set up a nonroot domain. For guidelines about which type to set up and in what order, see Chapter 13, "Setup Guidelines."

Servers

Every NIS+ domain is supported by a set of NIS+ *servers*. The servers store the domain's directories, groups, and tables, and answer requests for access from users, administrators, and applications. Each domain is supported by only one set of servers. However, a single set of servers can support more than one domain.

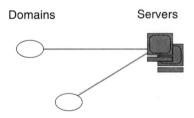

Remember that a domain is not an object, but only refers to a collection of objects. Therefore, a server that supports a domain is not actually associated with the domain, but with the domain's main *directory*.

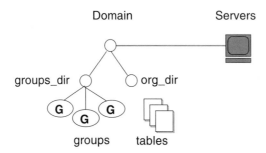

This connection between the server and the directory object is established during the process of setting up a domain. Although instructions are provided in Part 2, one thing is important to mention now: When that connection is established, the directory object stores the name and IP address of its server. This information is used by clients to send requests for service, as described later in this section.

Any workstation based on Solaris 2.3 can be an NIS+ server. The software for both NIS+ servers and clients is bundled into the Solaris 2.3 package. Therefore, any workstation that has Solaris 2.3 installed can become a server or a client, or both. What distinguishes a client from a server is the role it plays. If a workstation provides NIS+ service, it acts as an NIS+ server. If it requests NIS+ service, it acts as an NIS+ client.

Because of the need to service many client requests, a workstation that will act as an NIS+ server might be configured with more computing power and more memory than the average client. Because it needs to store NIS+ data, it might also have a larger disk. However, other than hardware to improve its performance, a server is not inherently different from an NIS+ client.

Two types of servers support an NIS+ domain: a master and its replicas.

The master server of the root domain is called the *root master* server. A namespace has only one root master server. The master servers of other domains are simply called master servers. Likewise, there are root replica servers and plain ol' replica servers.

Both master and replica servers store NIS+ tables and answer client requests. The master, however, stores the master copy of a domain's tables. The replicas store only duplicates. The administrator loads information into the tables in the master server, and the master server propagates it to the replica servers.

This arrangement has two benefits. First, it avoids conflicts between tables because only one set of master tables exists; the tables stored by the replicas are only copies of the masters. Second, it makes the NIS+ service much more available. If either the master or a slave is down, the other server can act as a backup and handle the requests for service.

How Servers Propagate Changes

An NIS+ master server implements updates to its objects immediately; however, it tries to "batch" several updates before it propagates them to its replicas. When a master server receives an update to an object, whether a directory, group, link, or table, it waits about two minutes for any other updates that may arrive. Once it is finished waiting, it stores the updates in two locations: on disk and in a *transaction log* (it has already stored the updates in memory).

The transaction log is used by a master server to store changes to the namespace until they can be propagated to replicas. A transaction log has two primary components: updates and timestamps.

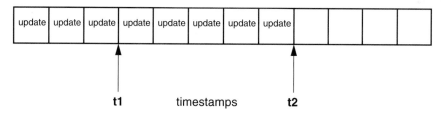

Transaction Log

An update is an actual copy of a changed object. For instance, if a directory has been changed, the update is a complete copy of the directory object. If a table entry has been changed, the update is a copy of the actual table entry. The timestamp indicates the time at which an update was made by the master server.

After recording the change in the transaction log, the master sends a message to its replicas, telling them that it has updates to send them. Each replica replies with the timestamp of the last update it received from the master. The master then sends each replica the updates it has recorded in the log since the replica's timestamp.

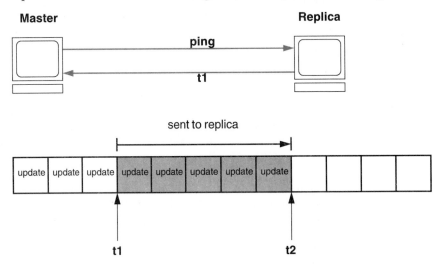

When the master server updates *all* its replicas, it clears the transaction log. In some cases, such as when a new replica is added to a domain, the master receives a timestamp from a replica that is before its earliest timestamp still recorded in the transaction log. If that happens, the master server performs a full *resynchronization*, or "resync." A resync downloads all the objects and information stored in the master down to the replica. During a resync, both the master and replica are busy. The replica cannot answer requests for information; the master can answer read requests, but cannot accept update requests. Both respond with a "Server Busy—Try Again" message.

Clients

An NIS+ client is a workstation that has been set up to receive NIS+ service. Setting up an NIS+ client consists of establishing security credentials, making it a member of the proper NIS+ groups, verifying its home domain, verifying its Switch configuration file and, finally, running the NIS+ initialization utility. (Complete instructions are provided in Chapter 17, "Setting Up an NIS+ Client.")

An NIS+ client can access any part of the namespace, subject to security constraints. In other words, if it has been authenticated and if it has been granted the proper permissions, it can access information or objects in any domain in the namespace.

Although a client can access the entire namespace, a client belongs to only one domain, which is referred to as its *home* domain. A client's home domain is usually specified during installation, but it can be changed or specified later. All the information about a client, such as its IP address and its credentials, is stored in the NIS+ tables of its home domain.

There is a subtle difference between being an NIS+ client and being listed in an NIS+ table. Entering information about a workstation into an NIS+ table does not automatically make that workstation an NIS+ client. It simply makes information about that workstation available to all NIS+ clients. That workstation cannot request NIS+ service unless it is actually set up as an NIS+ client.

Conversely, making a workstation an NIS+ client does not enter information about that workstation into an NIS+ table. It simply allows that workstation to receive NIS+ service. If information about that workstation is not explicitly entered into the NIS+ tables by an administrator, other NIS+ clients will not be able to get it.

When a client requests access to the namespace, it is actually requesting access to a particular domain in the namespace. Therefore, it sends its request to the server that supports the domain it is trying to access.

Here is a simplified representation:

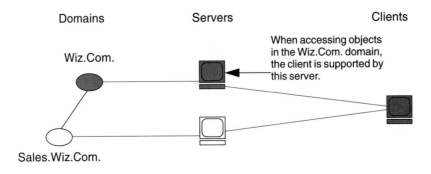

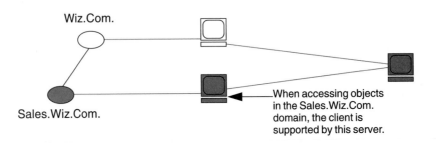

How does the client know which server is the supporting server? By a simple method of trial and error. Beginning with its home server, the client tries one server, then another, until it finds the right one. When a server cannot answer the client's request, it sends the client information to help it locate the right server. Over time, the client builds up its own cache of information and becomes more efficient at locating the right server. Following are the details of the process.

The Coldstart File and Directory Cache

When a client is initialized, it is given a *coldstart file*. A coldstart file gives a client a copy of a directory object that it can use as a starting point for contacting servers in the namespace. The directory object contains the address, public keys, and other information about the master and replica servers that support the directory. Normally, the coldstart file contains the directory object of the client's home domain.

A coldstart file is used only to initialize a client's *directory cache*. The directory cache, managed by an NIS+ facility called the *cache manager*, stores the directory objects that enable a client to send its requests to the proper servers.

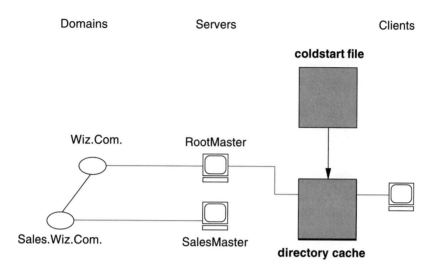

By storing a copy of the namespace's directory objects in its directory cache, a client can know which servers support which domains. Here is a simplified example[1]:

Domain	Directory Name	Supporting Server	IP Address
Wiz.Com.	Wiz.Com.	RootMaster	129.44.1.1
Sales.Wiz.Com	Sales.Wiz.Com.	SalesMaster	129.44.2.1
Eng.Wiz.Com.	Eng.Wiz.Com.	EngMaster	129.44.3.1
Intl.Sales.Wiz.Com.	Intl.Sales.Wiz.Com.	IntlSalesMaster	129.44.2.11

To keep these copies up-to-date, each directory object has a *time-to-live* field. Its default value is 12 hours. If a client looks in its directory cache for a directory object and finds that it has not been updated in the last 12 hours, the cache manager obtains a new copy of the object.

---

1. To view the contents of a client's cache, use the nisshowcache command, described in Chapter 24, "Administering NIS+ Directories."

You can change a directory object's time-to-live value with the `nischttl` command, as described in Chapter 24, "Administering NIS+ Directories." However, keep in mind that the longer the time to live, the higher the likelihood that the copy of the object will be out of date; the shorter the time to live, the greater the network traffic and server load.

How does the directory cache accumulate these directory objects? As mentioned above, the coldstart file provides the first entry in the cache. Therefore, when the client sends its first request, it sends the request to the server specified by the coldstart file. If the request is for access to the domain supported by that server, the server answers the request.

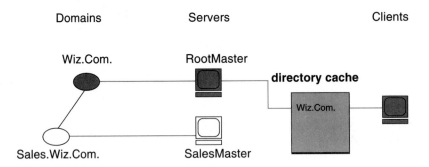

If the request is for access to another domain (e.g., Sales.Wiz.Com.), the server tries to help the client locate the proper server. If the server has an entry for that domain in its own directory cache, it sends a copy of the domain's directory object to the client. The client loads that information into its directory cache for future reference and sends its request to that server.

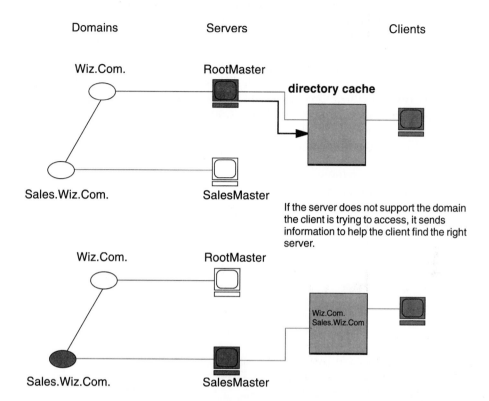

Domains   Servers   Clients

Wiz.Com.

RootMaster

directory cache

Sales.Wiz.Com.

SalesMaster

If the server does not support the domain the client is trying to access, it sends information to help the client find the right server.

Wiz.Com.

RootMaster

Wiz.Com.
Sales.Wiz.Com

Sales.Wiz.Com.

SalesMaster

In the unlikely event that the server does not have a copy of the directory object the client is trying to access, it sends the client a copy of the directory object for its own home domain, which lists the address of the server's parent. The client repeats the process with the parent server and keeps trying until it finds the proper server or until it has tried all the servers in the namespace. What the client does after trying all the servers in the domain is determined by the instructions in its Name Service Switch configuration file. See Chapter 5, "Understanding the Name Service Switch," for details.

Over time, the client accumulates in its cache a copy of all the directory objects in the namespace and, thus, the IP addresses of the servers that support them. When it needs to send a request for access to another domain, it can usually find the name of its server in its directory cache and send the request directly to that server.

An NIS+ Server Is Also a Client

An NIS+ server is also an NIS+ client. In fact, before you can set up a workstation as a server, you must initialize it as a client. The only exception is the root master server, which has its own unique setup process.

Thus, in addition to supporting a domain, a server also belongs to a domain. In other words, by virtue of being a client, a server has a home domain. Its host information is stored in the Hosts table of its home domain, and its DES credentials are stored in the Cred table of its home domain. Like other clients, it sends its requests for service to the servers listed in its directory cache.

An important point to remember is that—except for the root domain—a server's home domain is the *parent* of the domain the server supports.

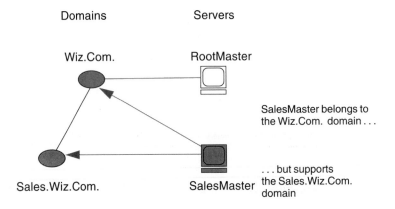

In other words, a server supports clients in one domain, but is a client of another domain. A server cannot be a client of a domain that it supports, with the exception of the root domain. The servers that support the root domain, because they have no parent domain, belong to the root domain itself.

For example, consider the following namespace:

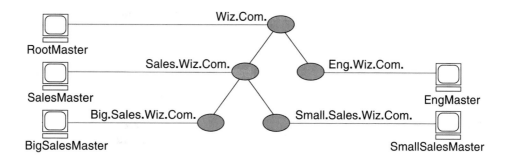

The chart below lists which domain each server supports and which domain it belongs to.

Server	Supports	Belongs to
RootMaster	Wiz.Com.	Wiz.Com.
SalesMaster	Sales.Wiz.Com.	Wiz.Com.
BigSalesMaster	Big.Sales.Wiz.Com.	Sales.Wiz.Com.
SmallSalesMaster	Small.Sales.Wiz.Com.	Sales.Wiz.Com.
EngMaster	Eng.Wiz.Com.	Wiz.Com.

Naming Conventions (to Dot or Not)

Objects in an NIS+ namespace can be identified with two types of names: *partially qualified* and *fully qualified*. A partially qualified name, also called a *simple* name, is simply the name of the object or any portion of the fully qualified name. If during any administration operation you enter the partially qualified name of an object or principal, NIS+ will attempt to expand the name into its fully qualified version. For details, see "*NIS+ Name Expansion*" on page 42.

A fully qualified name is the complete name of the object, including all the information necessary to locate it in the namespace, such as its parent directory, if it has one, and its complete domain name, *including a trailing dot.*

This description varies among different types of objects, so the conventions for each type, as well as for NIS+ principals, are described separately. This namespace is used as an example:

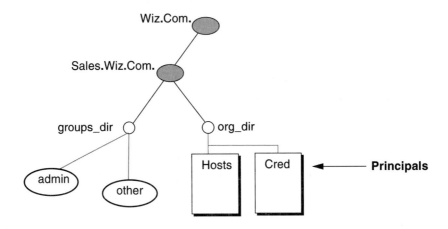

The fully qualified names for all the objects in this namespace, including NIS+ principals, are summarized in Figure 2-1.

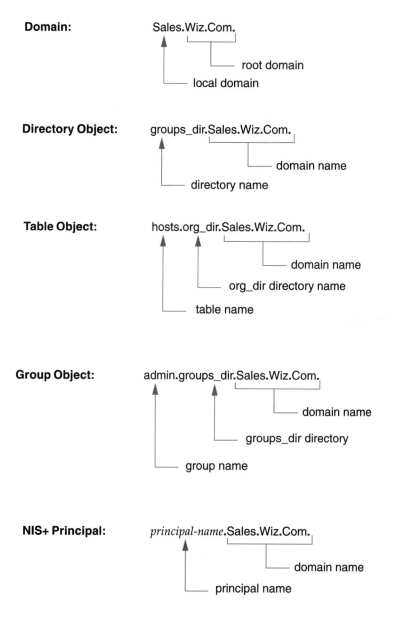

Domain: Sales.Wiz.Com.
— root domain
— local domain

Directory Object: groups_dir.Sales.Wiz.Com.
— domain name
— directory name

Table Object: hosts.org_dir.Sales.Wiz.Com.
— domain name
— org_dir directory name
— table name

Group Object: admin.groups_dir.Sales.Wiz.Com.
— domain name
— groups_dir directory
— group name

NIS+ Principal: *principal-name*.Sales.Wiz.Com.
— domain name
— principal name

Figure 2-1   Fully Qualified Names of Namespace Components

For domains

A fully qualified domain name is formed from left to right, starting with the local domain and ending with the root domain. For example:

> Wiz.Inc.Wiz.Com.
> Sales.Wiz.Inc.Sales.Wiz.Com.
> Intl.Sales.Wiz.Inc.Intl.Sales.Wiz.Com.

The first line above shows the name of the root domain. The root domain must always have at least two labels and must end in a dot. The second label can be an Internet domain name, such as Com. The second and third lines above show the names of lower-level domains.

For directory objects

A directory's simple name is simply the name of the directory object. Its fully qualified name consists of its simple name plus the fully qualified name of its domain (which always includes a trailing dot).

> groups_dir(simple name)
> groups_dir.Eng.Wiz.Com.(fully qualified name)

If you set up an unusual hierarchy in which several layers of directories do not form a domain, be sure to include the names of the intermediate directories. For example:

> lowest_dir.lower_dir.low_dir.MyStrangeDomain.Com.

The simple name is normally used from within the same domain, and the fully qualified name is normally used from a remote domain. However, by specifying search paths in a domain's NIS_PATH environment variable, you can use the simple name from remote domains (see "NIS+ Name Expansion" on page 42).

For tables and groups

Fully qualified table and group names are formed by starting with the object name and appending the directory name, followed by the fully qualified domain name. Remember that all system table objects are stored in an org_dir directory and all group objects are stored in a groups_dir directory. (If you create your own NIS+ tables, you can store them anywhere you like.) Here are some examples of group and table names:

> admin.groups_dir.Wiz.Inc.admin.groups_dir.Wiz.Com.
> admin.groups_dir.Sales.Wiz.Inc.admin.groups_dir.Sales.Wiz.Com.
> hosts.org_dir.Wiz.Inc.hosts.org_dir.Wiz.Com.
> hosts.org_dir.Sales.Wiz.Inc.hosts.org_dir.Sales.Wiz.Com.

For table entries

To identify an entry in an NIS+ table, you need to identify the table object and the entry within it. This type of name is called an *indexed* name. It has the following syntax:

[*column=value* , *column=value* , . . .] , *table-name*

Column is the name of the table column. *Value* is the actual value of that column. *Table-name* is the fully qualified name of the table object. Here are a few examples of entries in the Hosts table:

[addr=129.44.2.1,name=pine],hosts.org_dir.Sales.Wiz.Com.
[addr=129.44.2.2,name=elm],hosts.org_dir.Sales.Wiz.Com.
[addr=129.44.2.3,name=oak],hosts.org_dir.Sales.Wiz.Com.

You can use as few column-value pairs inside the brackets, as required to uniquely identify the table entry.

Some NIS+ administrative commands accept variations on this syntax. For details, see the `nistbladm`, `nismatch`, and `nisgrep` commands in Chapter 25, "Administering NIS+ Tables."

For NIS+ principals

NIS+ principal names are sometimes confused with secure RPC netnames. Both types of names are described in Chapter 4, "Understanding NIS+ Security." However, one difference is worth pointing out now because it can cause confusion: NIS+ principal names *always* end in a dot and secure RPC netnames *never* do.

olivia.Sales.Wiz.Com.(NIS+ principal name)
unix.olivia@Sales.Wiz.Com(secure RPC netname)

Also, even though credentials for principals are stored in a Cred table, neither the name of the Cred table nor the name of the `org_dir` directory is included in the principal name.

Accepted symbols

You can form namespace names from any printable character in the ISO Latin 1 set. However, the names cannot start with these characters:

@   < >   +   [ ]   -   /
=   .   ,   :   ;

To use a string, enclose it in double quotes. To use a quote sign in the name, quote the sign too (for example, to use `ol'yeller`, type `ol"'"yeller`). To include white space (as in `John Smith`), use double quotes within single quotes, like this:

```
'"John Smith"'
```

NIS+ Name Expansion

Entering fully qualified names with your NIS+ commands can quickly become tedious. To ease the task, NIS+ provides a name expansion facility. When you enter a partially qualified name, NIS+ attempts to find the object by looking for it under different directories. It starts by looking in the default domain. This is the home domain of the client from which you enter the command. If it does not find the object in the default domain, NIS+ searches through each of the default domain's parent directories in ascending order until it finds the object. It stops after reaching a name with only two labels. Here are some examples (assume you are logged onto a client that belongs to the Software.Big.Sales.Wiz.Com. domain).

```
mydir ─────────────────▶  mydir.Software.Big.Sales.Wiz.Com.
       expands into        mydir.Big.Sales.Wiz.Com.
                           mydir.Sales.Wiz.Com.
                           mydir.Wiz.Com.


hosts.org_dir ──────────▶  hosts.org_dir.Software.Big.Sales.Wiz.Com.
              expands into  hosts.org_dir.Big.Sales.Wiz.Com.
                           hosts.org_dir.Sales.Wiz.Com.
                           hosts.org_dir.Wiz.Com.
```

The NIS_PATH environment variable

You can change or augment the list of directories through which NIS+ searches by changing the value of the environment variable NIS_PATH. NIS_PATH accepts a list of directory names separated by colons.

```
setenv NIS_PATH directory1:directory2:directory3...
NIS_PATH=directory1:directory2:directory3...;export NIS_PATH
```

NIS+ searches through these directories from left to right. For example:

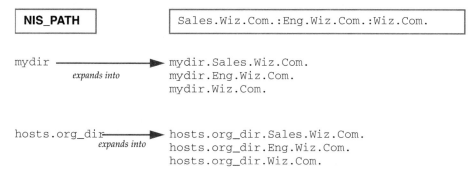

| NIS_PATH | Sales.Wiz.Com.:Eng.Wiz.Com.:Wiz.Com. |

```
mydir ───────────────► mydir.Sales.Wiz.Com.
        expands into    mydir.Eng.Wiz.Com.
                        mydir.Wiz.Com.


hosts.org_dir───────► hosts.org_dir.Sales.Wiz.Com.
        expands into   hosts.org_dir.Eng.Wiz.Com.
                       hosts.org_dir.Wiz.Com.
```

The NIS_PATH variable accepts a special symbol: $. You can append the $ symbol to a directory name or add it by itself. If you append it to a directory name, then NIS+ appends the default directory to that name. For example:

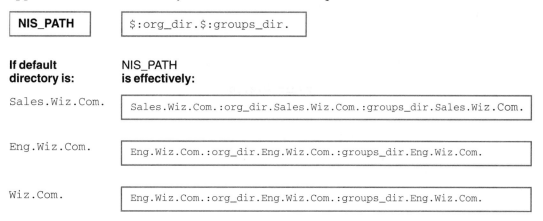

| NIS_PATH | $:org_dir.$:groups_dir. |

If default directory is:	NIS_PATH is effectively:
Sales.Wiz.Com.	Sales.Wiz.Com.:org_dir.Sales.Wiz.Com.:groups_dir.Sales.Wiz.Com.
Eng.Wiz.Com.	Eng.Wiz.Com.:org_dir.Eng.Wiz.Com.:groups_dir.Eng.Wiz.Com.
Wiz.Com.	Eng.Wiz.Com.:org_dir.Eng.Wiz.Com.:groups_dir.Eng.Wiz.Com.

If you use $ by itself (e.g., org_dir.$:$), NIS+ performs the standard name expansion described earlier: start looking in the default directory and proceed through the parent directories. In other words, the default value of NIS_PATH is $.

Understanding NIS+ Tables 3

NIS+ stores a wide variety of network information in tables. This chapter describes the structure of those tables and provides a brief overview of how they can be set up. Appendix A describes the information in each table.

NIS+ Table Structure

NIS+ tables provide several features not found in simple text files or maps. They have a column-entry structure, they accept search paths, they can be linked together, and they can be set up in several different ways. Although NIS+ provides 16 preconfigured system tables (see Table 3-1), you can create your own tables.

Table 3-1   NIS+ Tables

Table	Information in the Table
Hosts	Network address and hostname of every workstation in the domain.
Bootparams	Location of the root, swap, and dump partition of every diskless client in the domain.
Passwd	Password information about every user in the domain.
Cred	Credentials for principals who belong to the domain. (This table is described in Chapter 4, "Understanding NIS+ Security.")

Table 3-1   NIS+ Tables (Continued)

Table	Information in the Table
Group	The group password, group ID, and members of every UNIX group in the domain.
Netgroup	The netgroups to which workstations and users in the domain may belong.
Mail_Aliases	Information about the mail aliases of users in the domain.
Timezone	The time zone of every workstation in the domain.
Networks	The networks in the domain and their canonical names.
Netmasks	The networks in the domain and their associated netmasks.
Ethers	The Ethernet address of every workstation in the domain.
Services	The names of IP services used in the domain and their port numbers.
Protocols	The list of IP protocols used in the domain.
RPC	The RPC program numbers for RPC services available in the domain.
Auto_Home	The location of all users' home directories in the domain.
Auto_Master	Automounter map information.

These tables store a wide variety of information, ranging from user names to Internet services. Most of this information is generated during a setup or configuration procedure. For instance, an entry in the Passwd table is created when a user account is set up; an entry in the Hosts table is created when a workstation is added to the network; an entry in the Networks table is created when a new network is set up.

Since this information is generated from such a wide field of operations, much of it is beyond the scope of this manual. However, as a convenience, Appendix A summarizes the information contained in each column of the tables, providing details only when necessary to avoid confusion, such as when distinguishing groups from NIS+ groups and netgroups. For thorough explanations of the information, consult Solaris 2.3 system and network administration manuals.

The Cred table, because it contains only information related to NIS+ security, is described in Chapter 4, "Understanding NIS+ Security."

Columns and Entries

Although NIS+ tables store different types of information, they all have the same underlying structure; they are each made up of rows and columns (the rows are called "entries," or "entry objects").

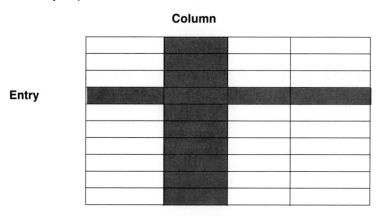

Column

Entry

A client can access information not just by a key, but by any column that is searchable. For example, to find the network address of a workstation named "baseball," a client could look through the hostname column until it found "baseball"—

**Hostname
Column**

		nose		
		grass		
		violin		
		baseball		

—then move along the baseball entry to find its network address.

	Address Column	Hostname Column		
		nose		
		grass		
		violin		
Baseball Row	129.44.1.2	baseball		

Because a client can access table information at the entry and column levels, in addition to the object level (that is, it can access the table as a whole), NIS+ provides security mechanisms for all three levels. For instance, an administrator could assign Read rights to everyone for a table at the object level, Modify rights to the owner at the column level, and Modify rights to the group at the entry level. Details about table security are provided in Chapter 4, "Understanding NIS+ Security."

Search Paths

A table contains information only about its *local* domain. For instance, tables in the Wiz.Com. domain contain information only about the users, clients, and services of the Wiz.Com. domain. The tables in the Sales.Wiz.Com. domain store information only about the users, clients, and services of the Sales.Wiz.Com. domain.

If a client in one domain tries to find information that is stored in another domain, it must provide a fully qualified name. As described in "NIS+ Name Expansion" on page 42, if the NIS_PATH environment variable is set up properly, the NIS+ service will do this automatically.

In addition, though, every NIS+ table can specify a *search path* that a server will follow when looking for information. The search path is simply an ordered list of NIS+ tables, separated by colons.

$$table : table : table \ldots$$

The table names in the search path don't have to be fully qualified; they can be expanded just like names entered in the command line. When a server cannot find information in its local table, it returns the table's search path to the client. The client uses that path to look for the information in every table named in the search path, in order, until it finds the information or runs out of names.

Here is an example that demonstrates the benefit of search paths. Assume the following domain hierarchy:

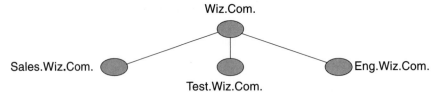

The Hosts tables of the lower three domains have the following contents:

Sales.Wiz.Com.	Test.Wiz.Com.	Eng.Wiz.Com.
127.0.0.1localhost	127.0.0.1localhost	127.0.0.1localhost
129.44.2.10vermont	129.44.4.10nebraska	129.44.3.10georgia
129.44.2.11maine	129.44.4.11oklahoma	129.44.3.11florida
129.44.2.12cherry	129.44.4.12corn	129.44.3.12orange
129.44.2.13apple	129.44.4.13wheat	129.44.3.13potato
129.44.2.14mailhost	129.44.4.14mailhost	129.44.3.14mailhost

Assume now that a user logged in to a client in the Sales.Wiz.Com. domain wants to log in remotely to another client. If that user does not provide a fully qualified name, it can remotely log in to only five workstations: vermont, maine, cherry, apple, and the mailhost.

Now assume that the search path of the Hosts table in the Sales.Wiz.Com. domain listed the Hosts tables from the Test.Wiz.Com. and Eng.Wiz.Com. domains.

    search path—hosts.org_dir.Test.Wiz.Com.:hosts.org_dir.Eng.Wiz.Com.

Now a user in the Sales.Wiz.Com. domain can enter something like rlogin oklahoma, and the NIS+ server will find it. It will first look for oklahoma in the local domain, but when it does not find a match, it will look in the Test.Wiz.Com. domain. How does the client know how to find the Test.Wiz.Com. domain? As described in Chapter 2, "Understanding the NIS+ Namespace," the information is stored in its directory cache. If the information is not stored in its directory cache, the client will obtain the information by following the process described in Chapter 2.

There is a slight drawback, though, to specifying a search path. If the user were to enter an incorrect name, such as rlogin potatoe, the server would need to look through three tables—instead of just one—before returning an error message. If you set up search paths throughout the namespace, an operation may end up searching through the tables in ten domains instead of just two or three. Another drawback is a performance loss from having many clients contact more than one set of servers when they need to access NIS+ tables.

You should also be aware that since "mailhost" is often used as an alias, when trying to find information about a specific mailhost, you should use its fully qualified name (e.g., mailhost.Sales.Wiz.Com.), or NIS+ will return *all* the mailhosts it finds in all the domains it searches through.

You can specify a table's search path by using the -p option to the nistbladm command, as described in Chapter 25, "Administering NIS+ Tables."

Ways to Set Up Tables

The second part of this book provides complete step-by-step instructions for setting up NIS+ tables, but here is an overview of the process. Setting up NIS+ tables involves three or four tasks:

1. Creating the org_dir directory
2. Creating the system tables
3. Creating nonsystem tables (optional)
4. Populating the tables with information

As described in Chapter 2, NIS+ system tables are stored under an org_dir directory. So, before you can create any tables, you must create the org_dir directory that will hold them. You can do this in two ways. You can use the nismkdir command or you can use the /usr/lib/nis/nissetup utility. The nismkdir command, described in Chapter 24, "Administering NIS+ Directories," simply creates the directory. The nissetup utility creates the org_dir and groups_dir directories and a full set of system tables.

The nissetup utility is the recommended way. It is described in the instructions for setting up the root domain and nonroot domains. To use it, follow the instructions either in Chapter 15, "Setting Up the Root Domain," or Chapter 19, "Setting Up a Nonroot Domain."

Another benefit of the nissetup utility is its capability to assign the proper access rights to the tables of a domain whose servers are running in NIS compatibility mode. When entered with the -Y flag, nissetup assigns Read permissions to the "Nobody" category of the objects it creates, allowing NIS clients, who are unauthenticated, to obtain information from the domain's NIS+ tables.

The 16 NIS+ system tables and the type of information they store are described in Appendix A. To create them, you could use the nistbladm command or the nissetup utility. The nistbladm utility creates and modifies NIS+ tables. You could, conceivably, create all the tables in a namespace with the nistbladm command, but you would have to do a lot more typing and you would have to know the correct column names and access rights. A much easier way is to use the nissetup utility.

To create a nonsystem table—that is, a table that has not been preconfigured by NIS+— use the nistbladm command, as described in Chapter 25, "Administering NIS+ Tables."

You can populate NIS+ tables in three ways: from NIS maps, from ASCII files (such as `/etc` files), and manually.

If you are upgrading from the NIS service, you already have most of your network information stored in NIS maps. You don't have to reenter this information manually into NIS+ tables; you can transfer it automatically with the `nisaddent` utility, as described in "How to Populate NIS+ Tables from NIS Maps" on page 239.

If you are not using another network information service but maintain network data in a set of `/etc` files, you don't have to reenter this information either. You can transfer it automatically, also using the `nisaddent` utility, as described in "How to Populate NIS+ Tables from Files" on page 234.

If you are setting up a network for the first time, you may not have much network information stored anywhere. In that case, you'll first need to find the information and then enter it manually into the NIS+ tables. You can do this with the `nistbladm` command, as described in Chapter 25, "Administering NIS+ Tables." You can also do it by entering all the information for a particular table into an *input file*—which is essentially the same as an `/etc` file—and then transferring the contents of the file with the `nisaddent` utility, as described in "How to Populate NIS+ Tables from Files" on page 234.

How Tables Are Updated

When a domain is set up, its servers receive their first versions of the domain's NIS+ tables. These versions are stored on disk, but when a server begins operating, it loads them into memory. When a server receives an update to a table, it immediately updates its memory-based version of the table. When it receives a request for information, it uses the memory-based copy for its reply.

Of course, the server also needs to store its updates on disk. Since updating disk-based tables takes time, all NIS+ servers keep *log files* for their tables. The log files are designed to temporarily store changes made to the table until they can be updated on disk. They use the table name as the prefix and append `.log`. For example:

```
hosts.log
bootparams.log
password.log
```

You should update disk-based copies of a table daily so that the log files don't grow too large and take up too much disk space. This process is called "checkpointing." To update log files, use the `nisping -C` command, described in Chapter 25, "Administering NIS+ Tables."

Understanding NIS+ Security   4

This chapter describes how NIS+ protects its namespace. The first section provides a simplified overview of the security process. More detailed descriptions are provided in the remaining two sections.

Overview of the Security Process

The security features of NIS+ protect the information in the namespace, as well as the structure of the namespace itself, from unauthorized access. Without these security features, any NIS+ client could obtain and change information stored in the namespace or even damage it.[1]

NIS+ security is provided by two means: *authentication* and *authorization*. Authentication is the process by which an NIS+ server identifies the NIS+ *principal* who sent a particular request. Authorization is the process by which a server identifies the access rights granted to that principal.

---

1. You can, of course, operate NIS+ without any security. Simply run the NIS+ servers at security level 0, as described in "About Server Security Levels" on page 56.

About NIS+ Principals

An NIS+ principal is the entity that submits a request for NIS+ service from an NIS+ client.[2] That entity may be someone who is logged in to the client as himself or herself, or it may be someone who is logged in as superuser. In the first instance, the request actually comes from the *client user*; in the second instance, the request comes from the *client workstation*. Therefore, an NIS+ principal can be a client user or a client workstation.

NIS+ principals are identified by their *credentials*. When a user is logged in to an NIS+ client as himself (or herself), his requests for NIS+ service include his *user* credentials.

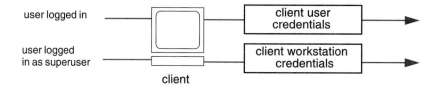

When a user is logged in to an NIS+ client as superuser, his request for service carries with it the *client workstation's* credentials. This distinction is important, since it is possible for a client request to be denied because it is coming from the right NIS+ client, but the wrong NIS+ principal.

NIS+ uses two types of credential: LOCAL and DES. (They are described later in this chapter, under the heading "NIS+ Authentication in Depth.") These credentials *authenticate* the NIS+ principal so that the server can determine whether the principal has been *authorized* to perform the requested operation.

About NIS+ Access Rights

NIS+ objects specify access rights for NIS+ principals in the same way that UNIX files specify permissions for UNIX users. Access rights specify the types of operations that NIS+ principals are allowed to perform on an NIS+ object.

---

2. It can also be the entity that supplies the NIS+ service from an NIS+ server. Keep in mind that all NIS+ servers are also NIS+ clients, so much of this discussion, though focused on clients, also applies to servers.

NIS+ operations vary among different types of objects, but they fall into four classes: Read, Modify, Create, and Destroy.   Every communication from an NIS+ client to an NIS+ server is, in effect, a request to perform one of these operations on a specific NIS+ object. For instance, when an NIS+ principal requests the IP address of another workstation, it is effectively requesting Read access to the Hosts table object, which stores that type of information. When a principal asks the server to add a directory to the NIS+ namespace, it is actually requesting Modify access to the directory's parent object.

NIS+ objects specify their access rights as part of their object definitions. (You can examine these by using the `niscat -o` command, described on page 339.) So, if the operation that a principal tries to perform on an object is *authorized* by the object's definition, the server performs it. If not, the request is denied.

There is one more wrinkle in this process. An object does not grant access rights directly to a particular principal. Instead, it grants access rights to four *classes of principal*: Owner, Group, World, and Nobody. The principal who happens to be the object's owner gets the rights granted to the Owner class. The principals who belong to the object's Group class get the rights granted to the Group[3] class. The World class encompasses all NIS+ principals that a server has been able to authenticate. Finally, the Nobody class is reserved for everyone, whether an authenticated principal or not. (Commands for working with access rights are described in Chapter 23, "Administering NIS+ Access Rights.") Figure 4-1 summarizes the entire process.

---

3. This is an NIS+ group, by the way, not a UNIX group or a netgroup. NIS+ groups are described on page 71.

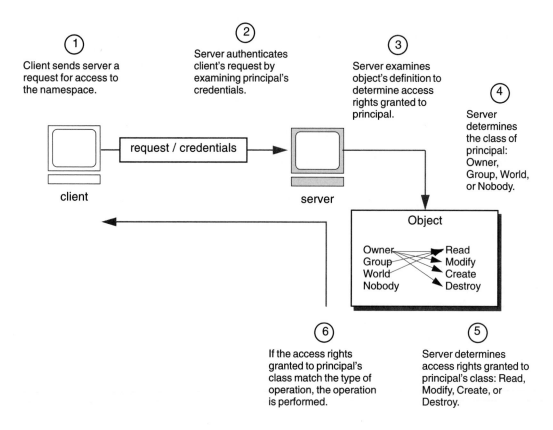

Figure 4-1   Summary of NIS+ Security Process

About Server Security Levels

NIS+ servers can operate at three security levels. These levels determine the types of credential a principal must submit for its request to be authenticated. They are described in Table 4-1.

Table 4-1 NIS+ Server Security Levels

Security Level	Description
0	Security level 0 is designed for testing and setting up the initial NIS+ namespace. An NIS+ server running at security level 0 grants any NIS+ principal full access rights to all NIS+ objects in the domain.

Table 4-1 NIS+ Server Security Levels (Continued)

Security Level	Description
1	Security level 1 is designed only for testing and debugging; in particular, to debug without the complications of DES authentication. Do not use it on networks to which untrusted clients may have access. Security level 1 authenticates requests that use either LOCAL or DES credentials. Requests that don't use any credentials at all are assigned only the access rights granted to the Nobody class.
2	Security level 2, the default, is the highest level of security currently provided by NIS+. It authenticates only requests that use DES credentials. Requests that use LOCAL credentials or none at all are assigned the access rights granted to the Nobody class. Requests that use invalid DES credentials are denied.

A Note About Setting Up NIS+ Security

Security cannot be added to an existing namespace. You cannot set up security and the namespace independently. For this reason, instructions for setting up security are woven through the steps used to set up the other components of the namespace, as described in Part 2 of this book.

NIS+ Authentication in Depth

Authentication is the mechanism used by an NIS+ server to verify the credentials of the NIS+ principal that has sent a request for NIS+ service. To explain the authentication mechanism, this section discusses the following topics:

- Types of credential
- Where credentials are stored
- How credential information is created by the administrator
- How credentials are created by the client
- How credentials are examined by the server
- The cached public keys

Types of Credential

NIS+ principals can have two types of credential: LOCAL and DES. A client user can have both types, but a client workstation can only have a DES credential.

Type of Credential	Client User	Client Workstation
LOCAL	YES	NO
DES	YES	YES

DES credential information can be stored only in the Cred table of the principal's home domain, regardless of whether that principal is a client user or a client workstation. LOCAL credentials, however, can be stored in any domain. In fact, in order to log in to a remote domain, a client user *must* store her LOCAL credentials in the Cred table of the remote domain.

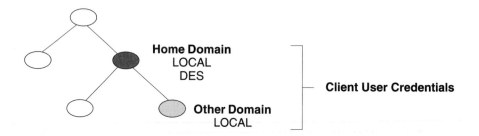

A LOCAL credential is simply the UID of an NIS+ principal. Since the UID of every workstation is zero, a LOCAL credential doesn't make sense for a client *workstation*; thus, it is allowed only for a client *user*.

A DES credential is more complex than a LOCAL credential, not only because of the information it requires, but because of the process involved in creating and verifying it. To understand how DES authentication works, you need to distinguish between the credential itself and the information that is used to create and verify it. To keep our terminology straight, we'll reserve the term *credential* for the former and use the term *credential information* for the latter. Thus, the credential is the magic bundle of numbers that is sent by the client to the server; the credential information is the data that is stored in the Cred table used by the client to generate the credential, and used by the server to verify the credential.

The DES credential itself consists of a principal's *secure RPC netname* plus a *verification* field.

DES Credential

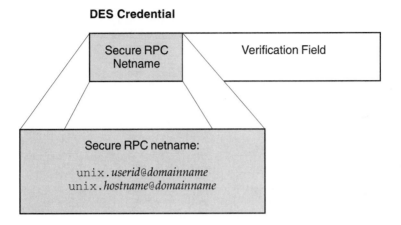

The secure RPC netname portion of the credential is the part used to actually identify the NIS+ principal. Every secure RPC netname begins with the prefix "`unix.`" If the principal is a client user, the second field in the netname is the user's UID. If the principal is a client workstation, the second field in the netname is the workstation's hostname. The last field is the principal's home domain.

If the Principal Is	The Domain Must Be
A client user	The domain that contains the user's password entry and DES credentials.
A client workstation	The domain name returned by executing the `domainname` command on that workstation.

A reminder about naming conventions: An NIS+ principal name *always* has a trailing dot, while a secure RPC netname *never* does.

The verification field of the credential is used to make sure the credential is not forged. It is generated from the *credential information* stored in the Cred table. This process is described later, in the sections titled "How Credential Information Is Created by the Administrator" and "How Credentials Are Created by the Client."

Where Credentials Are Stored

NIS+ credentials are stored in a *Cred* table. The Cred table is one of the 16 default NIS+ tables. Each domain has one Cred table, which stores the credentials of client workstations that belong to that domain and client users who are allowed to log in to them. The Cred tables are located in their domains' `org_dir` subdirectory.

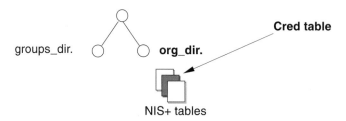

(You can view the contents of a Cred table with the `niscat` command, described in Chapter 25, "Administering NIS+ Tables.")

The Cred table has five columns:

NIS+ Principal Name	Authentication Type	Authentication Name	Public Data	Private Data
NIS+ principal name of a client user	LOCAL	UID	GID list	None
NIS+ principal name of a client user or client workstation	DES	Secure RPC netname	Public key	Encrypted private key

The second column, Authentication Type, determines the types of values found in the other four columns. If the authentication type is LOCAL, the other columns contain a client user's NIS+ principal name, UID, and GID; the last column is empty. If the authentication type is DES, the other columns contain an NIS+ principal's name, secure RPC netname, public key, and encrypted private key. These keys are used in conjunction with other information to encrypt and decrypt a DES credential, as described later in this section.

How Credential Information Is Created by the Administrator

Credentials for NIS+ principals can be created any time after their domain has been set up; in other words, once a Cred table exists. When a namespace is first set up, credentials are created first for the administrators who will support the domain. Once they have credentials, they can create credentials for other administrators, client workstations, and client users. Step-by-step instructions for creating NIS+ credentials are distributed throughout Part 2 and Part 3 of this manual. Here is a summary:

Chapter	Task/Step	See
Chapter 15	▼ How to Set Up the Root Domain	
	Step 10. Create DES credentials for the root master server.	page 225
	Step 16. Add your LOCAL credentials to the root domain.	page 229
	Step 17. Add your DES credentials to the root domain.	page 229
	Step 18. Add credentials for other administrators.	page 230
Chapter 17	▼ How to Set Up an NIS+ Client	
	Step 2. Create DES credentials for the new client workstation.	page 256
Chapter 19	▼ How to Set Up a Nonroot Domain	
	Step 8. Add credentials for other administrators.	page 281
Chapter 22	▼ How to Create Credentials for an NIS+ Principal	page 307

You could add credentials to your namespace simply by following the instructions listed above. However, understanding the process by which credentials are used may help you uncover mistakes in the setup process or troubleshoot problems that could arise later.

In all instances, the command used to create credentials is `nisaddcred`. (It is described completely in Chapter 22, "Administering NIS+ Credentials.") The `nisaddcred` command creates either LOCAL credentials or DES credential information.

When used to create LOCAL credentials, the command simply extracts the client user's UID (and GID) from the client's login record and places it in the domain's Cred table.

When used to create DES credential information, the command goes through a two-part process: forming the principal's secure RPC netname and generating the principal's private and public keys. Forming a secure RPC netname is easy; `nisaddcred` simply obtains the principal's userid from the password record, constructs a netname, and places it in the domain's Cred table. Generating the private and public keys takes a little more work.

To generate the private key, `nisaddcred` needs the principal's network password. So, when the `nisaddcred` command is invoked with the `des` argument, it prompts the principal for a network password. Normally, this password *is the same as the principal's login password.*[4] From this password the `nisaddcred` command generates a pair of random, but mathematically related, 192-bit authentication keys, using the Diffie-Hellman cryptography scheme. These keys are called the Diffie-Hellman key-pair, or simply "key-pair" for short.

One of these is the private key, the other is the public key. The public key is placed in the "Public Data" field of the Cred table. The private key is placed in the "Private Data" field, but only after being encrypted with the principal's network password.

nisaddcred

The principal's private key is encrypted as a security precaution because the Cred table, by default, is readable by all NIS+ principals, even unauthenticated ones.

How Credentials Are Created by the Client

When an NIS+ client sends a request to an NIS+ server, it does not know the security level at which the server is running, so it first sends along its DES credential. (This is the actual credential, not just the credential information.) If the DES credential fails because either the client or the server does not have the proper keys, the client tries a LOCAL credential. If the LOCAL credential fails, the client attempts again, without credentials, trying to qualify for the Nobody class.

---

4. If it is different, additional steps are required, as described on page 64.

To generate its DES credential, the client depends on the `keylogin` command, which must have been executed before the client tries to generate its credential. The `keylogin` command (often referred to simply as a "keylogin") is executed automatically by the client when an NIS+ principal logs in.[5] The purpose of the keylogin is to give the client access to its private key. The keylogin fetches the principal's private key from the Cred table, decrypts it with the principal's *network* password (remember that the private key was originally encrypted with the principal's network password), and stores it locally for future NIS+ requests.

`keylogin`

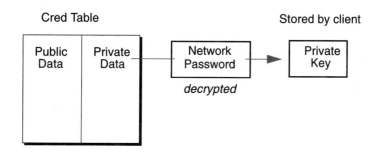

To generate its DES credential, the client still needs the public key of the server to which it will send the request. This information is stored in the client's directory cache (see "The Coldstart File and Directory Cache" on page 32). Once the client has this information, it can form the verification field of the credential. That is a complex process, but here is a simplified explanation.

First, the client uses its own private key and the server's public key to generate the DES key. It also generates a timestamp. It then encrypts the timestamp with the DES key and combines it with other credential-related information into the verification field.

---

5. It is not performed automatically if the client's login password is different from its network password.

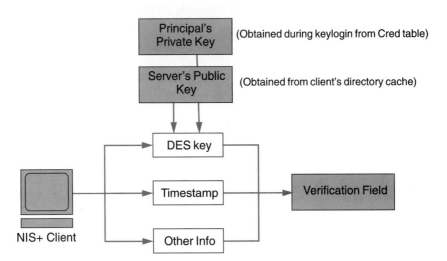

Principal's Private Key — (Obtained during keylogin from Cred table)

Server's Public Key — (Obtained from client's directory cache)

DES key

NIS+ Client

Timestamp

Other Info

Verification Field

To understand how a server examines these credentials, see "How Credentials Are Examined by the Server" on page 66.

If the Network Password Is Different from the Login Password

A principal's network password is usually the same as its login password, as mentioned earlier. They can, however, be different. If so, the following happens.

When the principal logs in to the client, the client attempts an automatic keylogin, as usual. In other words, the client fetches the principal's private key from the Cred table, decrypting it with the principal's login password. However, when the credential information was first stored in the Cred table, the private key was *encrypted* with the principal's *network* password. As a result, the private key cannot be decrypted by the client and cannot be used for authentication.

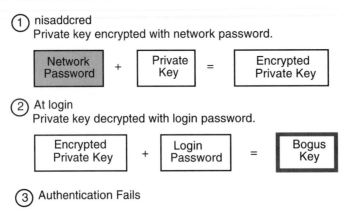

(1) nisaddcred
Private key encrypted with network password.

Network Password + Private Key = Encrypted Private Key

(2) At login
Private key decrypted with login password.

Encrypted Private Key + Login Password = Bogus Key

(3) Authentication Fails

To solve this problem, the NIS+ principal must give the NIS+ client a network password after he or she logs in. This procedure requires an explicit *keylogin*. In general, a principal must perform a keylogin any time he or she changes credentials. In this particular case, it should be after providing the `nisaddcred` command a network password that is different from the login password.

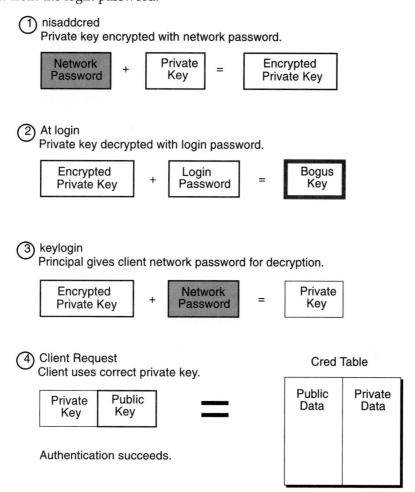

① nisaddcred
Private key encrypted with network password.

| Network Password | + | Private Key | = | Encrypted Private Key |

② At login
Private key decrypted with login password.

| Encrypted Private Key | + | Login Password | = | Bogus Key |

③ keylogin
Principal gives client network password for decryption.

| Encrypted Private Key | + | Network Password | = | Private Key |

④ Client Request
Client uses correct private key.

Cred Table

| Private Key | Public Key | = | Public Data | Private Data |

Authentication succeeds.

Instructions for performing a keylogin are provided on page 319.

How Credentials Are Examined by the Server

To decrypt the DES credential, the server essentially reverses the encryption process performed by the client. First, the server uses the secure RPC netname portion of the credential to look up the principal's public key in the Cred table. Then, using its own private key (keep in mind that servers, because they are also clients, have credentials too) and the principal's public key, it decrypts the DES key. Then it uses the DES key to decrypt the timestamp. If the timestamp is within a predetermined tolerance of the time the server received the message, the server authenticates the request.

This process satisfies the server. However, to let the client know that the information it receives indeed comes from a trusted server, the server encrypts the timestamp with the DES key and sends it back to the client.

LOCAL credentials are not verified. Instead, the NIS+ server gets the NIS+ principal name of the principal who sent the request by looking up the principal's UID in the third column of the Cred table.

The Cached Public Keys

Occasionally, you may find that even though you have created the proper credentials and assigned the proper access rights, some client requests are still denied. The most common cause of this problem is the existence of stale objects with old versions of a server's public key. You can usually correct this problem by running `nisupdkeys`, described on page 316, on the domain you are trying to access. The `nisupdkeys` command does just that. However, because some keys are stored in files or caches, `nisupdkeys` cannot always correct the problem. At times you might need to update the keys manually. To do that, you'll need to understand how a server's public key, once created, is propagated through namespace objects. The process generally has five stages of propagation:

- Stage 1—Server's public key is generated
- Stage 2—Public key is propagated to directory objects
- Stage 3—Directory objects are propagated into client files
- Stage 4—Public key is stored in replica's Cred table
- Stage 5—The server's public key is changed

Each stage is described below.

Stage 1—Server's public key is generated

An NIS+ server is first an NIS+ client. So, its public key is generated in the same way as any other NIS+ client's public key—with the `nisaddcred` command.

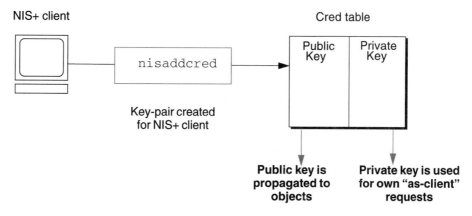

NIS+ client

Cred table

nisaddcred

Key-pair created
for NIS+ client

| Public Key | Private Key |

Public key is propagated to objects

Private key is used for own "as-client" requests

The public key is stored in the Cred table of the server's home domain, not in the table of the domain that the server will eventually support.

Stage 2—Public key is propagated to directory objects

Once you have set up an NIS+ domain and an NIS+ server, you can associate the server with a domain. This association is performed by the nismkdir command. When the nismkdir command associates the server with the directory, it also copies the server's public key from the Cred table to the domain's directory object. For example, assume the server is a client of the Wiz.Com. root domain and is made the master server of the Sales.Wiz.Com. domain.

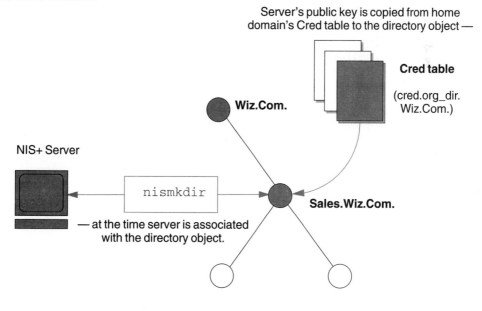

Server's public key is copied from home domain's Cred table to the directory object —

Cred table

(cred.org_dir. Wiz.Com.)

Wiz.Com.

NIS+ Server

nismkdir

Sales.Wiz.Com.

— at the time server is associated with the directory object.

Its public key is copied from the cred.org_dir.Wiz.Com. domain and placed in the Sales.Wiz.Com. directory object.

Stage 3—Directory objects are propagated into client files

All NIS+ clients are initialized with the `nisinit` utility, as described in Chapter 17, "Setting Up an NIS+ Client." Among other things, this utility creates a coldstart file, which it stores in the client's `/var/nis` directory. The coldstart file initializes the client's directory cache, a file that is also stored in `/var/nis`, by the name `NIS_SHARED_DIRCACHE`. The coldstart file contains a copy of the directory object of the client's domain. Since the directory object already contains a copy of the server's public key, the key is now propagated into the coldstart file of the client.

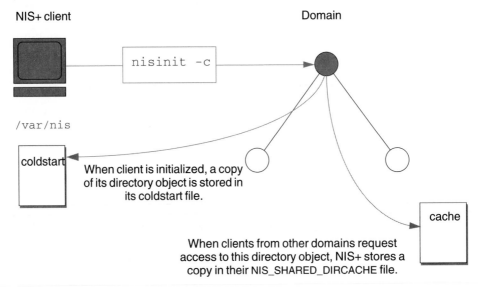

In addition, when a client makes a request to a server outside its home domain, a copy of the remote domains directory object is stored in the client's `NIS_SHARED_DIRCACHE` file. You can examine the contents of the client's cache by using the `nisshowcache` command, described on page 349. There is no NIS+ command that examines the contents of the coldstart file.

This is the extent of the propagation until a replica is added to the domain or until the server's key changes.

Stage 4—Public key is stored in replica's Cred table

When a replica server is added to a domain, the `nisping` command (described on page 350) is used to download the NIS+ tables, including the Cred table, to the new replica. Therefore, the original server's public key is now also stored in the replica server's Cred table.

Stage 5—The server's public key is changed

If, for any reason, you decide to create new DES credentials for the server (i.e., for the root identity on the server), its public key will change. As a result, the public key stored for that server in the Cred table will be different from those stored in the following locations:

- The Cred table of replica servers (for a few minutes only)

- The main directory object of the domain supported by the server (until its time to live expires)

- The `NIS_COLD_START` and `NIS_SHARED_DIRCACHE` files of every client of the domain supported by the server (until their time to live expires, usually 12 hours)

- The `NIS_SHARED_DIRCACHE` file of clients who have made requests to the domain supported by the server (until their time to live expires)

As indicated above, most of these locations will be updated automatically within a time ranging from a few minutes to 12 hours. To update the server's keys in these locations immediately, use the following commands:

Location	Command	See
Cred table of replica servers (instead of using `nisping`, you can wait a few minutes until the table is updated automatically)	`nisping`	page 350
Directory object of domain supported by server	`nisupdkeys`	page 316
`NIS_COLD_START` file of clients	`nisinit -H`	page 347
`NIS_SHARED_CACHE` file of clients	`niscachemgr`[a]	page 349

a. First kill the cache manager, then restart it with `niscachemgr`.

NIS+ Authorization in Depth

Access rights specify the type of operation that NIS+ principals, both authenticated and unauthenticated, can perform on an NIS+ object. Table 4-2 summarizes the four types of NIS+ access rights.

Table 4-2 NIS+ Access Rights

Access Right	Description
Read	Principal can read the contents of the object.
Modify	Principal can modify the contents of the object.
Destroy	Principal can destroy objects in a table or directory.
Create	Principal can create new objects in a table or directory.

These rights are granted by each object, not to a particular NIS+ principal, but to four different classes of NIS+ principal. These are called *authorization classes*.

Authorization Categories

To assign access rights, every NIS+ object uses four authorization classes: Owner, Group, World, and Nobody. An object can grant any number of access rights to each of these classes. For instance, an object could grant Read access to the World class, but Modify access only to the Group and Owner. Thus, any NIS+ principal that belonged to the World class could read the object, but only the NIS+ principals that belong to the Group and Owner class could modify the object. Each class is described below.

The object's Owner

The Owner is a single NIS+ principal. By default, an object's owner is the principal that created the object. However, an object's owner can cede ownership to another principal in two ways. One way is for the principal to specify a different owner at the time it creates the object (see "How to Override Defaults" on page 328). Another way is for the principal to change the ownership of the object after the object is created (see "nischown" on page 333).

Once a principal gives up ownership, it gives up all owner's access rights to the object and keeps only the rights the object assigns to either the Group, the World, or Nobody.

The object's Group

The object's Group is a single NIS+ group. An NIS+ group is simply a collection of NIS+ principals, grouped as a convenience for providing access to the namespace. The access rights granted to an NIS+ group apply to all the principals that are members of that group. By default, when an object is created, it is assigned the NIS+ principal's default group. (An object's Owner, however, does not need to belong to the object's Group.)

Information about NIS+ groups is *not* stored in the NIS+ Group table. That table stores information about UNIX groups. Information about NIS+ groups is stored in NIS+ group *objects*, under the `groups_dir` subdirectory of every NIS+ domain.

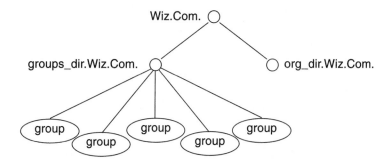

Instructions for administering NIS+ groups are provided in Chapter 21.

The World

The World is the class of all NIS+ principals that are authenticated by NIS+. Access rights granted to the World apply to all authenticated principals.

Nobody

Nobody is a class reserved for unauthenticated requests; that is, requests with no credentials. However, it does not apply to requests with invalid credentials. Requests that provide invalid credentials are not assigned the Nobody class; they are denied.

Where Access Rights Are Stored

An object's access rights are specified in its definition. (Note that this information is part of the object's *definition*; it is *not* an NIS+ table.)

Object's Owner	Object's Group Owner	Access Rights: Owner	Access Rights: Group	Access Rights: World	Access Rights: Nobody
The NIS+ principal that created the object or that was assigned ownership by the nischown command.	The NIS+ group owner of the object.	The access rights granted to the object owner.	The access rights granted to the principals in the object's group.	The access rights granted to any authenticated NIS+ principal.	The access rights granted to everyone, whether authenticated or not.

Access rights are displayed as a list of 16 characters, like this:

```
r---rmcdr---r---
```

Each character represents a type of access right. Thus, "r" represents Read, "m" represents Modify, "c" represents Create, "d" represents Destroy, and "-" represents no access rights. The first four characters represent the access rights granted to Nobody, the next four to the Owner, the next four to the Group, and the last four to the World.

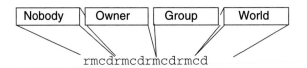

Note – Unlike UNIX filesystems, the first set of rights is for Nobody, not for the Owner.

How Access Rights Are Assigned

When you create an object, NIS+ assigns the object a default owner, group, and set of access rights. The default owner is the NIS+ principal who creates the object. The default group is the group named in the NIS_GROUP environment variable. Table 4-3 lists the default set of access rights.

Table 4-3 NIS+ Default Access Types

Nobody	Owner	Group	World
-	Read	Read	Read
-	Modify	-	-
-	Create	-	-
-	Destroy	-	-

NIS+ provides several different ways to change these default rights. The first is the NIS_DEFAULTS environment variable. That variable stores a set of security-related default values, one of which is access rights. The defaults stored in the NIS_DEFAULTS variable are assigned to every object that is created while they are in effect. If the value of this variable is changed on a particular client, any object created from that client will be assigned the new values. However, previously created objects will not be affected. Instructions for changing the NIS_DEFAULTS variable are provided in the section titled "How to Change Defaults" on page 327.

A second way to affect access rights is with the -D option that is available with several NIS+ commands. The -D option specifies the default values that will be applied to all the objects acted upon by the command. In other words, it overrides the default values stored by the NIS_DEFAULTS variable, but only for the object affected by that particular instance of the command. For instructions, see "How to Override Defaults" on page 328.

The third way is to explicitly change an object's access rights (or other security defaults), using one of the NIS+ commands designed for that purpose, such as nischmod. Instructions are provided in Chapter 23, "Administering NIS+ Access Rights."

NIS+ tables provide additional levels of security not provided by other types of NIS+ objects. As described in Chapter 3, information in an NIS+ table can be accessed by column or entry.

Column

Entry

In addition to the rights that can be assigned to the table as a whole, NIS+ allows you to assign access rights to the columns and entries of a table. Those rights can provide *additional* access, but they cannot restrict the access provided by the table as a whole. For instance, if the table provided Read rights to the World class, a column could give the World class Modify rights, but it could not restrict Read access to only the Owner or the Group.[6]

A column or entry can provide additional access in two ways: by extending the rights to additional principals or by providing additional rights to the same principals. Of course, both ways can be combined. Following are a couple of examples.

Assume a table object granted Read rights to the table's Owner.

```
                               Nobody   Owner    Group    World
      Table Access Rights  :   ----     r---     ----     ----
```

This would mean that only the table's owner could read the contents of the entire table. A principal who is not the owner would have no access. However, a particular entry in the table could also grant Read rights to the Group class.

```
                               Nobody   Owner    Group    World
      Table Access Rights  :   ----     r---     ----     ----
      Entry1 Access Rights :   ----     ----     r---     ----
```

---

6. Actually, it could assign Read rights to the Owner or the Group, but since the table already provides them to the World, the rights assigned by the column would have no effect on those assigned by the table object.

Although only the owner could read all the contents of the table, any member of the table's group could read the contents of that particular entry. Now, assume that a particular column granted Read rights to the World class.

```
                              Nobody   Owner    Group    World
     Table Access Rights   :  ----     r---     ----     ----
     Entry1 Access Rights  :  ----     ----     r---     ----
     Column1 Access Rights :  ----     ----     ----     r---
```

Members of the World class could now read that column *for all entries* in the table. Here is a representation of what would be displayed to members of the World class who tried to read the table (*NP* means "No Permission").

	Col 1	Col 2	Col 3
Entry 1	contents	*NP*	*NP*
Entry 2	contents	*NP*	*NP*
Entry 3	contents	*NP*	*NP*
Entry 4	contents	*NP*	*NP*
Entry 5	contents	*NP*	*NP*
Entry 6	contents	*NP*	*NP*
Entry 7	contents	*NP*	*NP*

Here is another example. Assume a table assigned Read rights to the Group.

```
                              Nobody   Owner    Group    World
     Table Access Rights   :  ----     ----     r---     ----
```

Any member of the group could read the contents of the entire table, but could not create, modify, or destroy them. However, a particular entry could assign the group Modify rights.

```
                              Nobody   Owner    Group    World
     Table Access Rights   :  ----     ----     r---     ----
     Entry1 Access Rights  :  ----     ----     -m--     ----
```

Members of the *entry*'s group could now modify the contents of the *entry*. However, they could still not destroy the entry. However, if a particular column assigned Create and Destroy rights to the Group—

```
                              Nobody   Owner    Group    World
     Table Access Rights   :  ----     ----     r---     ----
     Entry1 Access Rights  :  ----     ----     -m--     ----
     Col1 Access Rights    :  ----     ----     --cd     ----
```

—every member of an entry's group could create or destroy information about the entry as long as it was contained in that column.

How a Server Grants Access Rights to Tables

This process has already been described for access rights at the object level (see "Overview of the Security Process," starting on page 53). However, because of the overlapping rights of table objects, columns, and entries, it is worthwhile to go over how a server grants access to tables objects, entries, and columns during each type of operation: read, modify, destroy, and create.

Note, however, that at security level 0, a server enforces no access rights and all clients are granted full access rights to the table object.

As described earlier, after authenticating a request, an NIS+ server determines the type of operation and the object of the request. If that object is a directory or group, the server simply examines the object's definition and grants the request, provided the object has assigned the proper rights to the principal.   However, if the object is a table, the server follows a more involved process. The process varies somewhat depending on the operation, but it follows this general rule of thumb:

First, check rights at the table level.

Then, at the entry level.

Then, at the column level.

Following are detailed examples of the process involved in each type of operation. While going through them, keep in mind the four factors that a server must consider when deciding whether to grant access:

1.	The type of operation requested by the principal
2.	The table, entry, or column the principal is trying to access
3.	The authorization class the principal belongs to for that particular object
4.	The access rights that the table, entry, or column has assigned to the principal's authorization class

Granting access to read or modify a table

When a principal requests to read or modify the contents of a table (for example, by issuing the `niscat` or `nistbladm` command), an NIS+ server employs the following logic to grant access to the principal. For this example, assume that the principal is a member of the *group* named in the table's group authorization class and is trying to *read* or *modify* the entire table.

The server first checks the table object's rights. If the table grants Read access to the group, the principal is allowed to read all the contents of the table, and the server does not proceed to check rights of columns or entries. (The shaded boxes represent the columns and entries that the principal is allowed to read.)

Rights to Entire Table Granted to Group: READ				
	Col 1	Col 2	Col 3	Col 4
Entry 1				
Entry 2				
Entry 3				
Entry 4				
Entry 5				
Entry 6				
Entry 7				

If the table object does not grant Read access to the group, the server checks the access rights granted by the table entries the principal is trying to access.

If any of those entries grants its group Read rights and if the principal belongs to that group (which may be different from the table's group), the server allows the principal to read that entry's contents. Then it checks the rights granted by the next entry. (The shaded rows below represent the entries that have given the group Read rights.)

	Rights	Col 1	Col 2	Col 3	Col 4
Entry 1	READ				
Entry 2					
Entry 3	READ				
Entry 4					
Entry 5	READ				
Entry 6	READ				
Entry 7					

The server proceeds to check column rights only if none of the entries the principal has tried to access has granted the group Read rights.

If a server finds that no columns in the table have granted their group Read rights, it returns an error message stating that the principal does not have permission to access the object. However, if any column grants its group Read rights and if the principal belongs to that group (which may also be different from the table or even the entries' group), the server displays *the entries that specify the same group* but censors the columns that do not grant their group Read rights. Censored columns display the string *NP* (for "No Permission").

If all entries specified the same group, this would be displayed:

	Col 1	Col 2	Col 3	Col 4
Entry 1	READ	*NP*	READ	*NP*
Entry 2	READ	*NP*	READ	*NP*
Entry 3	READ	*NP*	READ	*NP*
Entry 4	READ	*NP*	READ	*NP*
Entry 5	READ	*NP*	READ	*NP*
Entry 6	READ	*NP*	READ	*NP*
Entry 7	READ	*NP*	READ	*NP*

However, if only some entries (e.g., 1, 3, 4, and 7) specified the same group, this would be displayed:

	Col 1	Col 2	Col 3	Col 4
Entry 1	READ	*NP*	READ	*NP*
Entry 2		*NP*		*NP*
Entry 3	READ	*NP*	READ	*NP*
Entry 4	READ	*NP*	READ	*NP*
Entry 5		*NP*		*NP*
Entry 6		*NP*		*NP*
Entry 7	READ	*NP*	READ	*NP*

Granting access to destroy table entries

When a principal requests to delete a table, the server checks the access rights granted to the principal by the table's `org_dir` directory. However, when a principal requests to delete a table entry, the server employs the following logic. Assume that the principal is a member of the group named in the table's group authorization class and that the principal is trying to delete entries 1 and 5.

If the table object grants its group Destroy rights, the principal is allowed to remove any entry from the table (columns cannot be removed). The server checks no further. If the table object does not grant the group Destroy rights, the server checks access rights at the entry level.

At the entry level, the server only checks the rights of the entries that the principal is trying to destroy; that is, 1 and 5. If one of those entries grants its group Destroy rights, and if the principal belongs to that group, the principal is allowed to delete that entry. If one of those entries does not grant the group Destroy rights, or if the principal does not belong to the entry's group authorization class, the principal is not allowed to delete the entry.

If no entries grant their group Destroy rights, an error message is returned, stating that the principal does not have permission to access the object.

Since no columns can be deleted from a table, the server does not check column access rights during a Destroy operation.

Granting access to create table entries

When a principal tries to create a table, the server checks the access rights granted to the principal by the `org_dir` directory under which the table will be created. However, when a principal tries to add new table entries to an existing table, the server employs the following logic. For this example, assume that the principal is a member of the group named in the table's group authorization class and that the principal is trying to add entries 8 and 9.

If the table object grants its group Create rights, the principal is allowed to add entries to the table (columns cannot be added). The server checks no further. However, if the object does not grant its group Create rights, the server checks whether the entry that the principal is trying to create already exists.

If the entry indeed exists, the server checks whether the table object has granted its group Modify rights. If it has, the server replaces the existing entry with the new one and checks no further. If the table has *not* granted its group Modify rights, the server checks rights at the entry level.

At the entry level, the server checks not whether the entry has granted the group Create rights but whether it has granted the group *Modify* rights. If the entry has granted Modify rights to its group and if the principal is a member of that group (which may not be the same as the table object's group), the server replaces the existing entry with the new one, and no further checking is done.

If the entry has not granted Modify rights to its group or if the principal is not a member of that group, an error message is returned, stating that the principal does not have permission to modify the object.

Since no columns can be added to a table, the server does not check column access rights during a Create operation.

Understanding the Name Service
Switch 5 ☰

The Name Service Switch, referred to as the "Switch," is not really part of NIS+, but it allows NIS+ clients (actually, clients of getXXbyYY() routines) to obtain their network information from one or more of these sources: NIS+ tables, NIS maps, the DNS Hosts table, and local /etc files. This chapter describes the Switch and what it can do. It has four sections:

About the Name Service Switch

An NIS+ client can obtain its information from one or more of the Switch's sources in place of, or in addition to, NIS+ tables. For example, an NIS+ client could obtain its hosts information from an NIS+ table, its group information from NIS maps, and its password information from a local /etc file. Plus, it could specify the conditions under which the Switch must use each source (see "Search Criteria" on page 83).

These choices are specified in a special configuration file called `nsswitch.conf`. This file is automatically loaded into every workstation's `/etc` directory by Solaris 2.3, along with three alternate versions:

- `/etc/nsswitch.nisplus`
- `/etc/nsswitch.nis`
- `/etc/nsswitch.files`

These alternate files contain the default Switch configurations used by the NIS+ service, NIS, and local files. (They are described later in this section.) No default file is provided for DNS, but you can edit any of these files to use DNS, as described in Chapter 20, "Setting Up the Name Service Switch."

When Solaris 2.3 is first installed on a workstation, the installer must select the workstation's default naming service: NIS+, NIS, or local files. During the installation itself, the corresponding configuration file is copied into the `/etc/nsswitch.conf` file.

You can change the sources of information used by an NIS+ client by creating your own customized configuration file and copying it over `/etc/nsswitch.conf`. Its syntax is described below, and instructions are provided in Chapter 20.

Format of the nsswitch.conf File

The `nsswitch.conf` file is essentially a list of 15 types of information and their sources, not necessarily in this order:

```
aliases:                    source(s)
bootparams:                 source(s)
ethers:                     source(s)
group:                      source(s)
hosts:                      source(s)
netgroup:                   source(s)
netmasks:                   source(s)
networks:                   source(s)
passwd: (includes shadow)   source(s)
protocols:                  source(s)
publickey:                  source
rpc:                        source(s)
services:                   source(s)

automount:                  source(s)

sendmailvars                source(s)
```

The information for the Auto_Home and Auto_Master tables is combined into one category, called "automount." The Timezone table does not use the Switch, so it is not included in the list.

A source can be any of the following:

Source	Description
files	A local file stored in the client's /etc directory (e.g., /etc/passwd
nisplus	An NIS+ table
nis	An NIS map
compat	Only for the Password and Group entries, supports the old-style "+" or "-" syntax in the /etc/passwd, /etc/shadow, and /etc/group files
dns	DNS, but only for the hosts entry

If an information type has only one source, the switch searches for the information in that source only. (If it does not find the information, it stops searching and returns a status message.[1])

If a table has more than one source, the Switch starts by searching for the information in the first source. If it does not find the information there, it tries the next source. It continues searching through the sources until it has tried them all.

If it still does not find the information, it stops searching and returns a status message. However, the Switch allows you to specify a different action, such as continuing to search for the information. This specification is done with *search criteria*.

Search Criteria

The Switch searches through the sources one at a time. If it finds the information it is looking for in the first source, it returns a successful status message and passes the information to the library routine that asked for it. If it does *not* find the information, it returns one of three unsuccessful status messages, depending on the reason for not finding the information, and moves to the next source.

---

1. That message is passed to the library routine that requested the information. What the routine does with the status message varies.

The four possible status messages are:

Status	Meaning
SUCCESS	The requested entry was found in the source.
UNAVAIL	The source is not responding or is unavailable.
NOTFOUND	The source responded with "No such entry."
TRYAGAIN	The source is busy; it might respond next time.

You can instruct the Switch to respond to status messages with either of these two actions:

Action	Meaning
return	Stop looking for the information.
continue	Try the next source, if there is one.

Default search criteria

The Switch's default search criteria are the same for every source. Described in terms of the status messages listed above, they are:

```
SUCCESS=return
UNAVAIL=continue
NOTFOUND=continue
TRYAGAIN=continue
```

You can change the default search criteria for any source, using the STATUS=action syntax shown above. Here is an example:

```
hosts:     nis
networks:  nis [NOTFOUND=return] files
protocols: nis [NOTFOUND=return] files
```

In the second line of the example above, when the switch searches for information in NIS maps and gets a NOTFOUND status message, instead of searching through the second source, it stops looking. It would search through files only if the NIS service were unavailable.

What if the syntax is wrong?

Client library routines contain compiled-in default entries that are used if an entry in the `nsswitch.conf` file is either missing or syntactically incorrect. These entries are the same as the default `nsswitch.conf` file.

The Name Service Switch assumes that the spelling of table and source names is correct. If you misspell a table or source name, the Switch uses the default values instead.

The default nsswitch.conf file

The default `nsswitch.conf` file shipped with Solaris 2.3 is actually a copy of the `nsswitch.nis` file, described below. You can change it to the NIS+ version by copying the `nsswitch.nisplus` file over the `/etc/nswitch.conf` file, as described in Chapter 20.

The Switch provides three alternate configuration files in addition to the default `/etc/nsswitch.conf` file. Each is described below.

The nsswitch.nisplus File

The `nsswitch.nisplus` configuration file specifies NIS+ as the primary source for all information except passwd, group, automount, and aliases. For those files, the primary source is local `/etc` files and the secondary source is an NIS+ table. The `[NOTFOUND=return]` search criterion instructs the Switch to stop searching the NIS+ tables if it receives a "No such entry" message from them. It searches through local files only if the NIS+ server is unavailable.

Here is a copy of the `nsswitch.nisplus` file with all the comments stripped out:

```
passwd:      files nisplus
group:       files nisplus

hosts:       nisplus [NOTFOUND=return]  files
services:    nisplus [NOTFOUND=return]  files
networks:    nisplus [NOTFOUND=return]  files
protocols:   nisplus [NOTFOUND=return]  files
rpc:         nisplus [NOTFOUND=return]  files
ethers:      nisplus [NOTFOUND=return]  files
netmasks:    nisplus [NOTFOUND=return]  files
bootparams:  nisplus [NOTFOUND=return]  files

publickey:   nisplus

netgroup:    nisplus

automount:   files nisplus
aliases:     files nisplus
```

DNS Forwarding for NIS+ Clients

NIS+ clients do *not* have implicit DNS-forwarding capabilities like NIS clients do. Instead, they take advantage of the Switch. To provide DNS-forwarding capabilities to an NIS+ client, change its hosts entry to:

```
hosts:   nisplus dns [NOTFOUND=return]  files
```

The nsswitch.nis File

The `nsswitch.nis` configuration file is almost identical to the NIS+ configuration file, except that it specifies NIS maps in place of NIS+ tables.

```
passwd:      files nis
group:       files nis

hosts:       nis [NOTFOUND=return] files
services:    nis [NOTFOUND=return] files
networks:    nis [NOTFOUND=return] files
protocols:   nis [NOTFOUND=return] files
rpc:         nis [NOTFOUND=return] files
ethers:      nis [NOTFOUND=return] files
netmasks:    nis [NOTFOUND=return] files
bootparams:  nis [NOTFOUND=return] files
publickey:   nis [NOTFOUND=return] files

netgroup:    nis

automount:   files nis
aliases:     files nis
```

Because the search order for passwd and group is "`files nis`," you don't need to place the "+" entry in the `/etc/passwd` and `/etc/group` files.

DNS Forwarding for NIS Clients

If an NIS client is using the DNS-forwarding capability of an NIS-compatible NIS+ server, its `nsswitch.conf` file should *not* have the following syntax for the hosts file:

```
hosts:   nis dns files
```

Since DNS forwarding automatically forwards host requests to DNS, the syntax shown above would cause the NIS+ server to forward unsuccessful requests to the DNS servers twice, impacting performance.

To take best advantage of DNS forwarding, use the default syntax for the `nsswitch.nis` file, as shown in the box above.

The nsswitch.files File

The nsswitch.files configuration file simply specifies local /etc files as the only source of information for the workstation.

```
passwd:       files
group:        files
hosts:        files
networks:     files
protocols:    files
rpc:          files
ethers:       files
netmasks:     files
bootparams:   files
publickey:    files

netgroup:     files^a

automount:    files
aliases:      files
services:     files
```

a. There is no "files" source for netgroup, so the client simply won't use it.

Part 2—Planning and Transition

Planning and Transition Guidelines

6 ☰

This chapter provides guidelines for planning the setup and administration of NIS+, whether from scratch—that is, without a transition from a previous network information service—or with a transition from NIS.

Planning Guidelines	Page 91
Transition Guidelines	Page 95

Planning Guidelines

Figure 6-1 suggests a planning process for a standard NIS+ setup. The blocks on the left represent the major planning activities, such as designing the final namespace and selecting security measures. The text in the middle describes the blocks. The large numbers on the right point to the chapters that provide planning guidelines for each block. All chapters are in Part 3 of this book.

A Summary Planning Sheet is provided at the end of this section, on page 94. If you fill it out, you will have much of the information you need to begin setting up your namespace. Additional copies are provided in Appendix B.

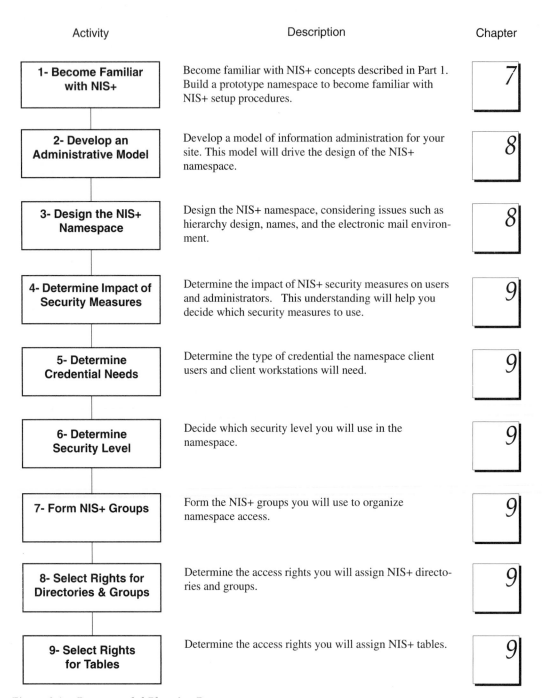

Activity	Description	Chapter
1- Become Familiar with NIS+	Become familiar with NIS+ concepts described in Part 1. Build a prototype namespace to become familiar with NIS+ setup procedures.	7
2- Develop an Administrative Model	Develop a model of information administration for your site. This model will drive the design of the NIS+ namespace.	8
3- Design the NIS+ Namespace	Design the NIS+ namespace, considering issues such as hierarchy design, names, and the electronic mail environment.	8
4- Determine Impact of Security Measures	Determine the impact of NIS+ security measures on users and administrators. This understanding will help you decide which security measures to use.	9
5- Determine Credential Needs	Determine the type of credential the namespace client users and client workstations will need.	9
6- Determine Security Level	Decide which security level you will use in the namespace.	9
7- Form NIS+ Groups	Form the NIS+ groups you will use to organize namespace access.	9
8- Select Rights for Directories & Groups	Determine the access rights you will assign NIS+ directories and groups.	9
9- Select Rights for Tables	Determine the access rights you will assign NIS+ tables.	9

Figure 6-1   Recommended Planning Process

Where To Get Information About the Namespace

NIS+ provides several commands that provide information about the data and objects in the namespace. Table 6-1 lists the commands.

Table 6-1 NIS+ Commands for Data and Objects in the Namespace

Command	Lists	See
niscat	Table contents	Chapter 25
niscat -o	Object properties of any NIS+ object (including a table entry)	Chapter 24
nisls	The contents and other particulars of a directory	Chapter 24
nislog	The contents of a transaction log	Chapter 24
nisshowcache	The contents of the directory cache	Chapter 24

Summary Table

When you have designed the namespace and selected its servers, types of credentials, groups, and access rights, you have gathered most of the information you will need to set up the namespace. You might want to summarize all this information in a worksheet that you can keep handy while you set up the namespace. Table 6-2 provides a sample worksheet that uses fictitious information for the Wizard, Inc. namespace. Appendix B, "Pre-Setup Worksheets," provides additional blank worksheets.

Table 6-2 Sample Pre-Setup Worksheet

Domain:	Wiz.Com.

Servers	Type	Name	Specifications
	Master	rootmaster	
	First Replica	rootreplica	
	Second Replica	rootreplica2	

Credentials	Type of Principal	Type of Credential
	Servers	DES
	Clients	DES
	Administrators	LOCAL and DES
	Users	LOCAL and DES

Rights	Types of Objects	Category & Rights				
	Directories	N	O	G	W	Use Defaults?
	`Wiz.Com.`	r---	rmcd	rmcd	r---	no
	`org_dir.Wiz.Com.`	r---	rmcd	rmcd	r---	no
	`groups_dir.Wiz.Com.`	r---	rmcd	rmcd	r---	no
	`Sales.Wiz.Com.`	r---	rmcd	rmcd	r---	no
	Groups	N	O	G	W	Description
	admin.Wiz.Com.	r---	rmcd	r---	r---	Admins who manage structure & security
	admin2.Wiz.Com.	r---	rmcd	r---	r---	Admins who manage information

Table 6-2 Sample Pre-Setup Worksheet (Continued)

Domain: | Wiz.Com.

Rights	Types of Objects	Category & Rights				
	Tables	N	O	G	W	Notes
	Hosts	r---	rmcd	rmcd	r---	
	Bootparams	r---	rmcd	rmcd	r---	
	Passwd	----	rmcd	rmcd	r---	Check column permissions.
	Cred	r---	rmcd	rmcd	r---	
	Networks	r---	rmcd	rmcd	r---	
	Netmasks	r---	rmcd	rmcd	r---	
	Ethers	r---	rmcd	rmcd	r---	
	Services	r---	rmcd	rmcd	r---	
	Protocols	r---	rmcd	rmcd	r---	
	RPC	r---	rmcd	rmcd	r---	
	Auto_Home	r---	rmcd	rmcd	r---	
	Auto_Master	r---	rmcd	rmcd	r---	

Transition Guidelines

Changing a site's network information service is never a simple task, because networked users and workstations are totally dependent on the service for communication. This and the accompanying chapters in Part 2 should help ease the transition by discussing the issues that an administrator must consider beforehand.

Differences Between NIS and NIS+

The transition from NIS to NIS+ is not only complex, but largely dependent on the differences between the two products. Understanding them is critical to a successful transition:

- Domain structure
- Interoperability
- Server configuration
- Information management
- Security

Domain Structure

As described in Chapter 1 of this book, the NIS domain structure addressed the administration requirements of client-server computing networks prevalent in the 1980s; in other words, client-server networks with a few hundred clients and a few multipurpose servers. The domain structure of NIS+ was designed to address the requirements of networks that range from 100 to 10,000 multivendor clients supported by 10 to 100 specialized servers located in sites throughout the world, connected to several "untrusted" public networks. It consists of hierarchical domains, similar to those of DNS.

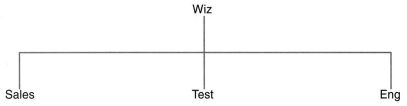

The NIS+ domain structure is described in Chapter 2 of this book.

Interoperability

NIS+ provides interoperability features for upgrading from NIS and for continuing the interaction with DNS originally provided by the NIS service:

- NIS compatibility mode
- Information transfer utility (`/usr/lib/nis/nisaddent`)
- Name Service Switch

The NIS compatibility mode enables an NIS+ server running Solaris 2.x to answer requests from NIS clients without interrupting service to NIS+ clients. Instructions for using it are provided throughout Part 3 of this book.

The `nisaddent` command enables transfer of information from NIS to NIS+ and back. It helps administrators keep NIS maps and NIS+ tables synchronized. Instructions for using it are provided in Chapter 16, "Setting Up NIS+ Tables."

The Name Service Switch, described in Chapter 5, "Understanding the Name Service Switch," allows an administrator to select the network information services, and their order, that a workstation can use.

Server Configuration

The NIS+ client-server arrangement is similar to those of NIS and DNS in that each domain is supported by a set of servers: a master and one or more replicas. The major difference between NIS and NIS+ servers, however, is the way they handle updates.

NIS updates are handled manually, and its maps need to be remade and propagated every time any information in the map changes. NIS+, however, accepts *incremental* updates to the replicas. Changes must still be made on the master server, but once made they are automatically propagated to the replica servers. They are made available to the entire namespace after they have been propagated to the replicas. You don't have to "make" any maps or wait for propagation. For more information, see "How Servers Propagate Changes" on page 29.

Information Management

NIS+ stores information in *tables* instead of maps or zone files. NIS+ provides 17 types of predefined, or *system*, tables.

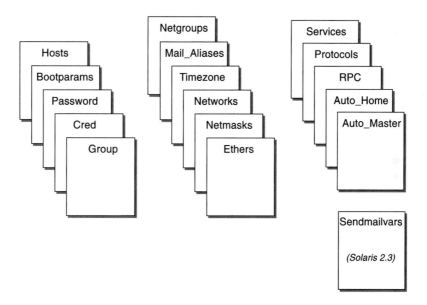

NIS+ tables provide two major improvements over the maps used by NIS. First, an NIS+ table can be accessed by any column, not just the first column (sometimes referred to as the "key"). This eliminates the need for duplicate maps, such as the hosts.byname and `hosts.byaddr` maps used by NIS. Second, the information in NIS+ tables has access controls at three levels: the table level, the entry level, and the column level. For more information about NIS+ tables, see Chapter 3, "Understanding NIS+ Tables."

Security

NIS+ security is provided by two means: *authentication* and *authorization*. Before clients can access anything in the namespace, they must be bona fide NIS+ clients and they must have the proper permission to access that information. Furthermore, requests for access to the namespace are honored only if they are implemented either through client library routines or through NIS+ administration commands, both of which are checked for authentication and authorization.

These security features have a significant impact on the NIS+ setup procedures. Instructions are provided throughout Part 3 of the book. For more information about NIS+ security, see Chapter 4, "Understanding NIS+ Security."

Suggested Transition Process

Figure 6-1 suggests a transition process. The blocks on the left represent the major transition planning activities, such as designing the final namespace and selecting security measures. The text in the middle describes the blocks. The large numbers on the right point to the chapters that provide planning guidelines for each block. Each planning activity is summarized in the remainder of this chapter. Detailed guidelines are provided in the remainder of Part 2.

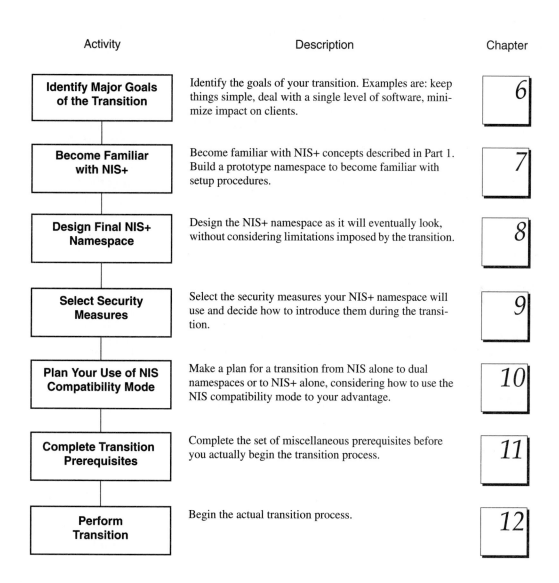

Activity	Description	Chapter
Identify Major Goals of the Transition	Identify the goals of your transition. Examples are: keep things simple, deal with a single level of software, minimize impact on clients.	6
Become Familiar with NIS+	Become familiar with NIS+ concepts described in Part 1. Build a prototype namespace to become familiar with setup procedures.	7
Design Final NIS+ Namespace	Design the NIS+ namespace as it will eventually look, without considering limitations imposed by the transition.	8
Select Security Measures	Select the security measures your NIS+ namespace will use and decide how to introduce them during the transition.	9
Plan Your Use of NIS Compatibility Mode	Make a plan for a transition from NIS alone to dual namespaces or to NIS+ alone, considering how to use the NIS compatibility mode to your advantage.	10
Complete Transition Prerequisites	Complete the set of miscellaneous prerequisites before you actually begin the transition process.	11
Perform Transition	Begin the actual transition process.	12

Figure 6-2   Recommended NIS to NIS+ Transition Process

1. Identify Major Transition Goals

Before you begin the transition, you might find it helpful to state the goals of your site's transition. Here are some typical goals.

Consider the Alternatives to Transition

Though this is not required, you could defer the upgrade to NIS+ until after your site has completed its transition to Solaris 2.x. Doing so would allow you to focus your resources on one transition effort at a time.

You could also upgrade to NIS+ before upgrading to Solaris 2.x, by using the Solaris 1.x NIS+ binaries, although this route is discouraged by SunSoft. These binaries were developed to enable sites to upgrade their network information service when they were unable to upgrade their servers to Solaris 2.x. There is no client-side NIS+ support for Solaris 1.x.

Keep Things Simple

You can take steps to simplify the transition. They will diminish the effectiveness of NIS+, but they will consume fewer servers and less administrative time. Once the transition is complete, you can change things to the way they were supposed to be. Here are some suggestions:

- Don't change domain names.
- Don't use any hierarchies; keep a flat NIS+ namespace.
- Use the NIS compatibility features.
- Use default tables and directory structures.
- Don't establish credentials for clients.

Deal with a Single Level of Software

Decide which version of both Solaris 2.x and NIS+ you will use for the transition. Since there are slight differences between versions, using multiple versions complicates the transition process needlessly. Pick one version of Solaris and use its corresponding version of NIS+.

Solaris 2.3 is recommended, since it has the most features (such as setup scripts) and is the most thoroughly tested. Make sure you compile a list of the SunOS™ patches (beyond the delivered FCS versions) that are required for normal operation and make sure that all servers and clients have the same patches loaded.

Minimize Impact on Clients

Minimizing impact implies two major considerations. First, the user should not notice any change in service. Second, the transition phase itself should cause minimal disruption to clients. To ensure the second consideration, be sure the administrators responsible for each domain migrate their clients to NIS+, rather than asking the clients themselves to implement the migration. This plan ensures that proper procedures are carried out, that procedures are consistent across clients, and that irregularities can be dealt with immediately by the administrator.

Miscellaneous "Don'ts"

- Don't change the services currently provided by NIS or the way it functions.
- Don't change the structure of DNS.
- Don't change the IP network topology.
- Don't upgrade applications that use NIS to NIS+; leave the migration to NIS+ APIs of the future.
- Don't consider additional uses for NIS+ during the implementation phase; add them later.

2. Become Familiar with NIS+

Familiarize yourself with NIS+, particularly with the concepts introduced in Part 1 of this book.

One of the best ways to become familiar with NIS+ is to build a prototype namespace. There is no substitute for hands-on experience with the product; administrators need the opportunity to practice in a forgiving test environment. The most important benefit of building the prototype might be a changed mind-set, with a different concept of name space structure and its implications. Remember that NIS+ is not simply an upgraded NIS; it is a completely different product.

Have the administrators who will convert your site from NIS to NIS+ build a small NIS+ namespace so they can become familiar with NIS+ before they have to deal with the added complications of a transition from NIS. When you set up the test domain, make small, manageable domains. For guidance, follow the suggestions in Chapter 7, "Building a Prototype NIS+ Namespace."

3. Design Your Final NIS+ Namespace

Design the final NIS+ namespace, following the guidelines in Chapter 8, "Designing the NIS+ Namespace." While designing the namespace, don't worry about limitations imposed by the transition from NIS. You can add those later, once you know what your final NIS+ goal is.

4. Select Security Measures

NIS+ security measures provide a great benefit to users and administrators, but they require additional knowledge and setup steps on the part of both users and administrators. They also require several planning decisions. Chapter 9, "Selecting NIS+ Security Measures," describes the implications of NIS+ security and the decisions you need to make for using it in your NIS+ namespace.

5. Decide How to Use NIS Compatibility Mode

The use of parallel NIS and NIS+ namespaces is virtually unavoidable in a transition. Because of the additional resources required for parallel namespaces, try to develop a transition sequence that reduces the amount of time your site uses dual services or the extent of dual services within the namespace (for example, convert as many domains as possible to NIS+ only).

Chapter 10, "Using NIS Compatibility Mode," explains the transition issues associated with the NIS compatibility mode and suggests a way to transition from NIS only, through NIS compatibility, to NIS+ alone.

6. Complete Prerequisites to Transition

In addition to all these planning decisions mentioned above, before you can implement your transition, you must complete several miscellaneous prerequisites, as described in Chapter 11, "Satisfying Prerequisites to Transition."

7. Implement the Transition

Chapter 12, "Implementing the Transition," provides a suggested series of steps to implement the transition you have just planned.

Building a Prototype NIS+
Namespace

7 ≡

The tasks described in this chapter build the following prototype namespace:

Test.Com.

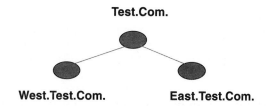

West.Test.Com.   **East.Test.Com.**

To build the prototype using the NIS+ commands, you *could* follow the instructions in the NIS+ documentation, but they are designed to cover a full-blown setup. A better way to become familiar with an NIS+ namespace is to build one in layers, starting with the skeleton directory structure, then adding information, then converting it to NIS compatibility, and only then adding real information and security. Following are four tasks to get you started. From then on, you will need to consult the complete NIS+ documentation.

▼ How to Set Up a Skeleton Namespace

This task builds a skeleton namespace. The purpose of building a skeleton namespace is to become familiar with the basic structure of NIS+ domains *without the clutter of real data and security procedures*. Once you are comfortable with the skeleton, you can throw it away and build a more realistic namespace, one that uses more complete NIS+ information and thorough security features.

To set up a skeleton namespace, follow the steps below; rootmaster is the name of the root master server.

1. **Set up the root domain.**
    The list of commands below is extracted from the complete root domain setup procedure provided in the NIS+ documentation.[1] These are all the commands you need to build the skeleton root domain:

    ```
    % su                        # Become superuser on the root master.
    # domainname Test.Com       # Change the root master's domain name.
    # nisinit -r                # Create the root directory.
    # rpc.nisd -r -S 0          # Start the NIS+ root daemon.
    # /usr/lib/nis/nissetup     # Create the NIS+ tables.
    ```

    Files created by these commands are placed in directories under /var/nis, which you can verify with the ls command. These files, however, are actually NIS+ objects, which are best examined with the niscat -o command.

    At this point, your NIS+ namespace looks like this:

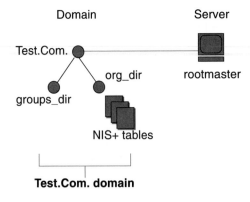

---

1. For a complete description of each command, see "Setting Up the Root Domain" in Chapter 15.

The combination of a directory object (Test.Com.), groups_dir and org_dir directories, and a set of NIS+ tables constitute an NIS+ domain. (In subsequent illustrations, they will be represented with a simple domain oval. In this and subsequent illustrations, the dotted lines between the server and the domain indicate that the server supports the domain. In this case, because it is the root domain, the server also belongs to the domain.)

2. **Create two clients for the root domain.**
   Be sure that each client has an entry for rootmaster in its /etc/hosts file. Then use these two commands for each client, while logged in to the client as superuser:[2]

```
# domainname Test.Com.           # Change the client's domain name.
# nisinit -c -H rootmaster       # Initialize the client.
```

Now your NIS+ namespace looks like this (assume that the clients were named "eastmaster" and "westmaster"):

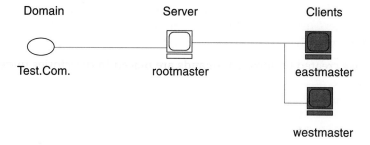

3. **Convert each client into an NIS+ server.**
   In an NIS+ namespace, all servers except the root master are created as clients. Once they have been initialized as clients, they can be converted to servers. Only then can they be associated with the domains they will support. This step converts them into servers:[3]

```
% su                             # Become superuser on the server.
# rpc.nisd -S 0                  # Start the NIS+ daemon.
```

---

2. These commands were extracted from the complete instructions in Chapter 17, "Setting Up an NIS+ Client."
3. These commands are extracted from Chapter 18, "Setting Up NIS+ Servers."

Now your NIS+ namespace looks like this (assume the new servers are named eastmaster and westmaster):

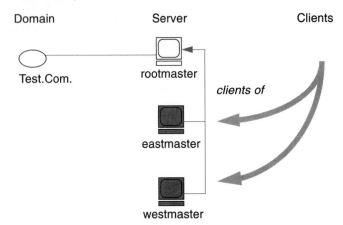

Observe that eastmaster and westmaster are still clients of rootmaster.

4. **Set up two nonroot domains and associate them with new servers.**
   NIS+ creates a nonroot domain and designates its master (or replicas) server in one step, with the nismkdir command, as shown below. Then the server's tables are created with the nissetup command. Do this for each server:[4]

```
% su                           # Become superuser on the new server.
# nismkdir -m westmaster \     # Create the new domain's main
    West.Test.Com.                 directory object and associate it with
                                   the new master server.

# /usr/lib/nis/nissetup \      # Create a set of NIS+ tables.
        West.Test.Com.
```

```
% su                           # Become superuser on the new server.
# nismkdir -m eastmaster \     # Create the new domain's main
    East.Test.Com.                 directory object and associate it with
                                   the new master server.

# /usr/lib/nis/nissetup \      # Create a set of NIS+ tables.
        East.Test.Com.
```

4. These steps are extracted from Chapter 19, "Setting Up a Nonroot Domain."

Now your NIS+ namespace looks like this:

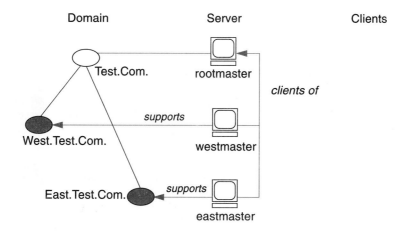

Although westmaster and eastmaster now support West.Test.Com. and East.Test.Com., they are still—and will continue to be—clients of the root domain, Test.Com.

5. **Add clients to each domain.**
   Now you can add clients to any domain in the hierarchy. Just make sure that each client has an entry for its master server in its /etc/hosts file. Use these commands for each client while logged in to the client as superuser:[5]

   ```
   # domainname <domainname>     # Change the client's domain name.
   # nisinit -c -H <master>      # Initialize the client.
   ```

---

5. These commands were extracted from the complete instructions in Chapter 17.

Now your NIS+ namespace looks like this:

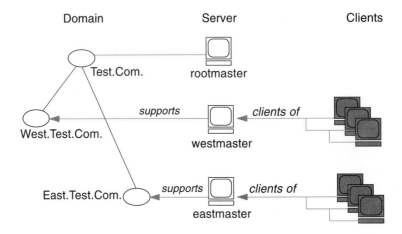

This is an insecure namespace; clients have no credentials and no keys, and the servers are running in the least secure mode.

6. **Test the skeleton namespace.**
   Become familiar with the operation of these NIS+ commands:[6]

Command	Description
niscat -o	Displays the object properties of an NIS+ object.
nisls	Lists the contents of an NIS+ directory object.
nismkdir	Creates an NIS+ directory or associates a new replica with an existing directory.
nisrmdir	Removes an NIS+ directory object from the namespace.
nisrm	Removes an nondirectory NIS+ object from the namespace.
rpc.nisd	Starts the NIS+ daemon on an NIS+ server.
nisinit	Initializes an NIS+ client (and also the NIS+ root master server).

---

6. These commands are described in the *"SunOS 5.x Administering NIS+ and DNS"* manual, in the chapter titled "Administering NIS+ Directories."

▼ How to Add a Replica Server to a Skeleton NIS+ Domain

This task adds a skeleton replica server (no security, no NIS compatibility) to a skeleton NIS+ domain. It is extracted from the complete setup procedures in Part 3 of this book.

1. **Set up the workstation as an NIS+ client.**
   Be sure that the client has an entry in its `/etc/hosts` file for the *master server of the domain to which it belongs—not the domain it will support*. Then use these commands:

```
% su                              # Become superuser on the client.
# domainname <domainname>         # Change the client's domain name.
# nisinit -c -H <master>          # Initialize the client.
```

   Be sure the server's domain name is the name of the domain the server *belongs to*, not the one it supports.

2. **Convert the client into an NIS+ server.**
   Just use the `rpc.nisd` command:

```
# rpc.nisd -S 0                   # Start the NIS+ daemon.
```

3. **Associate the new server with the domain it will support.**
   Log in to the NIS+ master server of the domain the new server will support. Then use the `nismkdir` command, as shown below:

```
# nismkdir -s <replica> \         # Associate the new replica with the
    <domain to be supported>        domain it will support.
# nisping -u \                    # Ping the new replica (to download the
    <domain to be supported>        master's tables to the replica).
```

If you added one replica to each domain, your skeleton NIS+ namespace would look like this:

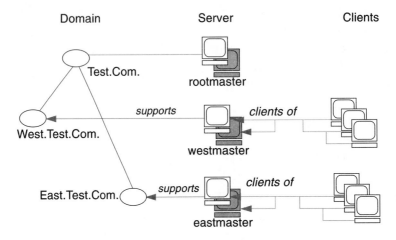

▼ How to Populate NIS+ Tables with Skeleton Data

This task describes how to add some test data to the NIS+ tables in a skeleton NIS+ domain. It ignores NIS+ security and NIS compatibility and does not work for the NIS+ automounter tables. It is extracted from the complete setup procedures in the NIS+ documentation.

You can populate NIS+ tables from text files or NIS maps. This task describes both ways. If you populate from text files, the text files must be formatted properly; the format used for /etc file versions of NIS maps will work. If you populate from NIS maps, the maps must be standard NIS maps from a standard NIS domain.

Use this task once for each domain.

1. **Log in to an NIS+ server and set the proper defaults.**
   NIS+ has several built-in defaults that work with normal security. Since the purpose of these skeleton tasks is to sidestep security temporarily, you also have to sidestep some of those defaults; namely, the permissions assigned to the Nobody category. To do this, use the command appropriate for your shell and change the access default so that it provides full rights to the Nobody category:

   ```
   access=n+rmcd
   ```

Here is an example:

```
% setenv access n+mcd
```

You can use the `nisdefaults` command to display the current value of the NIS+ defaults. Remember to reset the ACCESS environment variable back to its original setting once you start setting up a normal NIS+ domain.

2. **To populate from text files, use** `nisaddent -f`.
This example loads the file `hosts.txt` into the NIS+ Hosts table:

```
% /usr/lib/nis/nisaddent -f /etc/hosts.txt hosts
```

3. **To populate from NIS maps, use the** `-y` **option.**
This example loads the NIS map `hosts.byaddr` from the NIS domain NISWiz into the corresponding NIS+ table (which is the Hosts table):

```
% /usr/lib/nis/nisaddent -y NISWiz hosts.byaddr
```

You don't need to specify the corresponding NIS+ table; the software can figure that out.

The `nisaddent` command has three options: append, merge, and replace. By default it uses the append option. To experiment with the other two options, see the NIS+ documentation.

4. **Test the tables in the skeleton namespace.**
Become familiar with the operation of these NIS+ commands:[7]

Command	Description
nistbladm	Creates and deletes tables and operates on table entries. Establishes table paths.
niscat	Displays the contents of an NIS+ table.
nismatch	Searches through the contents of an NIS+ table.
nisgrep	Searches through the contents of an NIS+ table.
nisaddent	Adds information to NIS+ tables.

---

7. These commands are described in Chapter 25, "Administering NIS+ Tables."

▼ How to Set Up an NIS-compatible Skeleton Namespace

After becoming familiar with the process and commands for setting up a standard NIS+ namespace, throw away the namespace and rebuild it as an NIS-compatible domain. This task describes how. However, it still *ignores security* and provides only the most basic instructions. For complete instructions refer to Part 3 of this book.

For the steps below, assume that rootmaster is the name of the root master server.

Note – This task assumes you have already set up a standard NIS+ domain, as described earlier in this chapter.

1. **Clean out leftover NIS+ material and processes.**
   If the workstation you are working on was previously used as an NIS+ server or client, remove any files that might exist in /var/nis and kill the cache manager and NIS+ daemon, if either is still running. In this example, a coldstart file and a directory cache file still exist in /var/nis.

   ```
   rootmaster# ls /var/nis
   NIS_COLD_START      NIS_SHARED_CACHE
   rootmaster# rm -rf /var/nis/*
   rootmaster# ps -ef | grep nis_cachemgr
       root   295    260 10 15:26:58 pts/0   0:00 grep nis_cachemgr
       root   286      1 57 15:21:55 ?       0:01 /usr/sbin/nis_cachemgr
   rootmaster# kill -9 286
   ```

   This step makes sure that files left in /var/nis or directory objects stored by the cache manager are completely erased so they do not conflict with the new information generated during this setup process.

2. **Set up the root domain.**

The list of commands below is extracted from the complete root domain setup procedure provided in the NIS+ documentation.[8] These are all the commands you need to build the skeleton root domain:

```
% su                            # Become superuser on the root maste.
# nisinit -r                    # Create the root directory.
# rpc.nisd -r -Y -B -S 0        # Start the NIS+ root daemon.
# vi /etc/init.d/rpc            # Open the /etc/init.d/rpc file and change
                                #    # EMULYP="-Y"  to
                                #      EMULYP="-YB"

# /usr/lib/nis/nissetup -Y
```

In the `rpc.nisd` command, the `-r` option is used because this is a root domain, the `-Y` option makes this an NIS-compatible domain, the `-B` option supports the DNS forwarding capabilities of NIS, and the `-S 0` option selects no security.

When editing the `/etc/init.d/rpc` file, be sure to uncomment the EMULYP line after changing it.

3. **Create two clients for the root domain.**

Use the same clients that you used for this purpose in the original skeleton namespace setup. That way, all the prerequisites are satisfied. However, be sure to clean out leftover NIS+ material and kill the cache manager on the clients, as shown below:

```
# rm -rf /var/nis/*             # Clean out leftover NIS+ material.
# ps -ef | grep nis_cachemgr    # Find process ID of cache manager.

    (output)

# kill -9 <cachemgr id>         # Kill the cache manager.
# nisinit -c -H rootmaster      # Initialize the client.
```

---

8. For a complete description of each command, see Chapter 15, "Setting Up the Root Domain."

4. **Convert each client into an NIS-compatible NIS+ server.**
   Use the -Y and -B options to rpc.nisd:

   ```
   # rpc.nisd -Y -B -S 0          # Start the NIS+ daemon.
   # vi /etc/init.d/rpc           # Open the /etc/init.d/rpc file and change
                                  #      # EMULYP="-Y"   to
                                  #      EMULYP="-YB"
   ```

   As when setting up the root domain, be sure to edit the /etc/init.d/rpc file.

5. **Set up two nonroot domains and associate with new servers.**
   Do this for each server, from the root master:

   ```
   # nismkdir -m westmaster \     # Create the new domain's main
      West.Test.Com.                 directory object and associate it with
                                     the new master server.
   # /usr/lib/nis/nissetup -Y \   # Create a set of NIS-compatible NIS+
      West.Test.Com.                 tables.
   ```

   The nismkdir command is used in the usual way, but the nissetup command
   requires a -Y option.

6. **Add clients, replicas, and test data.**
   You can now add more NIS+ clients or use the ones already set up. Add replicas
   and populate the NIS+ tables with test data.

7. **Test the namespace's response to NIS client requests.**
   You can now add more NIS+ clients or use the ones that already exist. For selected
   NIS clients, designate the NIS-compatible NIS+ servers as their primary NIS
   servers and test the response.

Designing the NIS+ Namespace 8

This chapter provides general guidelines and recommendations for designing the final NIS+ namespace your site will have. It has four sections:

When designing the namespace, don't worry about limitations imposed by the transition from NIS. You can add those later, once you know what your final NIS+ configuration looks like.

Identify the Goals of Your Administrative Model

Select the model of information administration that your site will use. Without a clear idea of how information at your site will be created, stored, used, and administered, it is difficult to make the design decisions suggested in this section. You could end up with a design that is more expensive to operate than is necessary. You also run the risk of designing a namespace that does not suit your needs. Changing the namespace design after it has been set up is costly.

Design the Namespace Structure

Designing the NIS+ namespace is one of the most important transition tasks you can perform, since changing the domain structure after NIS+ has been set up is a time-consuming, complex job. It is complex because information, security, and administration

115

policies are woven into the domain structure of the namespace. Rearranging domains would require rearranging information, reestablishing security, and re-creating administration policies.

When designing the structure of an NIS+ namespace, consider the following factors:

- The domain hierarchy
- Domain names
- The electronic mail environment

The Domain Hierarchy

The essential benefit of the NIS+ domain hierarchy is that it allows the namespace to be divided into more easily managed components. Each component can have its own security, information management, and administration policies. A domain hierarchy is useful if you have more than 1,000 clients, if you want to set up different security policies for different groups of users, or if your sites are geographically distributed.

However, the hierarchical structure can present problems for some applications. In a hierarchy, all NIS+ servers except the root master reside in the domain above the domain of the clients they support. Some applications, basing their queries on the flat NIS domain structure, may expect the server to reside in the same domain that it supports.   For instance, if a nonroot NIS+ server were also used as an NFS server, it would not obtain its netgroup information from the domain it supports, but from the domain it belongs to: the parent domain. This separation of home domain and supported domains can also confuse users who try to log in remotely to the server to execute commands they cannot execute from their workstations.

A domain hierarchy also introduces the need for fully qualified names. In a single NIS namespace, all users could contact each other without the need for domain names. In an NIS+ domain hierarchy, users in one domain will not be able to contact users in another domain (to send a mail message, for instance) without using their fully qualified names.

You could, of course, use NIS+ search paths (described in Chapter 3, "Understanding NIS+ Tables"), which establish connections between NIS+ tables in different domains, but that eliminates some of the advantages of distinct domains and reduces the reliability of the NIS+ service.

Using a single-level hierarchy won't take advantage of several useful NIS+ features, but it will eliminate these kinds of problems.

To design a domain hierarchy, first make a map of how you expect the hierarchy to look when you are finished. The map will be a useful reference when you are in the middle of the setup procedure. As a minimum, you will need to consider the following issues:

- Organizational or geographical mapping
- Connection to higher domains
- Client support in the root domain
- Domain size vs. number of domains
- Number of levels
- Security operating levels
- Number of replica servers
- Information management

Organizational or geographical mapping

One of the major benefits of NIS+ is its capability to divide the namespace into smaller, manageable parts. You could create a hierarchy of organizations, such as those of the imaginary Wizard, Inc.

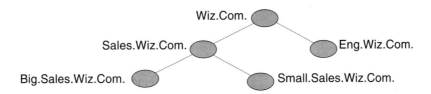

You could also organize the hierarchy by buildings instead of by organizations.

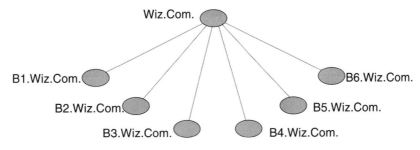

The scheme you select depends primarily on how you prefer to administer the namespace and how clients will tend to use the namespace. For example, if clients of Eng.Wiz.Com. will be distributed throughout the buildings of the Wizard Corporation, you shouldn't organize the namespace by building. Since the clients would need to constantly access other domains, you would need to add their credentials to the other domains and you would increase traffic flow through the root master server. A better scheme would be to arrange them by organization. On the other hand, building-sized domains are immune to the reorganizations that require organization-based domains to be restructured.

Don't be limited by the physical layout of the network, since an NIS+ namespace does not have to be congruent with the physical network—unless it has to support NIS clients (using NIS compatibility mode). The number of domains your namespace needs depends on the kind of hierarchy you select.

Also consider future expansion plans. Will today's NIS+ root domain end up beneath another NIS+ domain in the future? Making this change would entail a great deal of work, so you should try to avoid it. Try to estimate the need for future domains in the namespace and design a structure than can accommodate them without disruption.

Connection to higher domains

Consider whether the NIS+ namespace will be connected to higher domains, such as those of the Internet or DNS. If you currently use NIS under a DNS hierarchy, do you want to replace the NIS domains only or do you want to replace the entire DNS/NIS structure with an NIS+ namespace?

Client support in the root domain

In the two domain hierarchies illustrated above, are all the clients placed in domains beneath the root domain? Or do some belong to the root domain? Is the purpose of the root domain only to act as the root for its subdomains or will it support its own group of clients? You could place all clients in the lowest layer of domains and only those used for administration in the intermediate domains. For example, in the first illustration, all clients belong to the Big.Sales.Wiz.Com., Small.Sales.Wiz.Com., and Eng.Wiz.Com. domains, and only clients used for administration belong to the Wiz.Com. and Sales.Wiz.Com. domains.

Or, you could place the clients of general-purpose departments in higher-level domains. For example, in the second illustration, you could put the clients of the Facilities Department in the Wiz.Com. domain.

Domain size vs. number of domains

The NIS+ service was optimized for domains with 1,000 clients and a maximum of 10 replica servers. Such a domain would typically have 10,000 table entries. However, you might still prefer larger domains. For instance, one large domain requires less administration than multiple smaller domains. Large domains need fewer skilled administrators, since tasks can be automated more readily, thus lowering the administrative cost.

However, with smaller domains, in addition to optimized performance, you can customize tables more easily, and, with the smaller impact of any task, you can have much greater administrative flexibility.

When considering the number of domains in the hierarchy, use this chart as a guideline:

Size of Namespace	Number of Domains
1 to 1,000 workstations	1 domain
1,000 to 3,000 workstations	2 to 3 domains
Over 3,000 workstations	5 to 10 domains

Number of levels

The NIS+ service handles multiple levels of domains. Although the software can accommodate almost any number of levels, a hierarchy with too many levels would prove difficult to administer. For one thing, the names of objects could become long and unwieldy. You might also want to consider 20 the reasonable limit for the number of subdomains for any one domain, and 5 as the reasonable limit for the depth of the hierarchy.

Security operating levels

In most cases, you will run the namespace at security level 2. However, if you plan to use different security levels for different domains, you should identify them now. Chapter 4 provides more information about security levels.

Number of replica servers

A domain should have no more than 10 replica servers because of the increased network traffic and server load that occur when information updates are propagated to additional replicas. The optimal number of replicas depends on other factors as well:

- The physical location of the servers

- The number of subnets that the domain spans
- The support of NIS clients

The recommended minimum for servers is one master and one replica per domain, plus at least one replica for every subnet with NIS clients. Without an NIS+ server on the subnet, the NIS clients would be unable to reach the other NIS+ servers in the domain because they would not have their `netmask` information. An alternative is to maintain the `/etc/netmask` file on the NIS clients, but consider the administrative load.

Another alternative is to use "multihomed" servers. These are servers with more than one IP address. They can thus serve more than one subnet.

If the domain hierarchy that you design spans a WAN link, it would be prudent to replicate the domain on either side of the WAN link. Have a master server on one side and a replica on the other. This arrangement would enable clients on the other side of the link to continue with the NIS+ server even if the WAN link were temporarily disabled. However, it would change the administration model, since the replica would physically reside within the geographic perimeter of a different domain.

Information management

We recommend using a model of local administration within centralized constraints for managing the information in an NIS+ namespace. Information should be managed, as much as possible, from within its home domain, but according to guidelines or policies set at the global namespace level. This plan provides the greatest degree of domain independence while maintaining consistency across domains.

Domain Names

Consider name length and complexity. First, pick names that are descriptive. "Sales" is considerably more descriptive than "BW23A." Second, pick short names. You want to avoid appending something as odious as "EmployeeAdministrationServices.WizardCorporation" to object names when you administer the namespace.

A domain name is formed from left to right, starting with the local domain and ending with the root domain. For example:

Wiz.Com.
Sales.Wiz.Com.
Intl.Sales.Wiz.Com.

The first line above shows the name of the root domain. The root domain must always have at least two labels and must end in a dot. The second label can be an Internet domain name, such as Com. The second and third lines above show the names of lower-level domains.

Also consider implications for electronic mail domains, both within the company and via the Internet.

Depending on the migration strategy chosen, it could be a viable alternative to change domain names on NIS to the desired structure, then migrate to NIS+, domain by domain.

If your network is connected to the Internet, consider whether the domain name changes will require a new network name and number. If you plan to join the Internet, obtain the name and number from the Network Information Center.

The Electronic Mail Environment

Because NIS+ offers a domain hierarchy while NIS has a flat domainspace, changing to NIS+ can affect your mail environment. With NIS, only one mailhost is required. If you use a domain hierarchy for NIS+, you may need one mailhost for each domain in the namespace.

Therefore, the email addresses of clients who are not in the root domain will change. As a general rule, client email addresses can change when domain names change or when new levels are added to the hierarchy.

In Solaris 2.0, these changes required a great deal of work. Later releases provided several `sendmail` enhancements to make the task easier. In addition, the Solaris 2.3 version of NIS+ provides a Sendmailvars table. The `sendmail` program first looks at the Sendmailvars table, then examines the local `mail` file.

Be sure that mail servers reside in the NIS+ domain of those clients they support. Also, for performance, don't create search paths for mail servers to tables in lower-level domains.

Consider the impact of the new mail addresses on DNS. You may need to adjust the DNS MX records.

Select the Namespace Servers

Each NIS+ domain is supported by a set of NIS+ *servers*. The servers store the domain's directories, groups, and tables, and answer requests for access from users, administrators, and applications. Each domain is supported by only one set of servers. However, a single set of servers can support more than one domain.

Remember that a domain is not an object, but only refers to a collection of objects. Therefore, a server that supports a domain is not actually associated with the domain, but with the domain's main *directory*.

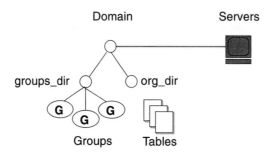

Any workstation based on Solaris 2.x can be an NIS+ server. The software for both NIS+ servers and clients is bundled together into the Solaris package. Therefore, any workstation that has Solaris 2.x installed can become a server, a client, or both. For performance, be sure the servers are SPARCstation™ IPXs or better.

When selecting the servers that will support the NIS+ namespace, consider the following factors:

- Supported domains
- Server load
- Time to live
- Disk space and memory requirements

Supported Domains

When selecting servers, differentiate between the requirements imposed by the NIS+ service and those imposed by the traffic load of your namespace.

The NIS+ service requires you to assign at least one server, the master, to each NIS+ domain. Although you can assign any number of replicas to a domain, we don't advise using more than ten per domain.[1] How many servers a domain requires is determined by the traffic load and the configuration of its servers.

---

1. An NIS+ server is capable of supporting more than one domain, but we don't advise this except in small namespaces or testing situations.

The traffic loads you anticipate will determine the total number of servers used to support the namespace, how much storage and processing speed each will require, and whether a domain needs replicas to ensure its availability. How can you determine how many servers you need?

A good way to begin is by assigning one master server to each domain in the hierarchy.

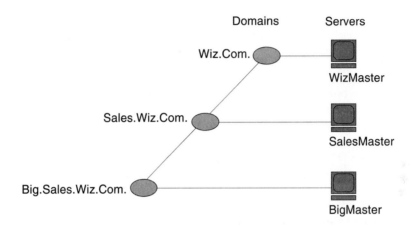

If certain domains must always be available, add replicas to them—one or more. We recommend always adding at least one replica to a domain. In small- to medium-sized domains, configurations with two to four replicas are normal.

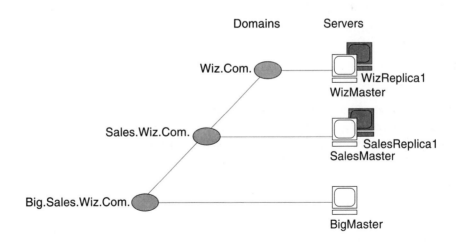

In organizations with many distributed sites, each site often needs its own subdomain. Often, the subdomain master is placed in a higher-level domain. As a result, there can be a great deal of traffic between point-to-point links. To alleviate this traffic, you can create replicas across the link. In this way, lookups are handled locally, while the only traffic traveling across point-to-point links is that between the master and replica servers (or updates made to the master from the other side of the link).

Server Load

NIS+ master servers require fewer replicas than NIS servers did, since NIS+ does not depend on broadcasts.

Putting replicas on both sides of a weak network link (such as optical or wide-area links) is recommended. If the link breaks and the networks are decoupled, both sides of the network can still obtain service.

Do not put more than ten replicas on one domain. If you have enough, put one on each subnet; otherwise, distribute the servers as best you can and optimize for the best performance. You don't need NIS+ servers on every subnet, unless they support NIS clients. Try to use fewer than 1,000 clients in a domain, keeping in mind that NIS+ clients create a higher load than NIS clients.

Disk Space and Memory Requirements

How much disk space you need depends on four factors:
- Disk space consumed by Solaris 2.3
- Disk space for /var/nis (and /var/yp)
- Amount of memory
- Swap space required for NIS+ processes

Solaris 2.3 can consume over 220 megabytes (Mbytes) of disk space, including OpenWindows™, depending on how much of it you install. This is an estimate; for exact numbers, see the Solaris 2.3 installation manual. You should also count the disk space consumed by other software the server may use. The NIS+ software itself is part of the Solaris 2.3 distribution, so it does not consume additional disk space.

NIS+ directory objects, groups, tables, and client information are stored in /var/nis. As a rule of thumb, /var/nis uses about 5 Kbytes of disk space per client. So, if a namespace has 1,000 clients, then /var/nis requires about 5 Mbytes of disk space. However, because transaction logs (also kept in /var/nis) can grow large, you may want additional space per client—we recommend an additional 10–15 Mbytes. In other words, for 1,000 clients, allocate 15–20 Mbytes for `/var/nis`. You can reduce this if you checkpoint transaction logs regularly. We recommend that you create a separate partition for `/var`.

If you will use NIS+ concurrently with NIS, allocate an equal amount of space for `/var/yp` to hold NIS maps that you may transfer from NIS. By the way, if you can, keep `/var/nis` on a separate partition; doing so will help during an OS upgrade.

Although 32 Mbytes is the minimum memory requirement for servers, we recommend that you equip servers of medium to large domains with at least 64 Mbytes.

You also need swap space equal to three times the size of the NIS+ server process—in addition to the server's normal swap space requirements. The size of the `rpc.nisd` process, as shown by the `ps -efl` command, can be misleading because it includes 256 Mbytes of address space reserved by the NIS+ transaction log. For the actual process size, subtract 256 Mbytes from the output of `ps`.

Most of this space is used when directories are checkpointed (with `nisping -C`), since during a checkpoint, an entire NIS+ server process is forked. In no case should you use less than 64 Mbytes of swap space.

Time to Live

A small detail that can affect server support, especially across wide-area networks, is the *time-to-live* value of directory objects. Once you understand how a directory object's time to live affects connections between clients and servers, you may want to customize the time-to-live values in your domains to match the needs of your namespace structure.

NIS+ clients get their NIS+ service from the NIS+ servers listed in their *directory cache*. The directory cache is initialized from a *coldstart file* during client setup (for a complete description, see Chapter 2). Once initialized, the directory cache accumulates information about each server the client contacts, dropping stale information over time.

This contact information is actually a copy of a directory object, which is what contains the server contact information. To keep the cache from growing large, every copy of the directory object has a *time to live*. The default is 12 hours. You can change a directory object's time-to-live value with the `nischttl` command. However, keep in mind that the longer the time to live, the higher the likelihood that the copy of the object will be out of date; and the shorter the time to live, the greater the network traffic and server load.

Determine Table Configurations

NIS+ tables provide several features not found in simple text files or maps. They have a column-entry structure, they accept search paths, they can be linked together, and they can be set up in several different ways. You can also create your own custom NIS+ tables. When selecting the table configurations for your domains, consider the following factors:

- Differences between NIS+ tables and NIS maps
- Use of custom NIS+ tables
- Table location
- Connections between tables

Differences Between NIS+ Tables and NIS Maps

NIS+ tables differ from NIS+ maps in many ways, but two of those differences are worth keeping in mind during your namespace design:

- NIS uses 17 standard tables
- NIS tables interoperate with /etc files differently

NIS+ Uses 17 Standard Tables

Review the 17 standard NIS+ tables to make sure they suit the needs of your site. They are listed in Table 8-1. Table 8-2 lists the correspondence between NIS maps and NIS+ tables.

Don't worry about synchronizing related tables. The NIS+ tables store essentially the same information as NIS maps, but they consolidate like information into a single table (for example, the NIS+ Hosts table stores the same information as the hosts.byaddr and hosts.byname NIS maps). Instead of key-value pairs, NIS+ tables use columns and rows.[2] Therefore, when you update any information (e.g., host information), you need to update it only in one place (e.g., Hosts table). You no longer have to worry about keeping that information consistent across related maps.

Note the new name of the automounter tables:

- auto_home (old name: auto.home)
- auto_master (old name: auto.master)

---

2. The information contained in the columns of NIS+ tables is described in the appendices to the *"SunOS 5.x Administering NIS+ and DNS"* manual.

The dots were changed to underscores because NIS+ uses dots to separate directories. Dots would cause NIS+ to misinterpret the table name.

To ease the transition from NIS to NIS+, you should also change the dots in your NIS automounter maps to underscores. You may also need to do this on your clients' automounter configuration files.

Table 8-1 The Seventeen NIS+ Tables

NIS+ Table	Information in the Table
Hosts	Network address and hostname of every workstation in the domain.
Bootparams	The location of the root, swap, and dump partition of every diskless client in the domain.
Passwd	Password information about every user in the domain.
Cred	Credentials for principals who belong to the domain.
Group	The group password, group id, and members of every UNIX group in the domain.
Netgroup	The netgroups to which workstations and users in the domain may belong.
Mail_Aliases	Information about the mail aliases of users in the domain.
Timezone	The timezone of every workstation in the domain.
Networks	The networks in the domain and their canonical names.
Netmasks	The networks in the domain and their associated netmasks.
Ethers	The Ethernet address of every workstation in the domain.
Services	The names of IP services used in the domain and their port numbers.
Protocols	The list of IP protocols used in the domain.
RPC	The RPC program numbers for RPC services available in the domain.
Auto_Home	The location of all users' home directories in the domain.
Auto_Master	Automounter map information.
Sendmailvars	The location of the mail domain used by `sendmail`.

Table 8-2 Correspondence Between NIS Maps and NIS+ Tables

NIS Map	NIS+ Table	Notes
auto.home	Auto_Home	
auto.master	Auto_Master	
bootparams	Bootparams	
ethers.byaddr	Ethers	
ethers.byname	Ethers	
group.bygid	Group	Not the same as NIS+ groups.
group.byname	Group	
hosts.byaddr	Hosts	
hosts.byname	Hosts	
mail.aliases	Mail_Aliases	
mail.byaddr	Mail_Aliases	
netgroup	Netgroup	
netgroup.byhost	Netgroup	
netgroup.byuser	Netgroup	
netid.byname	Cred	
netmasks.byaddr	Netmasks	
networks.byaddr	Networks	
networks.byname	Networks	
passwd.byname	Passwd	
passwd.byuid	Passwd	
protocols.byname	Protocols	
protocols.bynumber	Protocols	
publickey.byname	Publickey	
rpc.bynumber	RPC	
services.byname	Services	
ypservers		Not needed.

NIS+ has two new tables for which there are no corresponding NIS tables:

- Cred
- Sendmailvars

The Cred table stores the credentials of NIS+ principals. These credentials authenticate requests for NIS+ service. You won't need to transfer any data from NIS maps to the NIS+ Cred table. Information is created for that table just as credentials are created for NIS+ principals.

The Sendmailvars table stores the mail domain used by `sendmail`.

NIS+ Tables Interoperate with /etc Files Differently

The way NIS interacted with `/etc` files was controlled by the `/etc` files, using the `+/-` syntax. How NIS+ interacts with `/etc` files—or other network information services—is determined by the Name Service Switch. A configuration file located on every NIS+ client specifies the sources of information for that client: `/etc` files, DNS zone files, NIS maps, or NIS+ tables. The configuration file of NIS+ clients looks like this:

```
passwd:      files nisplus
group:       files nisplus

hosts:       nisplus [NOTFOUND=return] files
services:    nisplus [NOTFOUND=return] files
networks:    nisplus [NOTFOUND=return] files
protocols:   nisplus [NOTFOUND=return] files
rpc:         nisplus [NOTFOUND=return] files
ethers:      nisplus [NOTFOUND=return] files
netmasks:    nisplus [NOTFOUND=return] files
bootparams:  nisplus [NOTFOUND=return] files

publickey:   nisplus

netgroup:    nisplus

automount:   files nisplus
aliases:     files nisplus
```

In other words, for most types of information, the source is first an NIS+ table, then a `/etc` file. This arrangement replaces the `+/-` syntax used with NIS.

You can select from three versions of the Switch configuration file or you can create your own. For instructions, see the NIS+ documentation.

Use of Custom NIS+ Tables

Determine which nonstandard NIS maps you use and their purpose. Can they be converted to NIS+ or replaced with NIS+ standard maps?

Some applications may rely on NIS maps (e.g., Calendar Manager). Will they still function the same way with NIS+? Can they function correctly in a mixed environment?

To build a custom table in NIS+, use `nistbladm`. Remember that you cannot use dots in the table names.

If NIS+ is to support your custom NIS maps, create a "key-value" table. This table has only two columns, one the key, the other the value of the key. To support these tables, run the NIS+ servers in NIS compatibility mode. NIS clients notice no change.

Table Location

Deciding where in a domain structure to locate NIS+ tables is a complex decision, but here are some basic principles to keep in mind.

- Every domain must have access to every standard table
- Volatile, frequently accessed data should be located lower in the hierarchy, closer to where it is used most often
- Data that is accessed by several domains should be located higher in the hierarchy, unless the domains need to be independent
- The lower in the hierarchy you place data, the easier it will be to administer autonomously

Here is a diagram that summarizes these principles.

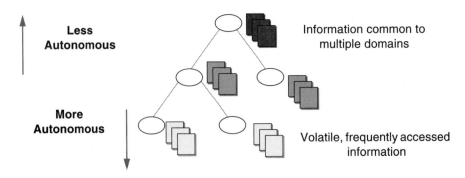

NIS maps are located in /var/yp/*domainname*. NIS+ tables are located in /var/nis/*domainname*.

Connections Between Tables

NIS+ tables contain information only about the resources and services in their home domain. If a client tries to find information that is stored in another domain, it must provide the other domain name. You can automate this "forwarding" by connecting the local table to the remote table. NIS+ tables can be connected in two different ways:

- Through *paths*
- Through *links*

(Note that only NIS+ clients can follow links and paths; NIS clients cannot.)

Paths

If information in a particular NIS+ table is often requested by clients in other domains, you may consider establishing a path from the local NIS+ table to the one in the other domain.

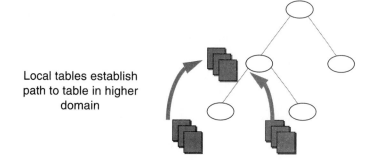

Local tables establish path to table in higher domain

Such a path would have two main benefits. First, it would save clients in lower domains the trouble of explicitly searching through a second table. Second, it would allow the administrator in the higher-level domain to make changes in one table and have that change affect clients in other domains. However, such a path could also hurt performance. Performance is especially affected when searches are unsuccessful, since the NIS+ service must exhaust searches through two tables instead of one.

You should also be aware that since "mailhost" is often used as an alias, when trying to find information about a specific mailhost, you should use its fully qualified name in the search path (e.g., `mailhost.Sales.Wiz.Com.`), or NIS+ will return *all* the mailhosts it finds in all the domains it searches through.

The path is established in the local table by means of the `-p` option to the `nistbladm` command. You can also establish a path using the `NIS_PATH` environment variable. To change a table's path, you must have Modify access to the table object. To find out what a table's search path is, use the `niscat -o` command (you must have Read access to the table).

Links

Links between tables produce an effect similar to paths, except that the link involves a search through only one table: the remote table. With a search path, NIS+ first searches the local table, and only if it is unsuccessful does it search the remote table. With a link, the search moves directly to the remote table. In fact, the remote table is a virtual replacement for the local table.

The benefit of links is that it allows a lower domain to access the information in a higher domain without the need to administer its own table.

To create a link, use the `nisln` command. You must have Modify rights to the table object.

Selecting NIS+ Security Measures　　　9 ≡

This chapter provides general guidelines and recommendations for making choices about security in your namespace. It has six sections:

Determine the Impact of Implementing NIS+ Security

Although NIS+ provides protection that NIS did not, it requires more administrative work. It may also require more work from clients who are not accustomed to performing keylogins. Furthermore, the protection provided by NIS+ is not 100% secure. Given enough computing power and the right knowledge, the DES keys can be broken. Nevertheless, NIS+ is an order of magnitude more secure than NIS.

Keeping these trade-offs in mind, consider the impact NIS+ security will have on both users and administrators before you decide how to use it.

How NIS+ Security Affects Users

NIS+ security is a benefit to users because it improves the reliability of the information they obtain from NIS+ and it protects their information from unauthorized access. However, it requires them to learn a bit about security and requires them to perform a few extra administrative steps.

Although NIS+ requires a network login, users are not required to perform one because the `login` command automatically retrieves the network keys for them. The secret key is normally made available to superusers in the `/etc/.rootkey` file. If a client user's NIS+ password is changed with the `nispasswd` command, the client user's credential information is automatically updated. A client workstation's password must be changed with the `chkey` command.

However, if your site allows users to maintain passwords in their local `/etc/passwd` files in addition to their network passwords and if these passwords are different, then users must perform a keylogin each time they log in. The reasons for this are explained in Chapter 4, "Understanding NIS+ Security."

How NIS+ Security Affects Administrators

Because NIS+ bundles the DES encryption mechanism for authentication, administrators who need secure operation do not need to purchase a separate encryption kit. However, administrators must train users to use the `keylogin` and `chkey` commands and to know when to use them.

Furthermore, setting up a secure NIS+ namespace is more complex than setting up one without any security. The complexity comes not only from the extra steps required to set up the namespace, but from the job of creating and maintaining credentials for all NIS+ principals. Administrators will also have to remove obsolete credentials, just as they remove dead account information from the Passwd and Hosts tables. Also, when servers' public keys change, administrators must update the keys throughout the namespace (using `nisupdkeys`). Administrators must also add LOCAL credentials for clients from other domains who want to log in remotely with proper authentication.

How NIS+ Security Affects Transition Planning

After you become familiar with the benefits and the administrative requirements of NIS+ security, you will have to decide whether to implement NIS+ security during or after the transition. We recommend that you use full NIS+ security even if you operate some or all servers in NIS compatibility mode. However, this choice entails a heavy administrative burden. If you prefer a simpler approach, add security slowly, after the transition is complete.

Alternatively, you could set up the NIS+ servers and namespace with NIS-compatible security, but skip creating credentials for NIS+ clients. The NIS+ clients would be relegated to the Nobody category, along with the NIS clients. This method reduces training and setup requirements, but it has the following drawbacks:

- Users lose the ability to update their network passwords

- Administrators and servers still require credentials

- "Visiting" administrators cannot be authenticated

Determine Credential Needs of the Namespace

NIS+ provides two types of credential: LOCAL and DES. All NIS+ principals need at least one of these credentials. If the namespace is running at security level 2 (the default), all NIS+ principals must have DES credentials in their home domain. In addition, all users (not workstations) must have LOCAL credentials in their home domains and in every other domain for which they need login access.

To determine the credential needs of your namespace, consider the following:

- Type of principal

- Type of credential

Type of Principal

NIS+ principals can be client users or the superuser identity on the client workstation.

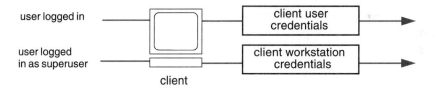

When you determine the credentials you need to create, make sure you know which type of principal the credential is for. For instance, when you set up an NIS+ client, you will create credentials for the client workstation, not for the client user. Unless credentials for the client user are created, the client user has only the access rights granted to the Nobody class. This scheme can work perfectly well if that's how you choose to set up your namespace. But, if you don't give any access rights to the Nobody class, the namespace won't be available to the client users.

Type of Credential

The type of credentials required in a namespace is determined primarily by the security level at which each domain is running. If a domain is to be operated in NIS compatibility mode (security level 0), no one needs credentials of any kind. If the domain is to operate at security level 1, any NIS+ principal that will have access rights, in addition to those granted to the Nobody class, needs LOCAL credentials. At security level 2, principals need DES credentials.

Select a Security Level

Although NIS+ servers can operate at three security levels, we do not recommend that you operate your domain at any level other than 2, except for initial setup, testing, or debugging.   If you use levels 0 or 1 for normal operation, any user, authenticated or not, can modify not only namespace information, but the structure of the namespace itself. For more information about security levels, see Chapter 4, "Understanding NIS+ Security."

Form NIS+ Groups

Different types of groups have proliferated throughout UNIX. Unfortunately, NIS+ creates one more type: the NIS+ group. Fortunately, its role is clear. An NIS+ group is used only as a means to provide NIS+ access rights to several NIS+ principals at one time. It is used only for NIS+ authorization.

After identifying the type of credentials you will need, you would normally try to select the access rights that are required in the namespace. To make that task easier, you should first determine how many administrative groups you will need. Will you create one group for the entire namespace or one group per domain? Using separate groups is useful if you want to assign them different rights.

To determine the number of groups you need, determine the classes of principals you will have in your namespace. Then, create a group for each class. You can also create groups of groups. For example, principals who are simple users of the namespace form one class of principal. They need only Read access to the tables in the namespace. On the other hand, principals who administer the namespace need much greater access rights. Some of them may perform only basic administration tasks, like adding user accounts, so they simply require Read and Modify rights to the namespace tables. Others, however, may actually set up or modify the namespace, so they will need Read, Modify, Create, and Delete rights to the entire namespace—or perhaps only to a single domain in the namespace.

You don't need a group for all the principals in the namespace, something like all.Wiz.Com., because the World class already accomplishes that.

Determine Access Rights to NIS+ Groups and Directories

After arranging your principals into groups, determine the kind of access rights granted by the objects in the namespace to those groups, as well as to the other categories of principal (Owner, World, and Nobody). Planning these assignments ahead of time helps you establish a coherent security policy. NIS+ provides different default access rights for different namespace objects. They are listed in Table 9-1.

Table 9-1 Default Access Rights for NIS+ Objects

Object	Nobody	Owner	Group	World
Root directory object	r---	rmcd	rmcd	r---
Nonroot directory object	----	rmcd	r---	r---
groups_dir directory objects	----	rmcd	rmcd	r---
org_dir directory objects	----	rmcd	rmcd	r---
NIS+ groups	----	rmcd	r---	r---
NIS+ tables (see "Determine Access Rights to NIS+ Tables" on page 138)	*varies*	*varies*	*varies*	*varies*

You can use the default rights or assign your own. If you assign your own, consider how the objects in your namespace will be accessed. Keep in mind that the Nobody class comprises all requests from NIS+ clients, whether authenticated or not. The World class comprises all authenticated requests from NIS+ clients. Therefore, if you don't want to provide namespace access to unauthenticated requests, don't assign any access rights to the Nobody class; reserve them only for the World class. On the other hand, if you expect some clients —via applications, for instance—to make unauthenticated Read requests, you can assign Read rights to the Nobody class. If you want to support NIS clients in NIS compatibility mode, make sure you assign Read rights to the Nobody class.

Also consider the rights each type of namespace object will assign to the NIS+ groups you specified earlier. Depending on how you plan to administer the namespace, you can assign all or some of the available access rights to the group. For instance, if only one administrator will create and modify the root domain, you should not assign the owning group Create and Destroy rights to the objects in the root domain. Instead, assign those rights only to the Owner of those objects. However, if several administrators may be involved in the setup process, put them all in a group and assign full rights to it. That method is easier than switching ownership back and forth.

Finally, the owner of an object should have full rights, although this is not as important if the group has such rights. A namespace is more secure if you give only the owner full rights, but easier to administer if you give the administrative group full rights.

Determine Access Rights to NIS+ Tables

NIS+ objects other than NIS+ tables are primarily structural. In other words, access to them is required primarily by NIS+ principals who administer the namespace. NIS+ tables, however, are a different type of object: They are informational. Access to NIS+ tables is required by all NIS+ principals and applications running on behalf of those principals. Therefore, their access requirements are a bit different.

Table 9-2 lists the default access rights assigned to NIS+ tables. If any columns provide rights in addition to those of the table, they are also listed. You can change these rights at the table and entry level with the nischmod command, and at the column level with the nistbladm -u command. The section below provides just one example of how to change table rights to accommodate different needs.

Table 9-2 Default Access Rights for NIS+ Tables and Columns

Table/Column	Nobody[a]	Owner	Group	World
Hosts table	r---	rmcd	rmcd	r---
Bootparams table	r---	rmcd	rmcd	r---
Passwd table	----	rmcd	rmcd	r---
name column	r---	----	----	----
passwd column	----	-m--	----	----
uid column	r---	----	----	----
gid column	r---	----	----	----
gcos column	----	-m--	----	----
home column	r---	----	----	----
shell column	r---	----	----	----
shadow column	----	----	----	----
Cred table	r---	rmcd	rmcd	r---
cname column	----	----	----	----
auth_type column	----	----	----	----
auth_name column	----	----	----	----
public_data column	----	-m--	----	----
private_data column	----	-m--	----	----
Networks table	r---	rmcd	rmcd	r---
Netmasks table	r---	rmcd	rmcd	r---
Ethers table	r---	rmcd	rmcd	r---
Services table	r---	rmcd	rmcd	r---
Protocols table	r---	rmcd	rmcd	r---
RPC table	r---	rmcd	rmcd	r---
Auto_Home table	r---	rmcd	rmcd	r---
Auto_Master table	r---	rmcd	rmcd	----

a. NIS-compatible domains give the Nobody class Read rights to the Passwd table at the table object level.

Protecting the Encrypted Password Field

As you can see in Table 9-2, Read access is provided to the Nobody class by all tables except the Passwd table. NIS+ tables give the Nobody class Read access because many applications that need to access NIS+ tables run as unauthenticated clients. However, if this were also done for the Passwd table, it would expose the encrypted Passwd column to unauthenticated clients.

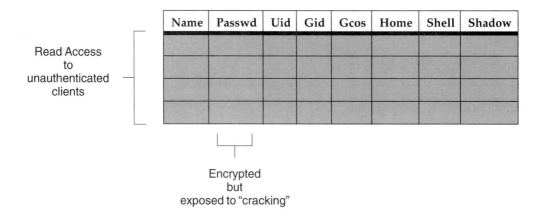

The setup pictured above is the default for NIS-compatible domains. NIS-compatible domains must give Nobody Read access to the Passwd column because NIS clients are unauthenticated and would otherwise be unable to access their Passwd column. Therefore, in an NIS-compatible domain, even though passwords are encrypted, they are vulnerable to decoding. They would be much more secure if they were not readable by anyone except their owner.

Standard NIS+ domains (not NIS compatible) can provide that extra level of security. From Solaris 2.3 on, the default setup (provided by `nissetup`) uses a column-based scheme to hide the passwd column from unauthenticated users while still providing access to the rest of the Passwd table.

At the table level, no unauthenticated principals have Read access. At the column level, they have Read access to every column except the passwd column.

All columns except passwd provide Read rights to the Nobody class

Name	Passwd	Uid	Gid	Gcos	Home	Shell	Shadow

At the table level,
NO rights are provided
to the Nobody class.

Passwd column
provides NO rights to the
Nobody class

How does an entry owner gain access to the passwd column? Entry owners have both Read and Modify access to their own entries. They obtain Read access by being a member of the World class. (Remember that at the table level, the World class has Read rights.) They obtain Modify access by explicit assignment at the column level.

```
                         Nobody    Owner    Group    World
    Passwd Table Rights  :  ----     rmcd     rmcd     r---
    Passwd Column Rights :  ----     -m--     ----     ----
```

Keep in mind that table Owners and entry Owners are rarely the same NIS+ principals. Thus, table-level Read access for the Owner does not imply Read access for the Owner of any particular entry.

As mentioned earlier, this is the default setup from Solaris 2.3 on. To use this scheme in earlier versions of Solaris, follow the instructions in the task titled "How to Limit Access to the Passwd Column" on page 245.

You can further restrict access to the passwd column by removing Read access at the table level from the World class and assigning it at the column level to the Owner and Group classes, as described in the task titled "How to Further Limit Access to the Passwd Column" on page 248.

Using NIS Compatibility Mode 10 ☰

Deciding whether and how to run NIS+ in parallel to NIS—and when to stop—is probably the second most difficult transition issue you will face. NIS+ provides several features that allow it to operate in parallel with NIS, most notably, the NIS compatibility mode.

The essential benefit provided by NIS compatibility is that it does not require any changes to NIS clients—they can be left as they are. The essential drawback is that it allows any unauthenticated client to obtain information from NIS+ tables. You will also eventually have to change those clients' domain names, and they will not be able to update their network passwords with the `yppasswd` command.

To help you plan your use of NIS compatibility mode, this chapter provides three sections:

An NIS Client's View of NIS Compatibility

An NIS client's view of the NIS+ namespace supported by servers running in NIS compatibility mode differs from the view of an NIS+ client in the following ways:

- NIS clients cannot follow NIS+ table paths or links or perform Read operations in other domains.

- Unsatisfied host requests by NIS clients can be forwarded to DNS if the NIS-compatible server has been set up with the -Y and -B options to rpc.nisd (see page 269). However, the same NIS-compatible server does not forward unsatisfied host requests for NIS+ clients. NIS+ clients must arrange for DNS forwarding through their nsswitch.conf file and by properly configuring their resolv.conf file.

- Although NIS+ clients can update entries in the namespace and perform operations such as updating a password (with the nispasswd command), NIS clients cannot make any updates directly to NIS-compatible NIS+ servers. For instance, an NIS client cannot use the yppasswd command to update a password in the NIS+ Passwd table.

- Although NIS+ clients can obtain service even if all the NIS+ servers on a local subnet are not responding (by directly contacting servers in other domains), NIS clients cannot look outside their subnet unless the names of servers outside their subnet have been explicitly identified with the ypset command.

- Because of the NIS+ authentication scheme, NIS+ clients can be sure that the response they receive comes from an authorized server. Because the NIS-compatible mode that NIS clients must use does not support the NIS+ authentication scheme, NIS clients do not have the same assurance as NIS+ clients.

- If an NIS-compatible NIS+ server does not respond to an NIS client, the client's yp_match() call continues to try to call until the server responds. When this happens, the NIS+ API returns an error message to the application.

Table 10-1 lists the NIS protocols that are supported by NIS+ servers in NIS compatibility mode.

Table 10-1 NIS Protocols Supported by NIS+ Servers in NIS Compatibility Mode

Protocols	Supported
NIS client V2 protocol	Yes
NIS server-to-server protocol	No
NIS client update protocol	No
NIS client V1 protocol	Not supported except for YPPROC_NULL, YPPROC_DOMAIN, and YPPROC_DOMAIN_NOACK

A Suggested Transition to NIS Compatibility Mode

Figure 10-1 illustrates how you can transition from an NIS-only namespace to a namespace that answers both NIS and NIS+ requests.

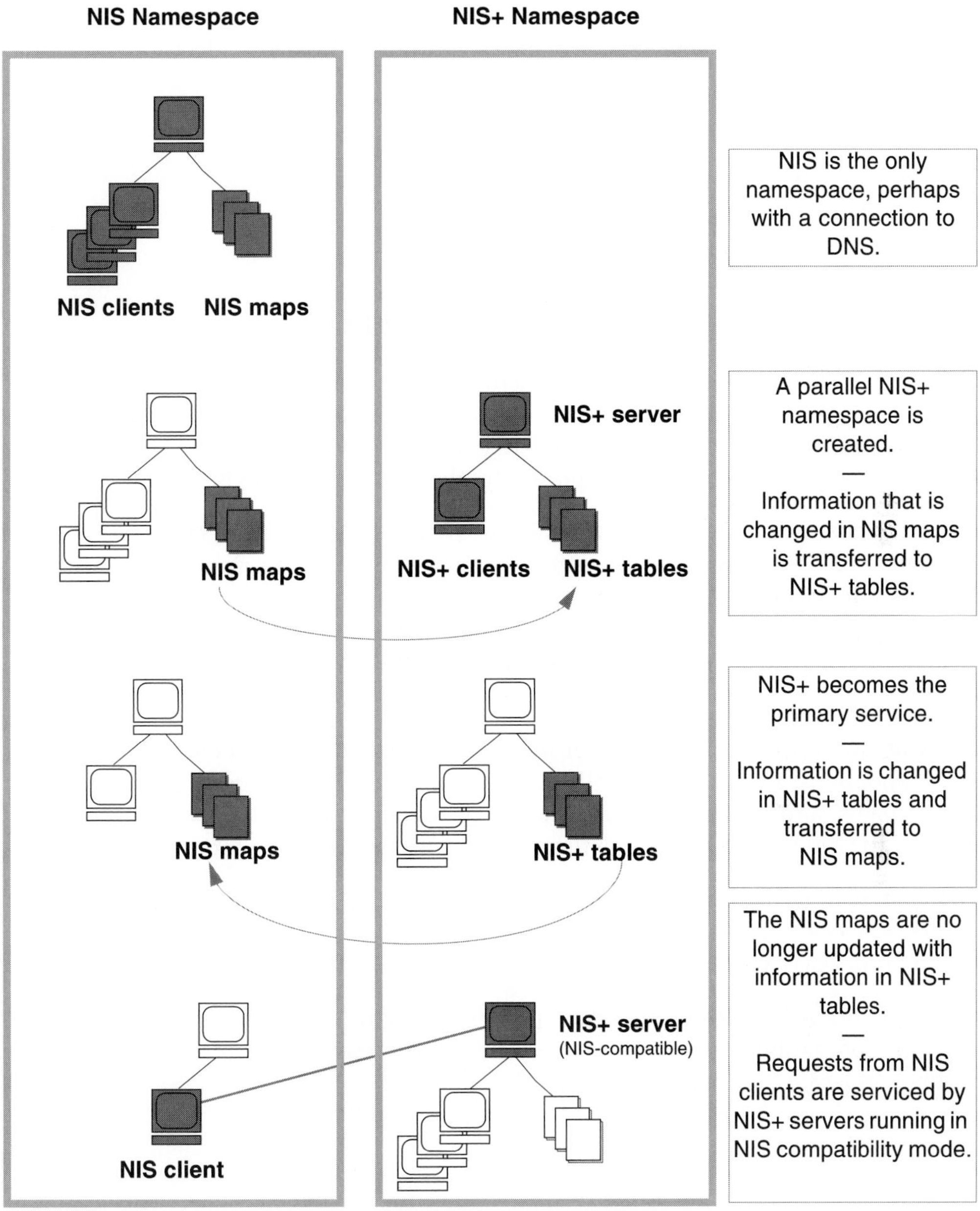

NIS Namespace   **NIS+ Namespace**

NIS clients   NIS maps

NIS is the only namespace, perhaps with a connection to DNS.

NIS maps

NIS+ server

NIS+ clients   NIS+ tables

A parallel NIS+ namespace is created.
—
Information that is changed in NIS maps is transferred to NIS+ tables.

NIS maps

NIS+ tables

NIS+ becomes the primary service.
—
Information is changed in NIS+ tables and transferred to NIS maps.

NIS client

NIS+ server
(NIS-compatible)

The NIS maps are no longer updated with information in NIS+ tables.
—
Requests from NIS clients are serviced by NIS+ servers running in NIS compatibility mode.

Figure 10-1   Transition to NIS Compatibility Mode

☰ 10

Planning the Transition to NIS Compatibility Mode

If you plan to use the NIS compatibility mode, make the following decisions:

- Select the domains that will be NIS-compatible
- Determine the configuration of NIS-compatible servers
- Decide how to transfer information between services
- Decide how to use the Name Service Switch
- Decide how to implement DNS forwarding

Select the Domains that Will Be NIS Compatible

Make a list of your NIS clients and map them to their eventual NIS+ domains. If the NIS+ domain running in NIS compatibility mode does not have the same name as its NIS clients' original NIS domain, you must change the NIS clients' domain name. Make it the same as the NIS+ domain being supported by the NIS-compatible NIS+ server.

Some NIS+ clients may want the capability to switch back and forth between the main NIS domain and the new NIS+ domain. Consider whether you can provide a script that helps them do this easily.

Determine the Configuration of NIS-compatible Servers

Take stock of your NIS servers, keeping in mind the requirements for your NIS+ servers. If you plan to eventually use them for the NIS+ service, upgrade them to the NIS+ recommendations. Identify which NIS servers will eventually be used to support which NIS+ domains, and in what capacity (master or replica). Remember that NIS+ servers belong to the domain *above* the one they support (except for the root domain servers).

If possible, plan to use your NIS+ servers only for NIS+. You may have to transfer other network services, such as DNS name services, home directories, and NFS, to servers not scheduled for NIS+ use.

If your network has machines that run operating systems other than Solaris, you can plan to use NIS compatibility mode indefinitely, or you can move those machines to their own domain—preferably in their own subnet.

Decide How to Transfer Information Between Services

To keep the information synchronized, be sure to make one namespace subordinate to the other. At first, the NIS namespace may be the dominant one, in which case you would make changes to the NIS maps and load them into the NIS+ tables. In effect, the NIS namespace would be the *master* database.

For instance, you could update the NIS+ tables nightly with the latest NIS information. If you are using NIS domains as the master source of information at your site, all changes made to the NIS+ tables between synchronization updates will be erased each time you propagate an NIS update. For instance, passwords that were changed with the nispasswd command will be overwritten by the previous NIS password, unless you have also changed the password with the yppasswd command.

Eventually, the NIS+ namespace will be dominant. In that case, make changes in the NIS+ tables and dump them back to the NIS maps.

The NIS+ command /usr/lib/nis/nisaddent transfers information between NIS maps and NIS+ tables, as summarized below.

NIS+ Command	Description
/usr/lib/nis/nisaddent -y	Transfers information from an NIS map to an NIS+ table.
/usr/lib/nis/nisaddent -d	Dumps information from an NIS+ table into a file, which can then be transferred into an NIS map with standard NIS utilities.

A Note About Changing Information in the Passwd Table

While using parallel namespaces, be sure to keep the information in the NIS+ Passwd table synchronized with the information in the NIS Passwd map. The nispasswd and yppasswd commands affect only their respective databases.

NIS+ uses the nispasswd command to change or display information stored in the NIS+ Passwd table. It is the equivalent of the yppasswd command for NIS. The nispasswd command provides capabilities that are similar to those offered by other commands. Table 10-2 summarizes their differences.

Table 10-2 Differences between NIS and NIS+ Password Commands

Command	Description
passwd	Changes information in the workstation's /etc/passwd and /etc/shadow files.
yppasswd	Changes information in the NIS password map. Has no effect on the NIS+ Passwd table.
nispasswd	Changes and displays information in the NIS+ Passwd table. When a principal's password is changed, nispasswd tries to update the principal's secret key in the Cred table. Its options are customized for the Passwd tables, making the command easier to use for that table than the nistbladm command. It also allows an administrator to lock and force passwords, tasks that nistbladm does not allow. This command does not change the shadow field of the Passwd table.
nistbladm	Creates, changes, and displays information about any NIS+ table, including the Passwd table. Although the nispasswd command is easier to use for the Passwd table, nistbladm allows you to do the following: - Create new entries. - Delete an existing entry. - Change the UID and GID fields in the Passwd table. - Change the LastChanged, Inactive, and Expired fields in the Shadow table. - Change access rights and other security-related attributes of the Passwd table. (Do *not* use it to change the passwords themselves, though.)
niscat	Can be used to display the contents of the Passwd table.

These differences mean that NIS clients being supported by NIS-compatible NIS+ servers will no longer be able to change their own passwords with the yppasswd command. Instead, properly authorized NIS+ administrators will have to change their passwords for them, using the nispasswd command.

However, while NIS serves as the master source of information, make sure you change NIS client passwords, using *both* the nispasswd and yppasswd commands. Otherwise, information changed in the NIS+ databases (with nispasswd) can be overwritten by information stored previously in the NIS maps.

If you are the owner of the Passwd table and have the proper credentials, you can change password information at any time and without constraints. However, if you are not the owner, you must comply with aging and construction constraints. When you attempt to change a password, if the old password has not aged sufficiently (i.e., number of days since last change is less than *min*), NIS+ will terminate and not carry out the change.

The new password must have at least six characters, but no more than eight. It must contain at least two letters and at least one number or special character. Make sure the password is not derived in any way from the user's login name. Also, make sure the new password has at least three characters that are different from the old password.

To use the `nispasswd` command, you must have the access rights appropriate for the operation.

This Operation	Requires These Rights	To This Object
Displaying information	Read	The Passwd entry
Changing information	Modify	The Passwd entry
Adding new information	Modify	The Passwd table

In domains set up in NIS compatibility mode, the permissions are slightly different: Permissions at the table object level provide Read access to the Nobody category.

To change table permissions, use the following NIS+ commands.

Command	Description
`nischmod`	Change access rights to a table object or table entry.
`nistbladm -u`	Change access rights to a table column.

Decide How to Use the Name Service Switch

In an NIS-compatible domain, you can use the Name Service Switch to do the following:

- Enable NIS clients to obtain service from NIS+
- Enable clients to switch between NIS and NIS+

Enable NIS Clients to Obtain Service from NIS+

NIS+ servers set up in NIS compatibility mode automatically respond to requests from NIS clients. However, the NIS clients must ask for the service. This service is set up at the client level with the Name Service Switch.

Since the Name Service Switch is not available in Solaris 1.x, DNS forwarding for NIS+ servers running in NIS compatibility mode is implemented on the server side.

Enable Clients to Switch Between NIS and NIS+

Some NIS+ clients may want the capability to switch back and forth between the main NIS domain and the new NIS+ domain. Consider whether you can provide a script that helps them do this easily.

Decide How to Implement DNS Forwarding

NIS servers forward DNS requests made from Solaris 1.x clients. NIS+ servers running in NIS compatibility mode provide DNS forwarding only in Solaris 2.3 releases (also in Solaris 2.2 releases, but as a patch). As a result, the NIS clients supported by NIS+ servers running Solaris 2.0 or 2.1 releases must have an /etc/resolv.conf file and the DNS resolver libraries installed locally before they are disconnected from their NIS servers.

Solaris 1.x clients being supported by Solaris 2.0 or 2.1 servers running in NIS compatibility mode will not be able to take advantage of DNS forwarding. You must upgrade them to Solaris 2.x.

If the DNS domains are repartitioned, you will need to redefine new DNS zone files; otherwise, no changes are required in the DNS environment. Clients, however, may require some adjustments to their /etc/resolv.conf files or their /etc/nsswitch.conf files. A client, if it is also a DNS client, can set up its Switch configuration file to search for information in either DNS zone files or NIS maps, in addition to NIS+ tables.

DNS Forwarding for NIS+ Clients

NIS+ clients do *not* have implicit DNS-forwarding capabilities like NIS clients do. Instead, they take advantage of the Switch. To provide DNS-forwarding capabilities to an NIS+ client, change its hosts entry to:

```
hosts:   nisplus dns [NOTFOUND=return] files
```

DNS Forwarding for NIS Clients

If an NIS client is using the DNS-forwarding capability of an NIS-compatible NIS+ server, its nsswitch.conf file should *not* have the following syntax for the hosts file:

```
hosts:   nis dns files
```

Since DNS forwarding automatically forwards host requests to DNS, the syntax shown would cause the NIS+ server to forward unsuccessful requests to the DNS servers twice, impacting performance.

In addition, NIS clients running Solaris 1.x must have a resolver library. Be sure to install the `shlib_custom` software category.

Comparison of NIS+ and NIS Commands

The following tables summarize differences between NIS and NIS+ commands. Table 10-3 identifies the NIS commands supported or not supported in Solaris 2.x; Table 10-4 compares NIS and NIS+ commands.

Table 10-3 Solaris 2.x Support of NIS Commands

Command Type	Supported	Not Supported
Utilities	ypinit ypxfr ypcat ypmatch yppasswd ypset ypwhich	yppush yppoll ypchsh ypchfn ypmake
Daemons	ypbind	ypserv ypxfrd rpc.ypupdated rpc.yppasswd
NIS API	yp_get_default_ domain() yp_bind() yp_unbind() yp_match() yp_first() yp_next() yp_all() yp_master() yperr_string() ypprot_err()	yp_order() yp_update()

Table 10-4 Comparison of NIS and NIS+ Commands

NIS Server	NIS-Compatible NIS+ Server	NIS+ Server
ypcat	ypcat	niscat
ypwhich -m	ypwhich -m	niscat -o
ypmatch	ypmatch	nismatch/nisgrep
yppasswd	--	nispasswd
ypbind	ypbind	--
yppoll	--	--
ypset	--	--
ypxfr	--	--
makedbm	--	nisaddent
ypinit -m ypinit -s	ypinit -c	--
ypserv	rpc.nisd -Y	rpc.nisd
ypserv -B	rpc.nisd -Y -B	--
ypxfrd	--	--
rpc.updated	--	--
rpc.yppasswd	--	--
yppush	--	nisping
ypmake	--	nissetup, nisaddent

Satisfying Prerequisites to Transition

This chapter describes several miscellaneous tasks that must be carried out before beginning the transition to NIS+:

Gauge the Impact of NIS+ on Other Systems

Carry out a formal introduction, testing, and familiarization program at your site, not only to train administrators, but to uncover dependencies of other systems or applications on NIS that will be affected by a transition to NIS+.

For instance, some applications, such as Calendar Manager, may rely on the maps in the NIS service. Will they function with NIS+ tables? If so, what access rights do they need? How will their need for access affect your overall security plan? If they must depend on the NIS service, how will you make sure they function in a mixed environment?

What nonstandard NIS maps are being used throughout your site? Can you convert them to NIS+ tables or create nonstandard NIS+ tables to store their information? Be sure to check their access rights.

Does your site use any locally built applications that depend on NIS?

How will application licensing products interact with NIS+?

How will the network installation procedures be affected by the transition to NIS+? Figure out what changes they require, if any.

Gauging the impact of NIS+ on your site administrative practices will help uncover potential roadblocks.

Train Administrators

Another goal of the introduction and familiarization program is to give the administrators at your site an opportunity to become familiar with the concepts and procedures of NIS+. Classroom instruction alone is insufficient. Administrators need a chance to work in a harmless test environment. The training should consist of the following:

- A formal NIS+ concepts and administration course
- Basic NIS+ troubleshooting information and practice
- Information about your site's implementation strategy and plans

Write a Communications Plan

Prepare a plan to communicate your intentions to users long before you actually begin converting clients to NIS+. Tell them about the implementation plan and give them a way to obtain more information. As mentioned in Chapter 1, a typical transition goal is to keep the impact of the transition on clients to a minimum, but users will nevertheless become concerned about the upcoming change. Send out regular electronic mail notices, conduct informative seminars, and designate either electronic mail aliases or individuals to which users can send questions.

Identify Required Conversion Tools and Processes

Consider creating or obtaining transition tools to help with the implementation. If your site already uses automated tools to administer individual systems or network services, consider porting them to operate under the versions of Solaris and NIS+ that you will be using for the transition. Here are some suggestions.

- A script to convert users to NIS+

- A check script to verify the correctness of a user's NIS+ environment

- A script to reinstall NIS (not NIS+) in case you encounter failures during the transition

- Backup and recovery scripts and processes

- Scripts that automate the administration of large volatile tables, such as Hosts and Passwd

- Crontab entries for routine NIS+ maintenance

- Procedures for notification of outages

- Options for selecting alternate service

Scripts such as these will make sure the transition is carried out uniformly across domains, they will speed up the transition, and they will reduce complaints and callbacks.

You should also prepare a set of standard configuration files and options, such as nsswitch.conf, that everyone across the namespace can use.

Identify Administrative Groups Used for Transition

Be sure that the NIS+ groups created as part of your namespace design (see "Form NIS+ Groups" on page 136) correspond to the administrative resources you have identified for the transition. It is possible that you could require a set of NIS+ groups for the transition different from that for routine operation of an NIS+ namespace. Consider adding remote administrators to your groups in case you need their help in an emergency.

Remember to make sure that group members have the proper credentials, that namespace objects grant the proper access rights to groups, and that the right group is identified as the group owner of the right namespace objects.

Table 11-1 summarizes commands that operate on NIS+ groups and group permissions.

Table 11-1 Commands for NIS+ Groups and Group Permissions

Command	Description
nisgrpadm	Create or delete groups, add, change, or delete members.
niscat -o	Display the object properties of an NIS+ group.
nissetup	Create, among other things, the directory in which a domain's groups are stored: groups_dir.

Table 11-1 Commands for NIS+ Groups and Group Permissions (Continued)

Command	Description
nisls	List the contents of the groups_dir directory; in other words, all the groups in a domain.
nischgrp	Assign a group to any NIS+ object.
nisdefaults	List, among other things, the group that will be assigned to any new NIS+ object.
NIS_GROUP (env. var.)	Override the value of nisdefaults for the shell in which it is set.
nischmod	Change an object's access rights.
nischown	Change the owner of an NIS+ object.
nischgrp	Change the group owner of an NIS+ object.
nistbladm -c, -u	Change access rights to NIS+ table columns.
nisdefaults	Display the current NIS+ defaults.

Determine Who Will Own the Domains

To take complete advantage of the features inherent in a domain hierarchy, distribute the ownership of domains to the organizations they are dedicated to supporting. That ownership will free the administrators of the root domain from performing rudimentary tasks at the local level.

Once you know who owns what, you can provide guidelines for creating administrative groups and setting their access rights to objects.

Consider how to coordinate the ownership of NIS+ domains with the ownership of DNS domains. Here are some guidelines.

- The administration of the DNS domain structure remains the responsibility of the highest-level administrative group at the site.
- This same administrative group also owns the top-level NIS+ domain.
- Responsibility for the administration of lower-level DNS and NIS+ domains is delegated to individual sites by the top-level administrative group. If the NIS+ domains will be created along the same principles as the DNS domains (for instance, organized geographically), this delegation will be simple to spell out.

Determine Resource Availability

Determine what administrative resources will be required for the implementation. These will be above and beyond the resources required for normal operation of NIS+. A transition involving a long period of NIS+/NIS compatibility may require additional resources.

Consider not only the task of implementing the namespace design, but also of converting the numerous clients and dealing with special requests or problems. Keep in mind that NIS+ has a steep learning curve. Administrators may be less efficient for a while at performing support functions with NIS+ than they were with NIS. We recommend not only formal training, but extensive lab sessions with hands-on experience.

Finally, even after the transition is complete, administrators will require extra time to become as familiar with the everyday workflow of supporting NIS+ as they were with those of NIS.

Also consider the hardware resources. NIS servers are often used to support other network services such as routing, printing, and file management. Because of the potential load on an NIS+ server, we recommend that you use dedicated NIS+ servers. Doing so simplifies the transition because it simplifies troubleshooting and performance monitoring. Of course, you incur the cost of additional systems. How many servers you will need and what their configurations should be is described in Chapter 8, "Designing the NIS+ Namespace."

Remember, these servers are required *in addition to* the NIS servers. Although the NIS servers may be decommissioned or recycled after the transition is complete, the NIS+ servers will continue to be used.

Resolve Conflicts Between Login Names and Hostnames

The NIS+ authentication scheme does not allow workstations and users to share names within a domain. Although it gives login names precedence, NIS+ does not distinguish hostnames from login names, so if the same name is used for both, you'll run into problems with permissions and the automounter tables. You may need to alias the duplicate hostnames.

You'll need these procedures before the implementation can begin, but you should also adapt them later for checking new workstations and users during routine NIS+ operation.

Remove the "." From NIS Map Names

NIS+ automounter tables have replaced the "." in their names with underscores. However, you need to make this change to the NIS maps that you will use during the transition. If you don't, NIS+ will confuse the "." in the name with the periods that distinguish domain levels in object names. Be sure to convert the "." to underscores for *all* NIS maps, not just those of the automounter.

11

Document the Existing NIS Namespace

Documenting your current configuration will give you a clear point of departure for the transition. Document your existing NIS namespace, at a minimum, listing the following:

- Name and location of all current NIS domains and networks
- Hostname and location of all current NIS servers, both master and slave
- Configuration of all current NIS servers, including:
  - Hostname
  - CPU type
  - Memory size
  - Disk space available
  - Name of administrators with root access
- Nonstandard NIS maps

Map the list of your NIS clients to their eventual NIS+ domains. Determine whether they will need to be upgraded to Solaris 2.3 or whether they will use the Solaris 1.x distribution of NIS+.

Create a Conversion Plan for the NIS Servers

Take stock of your NIS servers. Although you can recycle them after the transition is complete, keep in mind that you will go through a stage in which you will need servers for *both* services. Therefore, you cannot simply plan to satisfy all your NIS+ server needs with your existing NIS servers.

You might find it helpful to create a detailed conversion plan for NIS servers, identifying the NIS servers that will be used for NIS+ and when they will be converted. We do not recommend that you salvage NIS servers during the transition, since this can impact the stability of the namespace. The implementation is most stable when you check the operation of the entire namespace as a whole before you convert any clients to NIS+.

Map each server to its eventual NIS+ domain and identify its capacity (master or replica). Once you have identified the servers you plan to convert to NIS+ service, upgrade them to NIS+ requirements (see "Disk Space and Memory Requirements" on page 124).

Implementing the Transition 12 ☰

Once you have performed the tasks described in the previous chapters, most of your hard work is done. Now all you have to do is set up the namespace you designed and add the clients to it. This chapter describes how to do that. Before performing these steps, be sure you have verified that all your pretransition tasks are completed and that users at your site are aware of your plans.

If you are running separate NIS+ domains under DNS domains, you will set up one NIS+ namespace under each DNS domain. After you have set up a complete NIS+ namespace under the first DNS domain and have verified that everything is working right, then you can set up the other NIS+ namespaces in parallel.

Here are the major implementation steps:

Phase I—Set Up the NIS+ Namespace

Set up the namespace with full DES authentication, even if the domains will operate in NIS compatibility mode. Use either the NIS+ setup commands or the NIS+ scripts, both described in Part 3 of this book. Whichever method you choose, make sure to perform the following steps.

1. **Set up the root domain.**
   If you are going to run the root domain in NIS compatibility mode, be sure to use the `-Y` versions of `rpc.nisd` and `nissetup`.

2. **Populate the root domain tables.**
   You can transfer information from NIS maps or text files, using the `nispopulate` script or the `nisaddent` command. Of course, you can also create entries one at a time, using `nistbladm`.

3. **Set up clients of the root domain.**
   Set up about 15–20 clients in the root domain so that you can test its operation properly. Be sure to use full DES authentication. Some of these clients will later be converted to root replica servers. Some will serve as workstations for the administrators who support the root domain.

4. **Create or convert site-specific NIS+ tables.**
   If the new NIS+ root domain will require custom, site-specific NIS+ tables, create them with the `nistbladm` command. Transfer NIS data into them with the `nisaddent` command. Make sure to propagate them to the replicas, using `nisping -C`.

5. **Add administrators to the root domain groups.**
   Use the `nisgrpadm` command. Be sure to give the administrators both LOCAL and DES credentials, using the `nisaddcred` command. Make their workstations clients of the root domain and give them DES credentials.

6. **Update the Sendmailvars table, if necessary.**
   If your email environment has changed as a result of the new domain structure, populate the root domain's Sendmailvars table with the new entries.

7. **Set up root domain replicas.**
   Remember to first convert the clients into servers (use `rpc.nisd` with `-Y` and `-Y` for NIS compatibility and `-B` for DNS forwarding), then associate the servers with the root domain. Use either the `nisserver` script with `-R` or the `nismkdir -s` command.

8. **Test the root domain's operation.**
   Develop a set of installation-specific test routines to verify a client's operation after the switch to NIS+. This speeds the transition work and reduces complaints. We recommend that you operate this domain for about a week before you begin converting other users to NIS+.

9. **Set up the remainder of the namespace.**
   Do not convert any more clients to NIS+, but go ahead and set up all the other domains beneath the root domain. This includes setting up their master and replica servers. Be sure to test each new domain as thoroughly as you tested the root domain until you are sure your configurations and scripts work properly.

10. **Test the operation of the namespace.**
    Test all operational procedures for maintenance, backup, recovery, and other scenarios. Be sure to test the information sharing process among all domains in the namespace. Do not proceed to the next phase until the entire NIS+ operational environment has been verified.

11. **Customize the security configuration of the NIS+ domains.**
    This step may not be necessary if everything is working fine, but if you want to protect some information from unauthorized access, you could change the default permissions of NIS+ tables so that even NIS clients would be unable to access them. You might also want to rearrange the membership of NIS+ groups and the permissions of NIS+ structural objects to align with administrative responsibilities.

Phase II—Connect the NIS+ Namespace to Other Namespaces

12. **Connect the root domain to the DNS namespace** (optional).
    An NIS+ domain can be connected to the Internet via its NIS+ clients, using the Name Service Switch, described below. The client, if it is also a DNS client, can set up its Switch configuration file to search for information in either DNS zone file—in addition to NIS maps or NIS+ tables.

    In order to do this, be sure each client's `/etc/nsswitch.conf` and `/etc/resolv.config` files are configured properly. The `/etc/nsswitch.conf` file is the client's Name Service Switch configuration file. The `/etc/resolv.config` lists the names of the client's DNS servers.

13. **Test the joint operation of NIS+ with DNS.**
    Be sure that requests for information can pass between the namespaces without difficulty.

14. **If operating NIS+ in parallel with NIS, test the transfer of information.**
    Use either the `nispopulate` script or the `nisaddent` command to transfer information back and forth between namespaces. Use scripts to automate this process. Establish policies for keeping tables synchronized; in particular, the Hosts and Passwd tables. Test the tools used to maintain consistency between the NIS and NIS+ environments. Decide when to make the NIS+ tables dominant.

15. Test operation of NIS+ with both DNS and NIS.
Although each namespace may operate perfectly with the other, you should test all three together to make sure the added links don't create problems.

Phase III—Make the NIS+ Namespace Fully Operational

16. Convert clients to NIS+.
Do this one workgroup at a time, and convert all workgroups in a subnet before starting on those of another subnet. That way, when you convert all the clients in a subnet, you can eliminate the NIS service on that subnet. Run the verification script after converting each client to make sure that the conversion worked properly. That verification script should inform the user about the support structure that can help with problems and how to report them.

The actual steps required depend on the site. Use the `nisclient` script or follow the instructions in Part 3. However, if the client is also a DNS client, check its `/etc/resolv.conf` and `/etc/nsswitch.conf` files to make sure they reflect the way you want the namespaces to interoperate.

A client conversion script can save you conversion time. For instance, instead of changing every client's domain name manually, you could insert that change into the client script. Other changes could be editing a client's `sendmail` configuration, DNS configuration, or the name service switch configuration file, adding site-specific environment variables, and even rebooting the client workstation.

You can also save time if your site has a shared, mounted central directory similar to `/usr/local`. You could put the script in the central directory and, on the day of conversion, send mail to clients asking them to run the script as root before leaving for the day.

17. Monitor the status of the transition.
Be sure to monitor the progress of the transition as clients are being converted. Track the progress against your plan; track all serious complications not anticipated in the planning stages. Post your status so that interested parties can access it at any time.

18. Decommission NIS servers.
As all the clients on a subnet are converted to NIS+, decommission the NIS servers. If a particular subnet has some clients that require NIS service, use the NIS compatibility feature of the NIS+ servers, but do not retain the NIS servers.

19. **Evaluate NIS+ Performance.**

    Once the implementation is complete, evaluate the performance of the NIS+ service.

20. **Optimize the NIS+ environment.**

    Based on the results of your performance evaluation, modify the NIS+ environment as needed. These improvements could be as simple as adding selected replicas in domains with high loads or as involved as rearranging the storage of NIS+ information for a group of domains.

21. **Upgrade old domain names.**

    If, for the sake of simplicity, you did not change old domain names during the transition, then upgrade them now to the new NIS+ naming scheme. For instance, if you left some domains with geographic labels while you converted to an organizational hierarchy, change the geographic names to their organizational versions.

Phase IV—Upgrade NIS-compatible Domains

22. **Convert the last NIS clients to NIS+.**

    As soon as you can, eliminate the need for NIS-compatible NIS+ domains. Upgrading the last NIS clients to NIS+ will allow you to take advantage of NIS+ security features. Remember to do the following:

    - Edit `/etc/defaultdomain` if domain name is different
    - Edit `/etc/nsswitch.conf` file
    - Initialize the client with `nisinit -C`
    - If the client is also a DNS client, edit the `/etc/resolv.conf` file
    - Create credentials for the client user and client workstation

23. **Adjust your security configuration.**

    Once you have no more NIS clients, you can restart the NIS+ servers in standard mode, eliminating the security hole caused by NIS compatibility. If you did not create credentials for NIS+ principals before, do that now. You'll also need to make sure you have restricted access to unauthenticated principals.

24. **Establish miscellaneous evaluation and improvement programs.**

    Evaluate operational procedures to determine which ones can be improved; in particular, procedures used to recover from problems. Plan for new NIS+ releases and possible functional enhancements. Track the development of SunOS components that might require new NIS+ tables. Look for automated tools that allow you to perform NIS+ administration functions more efficiently. Finally, work with internal developers to help them take advantage of the NIS+ API.

This step completes the transition.

Part 3—Setting Up NIS+

13   *Setup Guidelines*
This chapter suggests two setup sequences, one using standard NIS+ commands, the other using the NIS+ scripts.

14   *Setting Up an NIS+ Namespace, Using the NIS+ Scripts*
This chapter provides step-by-step instructions for setting up an NIS+ namespace, using the NIS+ scripts.

15   *Setting Up the Root Domain*
This chapter provides step-by-step instructions for setting up the root domain, whether NIS-compatible or standard NIS+.

16   *Setting Up NIS+ Tables*
This chapter provides step-by-step instructions for populating NIS+ tables, whether in the root domain or a subdomain, with information from input files or NIS maps.

17   *Setting Up an NIS+ Client*
This chapter provides step-by-step instructions for setting up an NIS+ client. The instructions apply to clients in the root domain and in nonroot domains.

18   *Setting Up an NIS+ Server*
This chapter provides step-by-step instructions for setting up a generic NIS+ server, which can later be assigned to any role except that of root master.

19   *Setting Up a Nonroot Domain*
This chapter provides step-by-step instructions for creating and setting up a nonroot domain, including designating its master and replica servers.

20   *Setting Up the Name Service Switch*
This chapter provides step-by-step instructions for setting up the Name Service Switch for use with NIS+, NIS, and DNS, as well as to provide backward compatibility with the +/- syntax.

Setup Guidelines 13 ≡

You can set up NIS+ with the standard NIS+ commands or with the NIS+ scripts (Solaris 2.3 or subsequent releases). This chapter provides a recommended setup procedure for both techniques:

Recommended Setup Sequence—Standard	Page 167
Recommended Setup Procedure—Scripts	Page 169

Recommended Setup Sequence—Standard

Figure 13-1 summarizes the recommended setup procedure. The blocks on the left represent the major setup activities, such as setting up the root domain or setting up a client. The text in the middle describes the blocks. The chapter numbers and tasks on the right point to the instructions that describe how to carry out each block.

The order of activities shown in Figure 13-1 is not mandatory. You could set up your namespace differently. However, the individual tasks would remain the same; only their order would change.

Activity	Description	Chapter	Task
1- Set Up Root Domain	Create the root domain; set up and initialize the root master server. Create root domain administration group and administrator credentials.	**15**	▼ How to Set Up the Root Domain
2- Populate Tables	Populate the NIS+ tables of the root domain from text files.	**16**	▼ How to Populate NIS+ Tables from Files
3- Set Up Root Domain Clients	Create credentials for clients of the root domain and set up the clients. Some of them will subsequently be converted into servers.	**17**	▼ How to Set Up an NIS+ Client
4- Set Up Servers	Convert some clients of the root domain into servers. Some will later become root replicas, others will support lower-level domains.	**18**	▼ How to Set Up an NIS+ Server
5- Designate Root Replicas	Designate one or more of the servers just set up as a replica of the root domain.	**18**	▼ How to Add a Replica to an Existing Domain
6- Set Up Nonroot Domain	Set up a new domain. Designate previously set-up servers as its master and replica(s). Create its administration group and administration credentials.	**19**	▼ How to Set Up a Nonroot Domain
7- Populate Tables	Populate the NIS+ tables of the new domain from text files.	**16**	▼ How to Populate NIS+ Tables from Files
8- Set Up Domain Clients	Create credentials for clients of the new domain and set them up. Some of them will subsequently be converted into servers for lower-level domains.	**17**	▼ How to Set Up an NIS+ Client
9- Set Up Servers for Lower Level	If the domain will have lower-level domains, convert some of its clients into the servers that will later become masters and replicas of the lower levels.	**18**	▼ How to Set Up an NIS+ Server
10- Set Up Other Domains	Set up other domains, whether parallel to the new domain or beneath it, by repeating blocks 6 through 9.		

Figure 13-1   Recommended NIS+ Setup Procedure—Standard

Recommended Setup Procedure—Scripts

Figure 13-2 summarizes the recommended generic setup procedure. The left column lists the major setup activities, such as setting up the root domain or creating a client. The text in the middle describes the activities. The third column lists the script or NIS+ command that accomplishes each step.

Activity	Description	Script and NIS+ Command
1- Set Up Root Domain	Create the root domain. Set up and initialize the root master server. Create the root domain administration group.	`nisserver`
2- Populate Tables	Populate the NIS+ tables of the root domain from text files or NIS maps. *Create credentials for root domain clients. Create administrator credentials.*	`nispopulate` `nisgrpadm` `nisping`
3- Set Up Root Domain Clients	Set up the client machines. (Some of them will subsequently be converted into servers.) *Initialize users as NIS+ clients.*	`nisclient`
4- Enable Servers	Enable some clients of the root domain to become servers. Some servers will later become root replicas, others will support lower-level domains.	`rpc.nisd`
5- Set Up Root Replicas	Designate one or more of the servers you just set up as a replica of the root domain.	`nisserver`
6- Set Up Nonroot Domain	Create a new domain. Designate previously enabled server as its master. Create its administration group and administration credentials.	`nisserver`
7- Populate Tables	Create credentials for clients of the new domain. Populate the NIS+ tables of the new domain from text files or NIS maps.	`nispopulate`
8- Set Up Domain Clients	Set up the clients of the new domain. (Some may subsequently be converted into servers for lower-level domains.) Initialize users as NIS+ clients.	`nisclient`
9- Set Up Servers for Lower Level	If the namespace will have lower-level domains, convert some of the second-level domain's clients into the servers that will later become masters and replicas of the lower levels.	`nisserver`
10- Set Up Other Domains	Set up other domains, whether at the same level as the new domain or beneath it, by repeating activities 6 through 9.	

Figure 13-2 Recommended NIS+ Setup Procedure—Scripts

Setting Up an NIS+ Namespace, Using the NIS+ Scripts   14 ≡

This chapter shows you how to set up a basic NIS+ namespace using the scripts `nisserver`, `nispopulate`, and `nisclient` in combination with a few NIS+ commands. Setting up NIS+ will be much simpler if you use these scripts than if you use the NIS+ commands described in the remainder of Part 3. The NIS+ setup scenarios described below use the scripts' default values.

This chapter provides step-by-step procedures for the following tasks:

See the `nisserver`(1M), `nispopulate`(1M), and `nisclient`(1M) man pages for complete descriptions of the scripts.

What the NIS+ Scripts Won't Do

While the NIS+ scripts reduce the effort required to create an NIS+ namespace, the scripts do not completely eliminate the need to use NIS+ commands, since they implement only a subset of NIS+ features.

The `nisserver` script will set up an NIS+ server only with the standard default tables and permissions (authorizations). This script does *not*:

- Set special permissions for tables and directories
- Add extra NIS+ principals to the NIS+ admin group
- Create private tables
- Start the `rpc.nisd` daemon on remote servers, which is required to complete server installation

The `nisclient` script does not set up an NIS+ client to resolve hostnames using DNS. You need to explicitly set DNS for clients that require this option.

Script Prerequisites

Before you use the scripts:

- Plan your NIS+ layout
- Choose a root server machine
- Choose a root domain name
- Choose your client machines

Note – The machine that will be designated the root server must be up and running, and you must have superuser access to it.

Creating a Sample NIS+ Namespace with Scripts

The procedures in this chapter show you how to create a sample NIS+ namespace. The sample NIS+ namespace will be created from `/etc` files and NIS maps. This sample shows you how to use the scripts both when your site is not running the Network Information Service (NIS) and when NIS is running at your site.

Note – Your site's actual NIS+ namespace and its domain hierarchy will probably differ from the sample namespace's, and yours will probably contain a different number of servers, clients, and domains. Do not expect to have any resemblance between your final domain configuration or hierarchy and the sample one. The sample namespace is merely an illustration of how to use the NIS+ scripts. Once you have created this sample namespace, you should have a clear idea about how to create domains, servers, and clients at your site.

The sample namespace will contain the following components:

- A root master server (for the Wiz.com. domain)
- Four clients:
    - The first client will become a root replica (for the Wiz.com. domain)
    - The second client will become a master server for a new subdomain (for the Subwiz.Wiz.com. domain)
    - The third client will become a nonroot replica server of the new subdomain (for the Subwiz.Wiz.com. domain)
    - The fourth client will remain solely a client of the root domain (Wiz.com.)
- Two clients of the subdomain (Subwiz.Wiz.com.)

This scenario shows the scripts being used to set up NIS+ at a site that uses both system information files, such as /etc/hosts, and NIS maps to store network service information. The sample NIS+ namespace uses such a mixed site purely for example.

Figure 14-1 shows the layout of the sample namespace. When you finish creating the sample domain, it should resemble the NIS+ domain in this figure. Notice that some machines are simultaneously servers and clients.

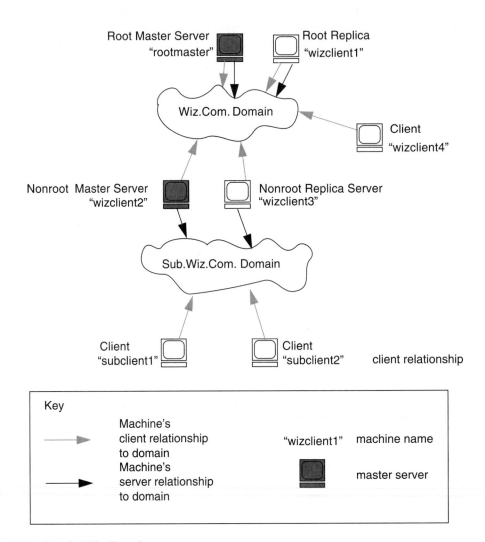

Figure 14-1   Sample NIS+ Domain

Summary of NIS+ Scripts Command Lines

Table 14-1 contains the generic sequence of NIS+ scripts and commands you will use to create the NIS+ domains shown in Figure 14-1. Subsequent sections describe these command lines in detail. After you are familiar with the tasks required to create NIS+

domains, servers, and clients, use Table 14-1 as a quick reference guide to the appropriate command lines. Table 14-2 on page 210 is a summary of the actual commands with the appropriate variables that you will type to create the sample NIS+ namespace.

Table 14-1   NIS+ Domains Setup Command Lines Summary

Purpose	On Which Machine	Command Line

Include `/usr/ lib/nis` in root's path; C shell or Bourne shell.	Root master server and client machines as superuser	`setenv PATH $PATH:/usr/lib/nis`
		or
		`PATH=$PATH:/usr/lib/nis; export PATH`

Create a root master server without or with YP (NIS) compatibility.	Root master server as superuser	`nisserver -r -d` *newdomain.* or `nisserver -Y -r -d` *newdomain.*
Populate the root master server tables from files or from NIS maps.	Root master server as superuser	`nispopulate -F -p` */files* `-d` *newdomain.* or `nispopulate -Y -d` *newdomain.* `-h` *NIS_servername* `-a` *NIS_server_ipaddress* `-y` *NIS_domain*
Add additional users to the NIS+ admin group.	Root master server as superuser	`nisgrpadm -a admin.`*domain.* *name.domain.*
Make a checkpoint of the NIS+ database.	Root master server as superuser	`nisping -C` *domain.*
Initialize a new client machine.	Client machine as superuser	`nisclient -i -d` *domain.* `-h` *rootmaster*
Initialize user as an NIS+ client.	Client machine as user	`nisclient -u`

Start the `rpc.nisd` daemon—required to convert a client to a server without or with NIS (and DNS) compatibility.	Client machine as superuser	`rpc.nisd`
		or
		`rpc.nisd -Y`
		or
		`rpc.nisd -Y -B`

Table 14-1 NIS+ Domains Setup Command Lines Summary (Continued)

Purpose	On Which Machine	Command Line
Convert a server to a root replica.	Root master server as superuser	`nisserver -R -d` *domain.* `-h` *clientname*
Convert a server to a nonroot master server.	Root master server as superuser	`nisserver -M -d` *newsubdomain.domain.* `-h \` *clientmachine*
Populate the new master server tables from files or from NIS maps.	New subdomain master server as superuser	`nispopulate -F -p` */subdomaindirectory* `-d \` *newsubdomain.domain.* or `nispopulate -Y -d` *newsubdomain.domain.* `-h \` *NIS_servername* `-a` *NIS_server_ipaddress* `-y` *NIS_domain*
Convert a client to a master server replica.	Subdomain master server as superuser	`nisserver -R -d` *subdomain.domain.* `-h` *clientname*
Initialize a new client of the subdomain. Clients can be converted to subdomain replicas or to another server.	New subdomain client machine as superuser	`nisclient -i -d` *newsubdomain.domain.* `-h \` *subdomainmaster*
Initialize user as an NIS+ client.	Client machine as user	`nisclient -u`

Setting Up NIS+ Root Servers with Scripts

Setting up the root master server is the first activity towards establishing an NIS+ domain. This section shows how to set up a root master server using the `nisserver` script with default settings. The root master server will use the following defaults:

- Security level 2 (DES)—the highest level of NIS+ security
- NIS (YP) compatible set to `OFF` (instructions for setting NIS (`yp`) compatibility are included)
- System information files (`/etc`) or NIS maps as the source of network services information
- `admin.`*domainname* as the NIS+ group

Note – The `nisserver` script modifies the Name Service Switch file for NIS+ when it sets up a root master server. The `/etc/nsswitch.conf` file may be changed later.

Prerequisites to Running `nisserver`

While the `/etc/passwd` file on the machine you want to be root master server usually contains an entry for root, check to see that this is the case.

You need the following information:

- The superuser password of the workstation that will become the root master server
- The name of the new root domain

In the following example, the machine that will be designated the root master server is called `rootmaster`, and Wiz.com. will be the new root domain.

▼ How to Create a Root Master Server (Scripts)

1. **Set the superuser's** `PATH` **variable to include** `/usr/lib/nis`.
   Either add this path to root's `.cshrc` or `.profile` file or set the variable directly with either of the following commands. The first example shows the C shell command; the second example shows the Bourne shell command.

   ```
   rootmaster# setenv PATH $PATH:/usr/lib/nis

   rootmaster# PATH=$PATH:/usr/lib/nis; export PATH
   ```

2. **Type the following as superuser (root) to set up a root master server.**
   The `-r` option indicates that a root master server should be set up. The `-d` option specifies the NIS+ domain name.

   ```
   rootmaster# nisserver -r -d Wiz.com.
   This script sets up this machine "rootmaster" as a NIS+
   Root Master Server for domain Wiz.com.

   Domainname              : Wiz.com.
   NIS+ Group              : admin.Wiz.com.
   YP compatibility        : OFF
   Security level          : 2=DES

   Is this information correct? (Y or N)
   ```

NIS+ Group" refers to the group of users who are authorized to modify the information in the Wiz.com. domain. (Domain names always end with a period.) Modification includes deletion. `admin.`*domainname* is the default name of the group. See "How to Change Incorrect Information (Scripts)" on page 180 for instructions on how to change this name.

"YP compatibility" (NIS compatibility) refers to whether an NIS+ server will accept information requests from NIS clients. When set to `OFF`, the default setting, the NIS+ server will not fulfill requests from NIS clients. When set to `ON`, an NIS+ server will fulfill such requests. You can change the NIS compatibility setting with this script. See "How to Change Incorrect Information (Scripts)" on page 180.

Note – This script sets machines only to security level 2, the highest level of NIS+ security. You cannot change the security level when using this script. After the script has completed, you can change the security level with the appropriate NIS+ command.

---

3. **Type y (if the information shown on the screen is correct).**
   Typing n causes the script to prompt you for the correct information. (See "How to Change Incorrect Information (Scripts)" below for what to do if you type n.)

   ```
   Is this information correct? (Y or N) y

   This script will set up your machine as a Root Master server for
   domain Wiz.com.

   Do you want to continue? (Y or N)
   ```

4. **Type y to continue the NIS+ setup.**
   (Typing n safely stops the script.) If you interrupt the script after you have chosen y and while the script is running, the script stops running; whatever it has so far created is retained. The script does not do any automatic recovery or cleaning up. You can always rerun this script.

   ```
   Do you want to continue? (Y or N) y

   setting up domain information "Wiz.com." ...

   setting up switch information ...

   running nisinit ...
   This machine is in the Wiz.com. NIS+ domain.
   Setting up root server ...
   All done.
   ```

```
Do you want to continue? (Y or N) y

starting root server at security level 0 ...

running nissetup ...
org_dir.Wiz.com. created
groups_dir.Wiz.com. created
passwd.org_dir.Wiz.com. created
group.org_dir.Wiz.com. created
auto_master.org_dir.Wiz.com. created
auto_home.org_dir.Wiz.com. created
bootparams.org_dir.Wiz.com. created
cred.org_dir.Wiz.com. created
ethers.org_dir.Wiz.com. created
hosts.org_dir.Wiz.com. created
mail_aliases.org_dir.Wiz.com. created
sendmailvars.org_dir.Wiz.com. created
netmasks.org_dir.Wiz.com. created
netgroup.org_dir.Wiz.com. created
networks.org_dir.Wiz.com. created
protocols.org_dir.Wiz.com. created
rpc.org_dir.Wiz.com. created
services.org_dir.Wiz.com. created
timezone.org_dir.Wiz.com. created

adding credential for rootmaster.Wiz.com...
Enter login password:
```

The `nissetup` command creates the directories for each NIS+ table.

5. **Type your machine's root password at the prompt, then press Return.**
   In this case, the user typed the `rootmaster` machine's root password.

```
Wrote secret key into /etc/.rootkey

setting NIS+ group admin.Wiz.com. ...

restarting root server at security level 2 ...

The system is now configured as a root server for domain Wiz.com.
You can now populate the standard NIS+ tables by using the
nispopulate or /usr/lib/nis/nisaddent commands.
```

Your root master server is now set up and ready for you to populate the NIS+ standard tables. To continue with populating tables, skip to "Populating NIS+ Tables with Scripts" on page 181.

▼ How to Change Incorrect Information (Scripts)

If you typed n because some or all of the information returned to you was wrong in step 2 in the above procedure, you will see the following:

```
Is this information correct? (Y or N) n
Domainname: [Wiz.com.]
```

1. **Press Return if Domainname is correct; otherwise, type the correct domain name and press Return.**
    In this example, Return was pressed, confirming that the desired domain name is Wiz.com. The script then prompts for the NIS+ Group name.

```
Is this information correct? (Y or N) n
Domainname: [Wiz.com.]
NIS+ Group: [admin.Wiz.com.]
```

2. **Press Return if NIS+ Group is correct; otherwise, type the correct NIS+ Group name and press Return.**
    In this example, the name was changed. The script then prompts for YP (NIS) compatibility.

```
NIS+ Group: [admin.Wiz.com.] netadmin.Wiz.com.
YP compatibility (0=off, 1=on): [0]
```

3. **Press Return if you do not want NIS compatibility; otherwise, type 1 and press Return.**
    In this example, Return was pressed, confirming that NIS-compatibility status is correct. Once again, the script asks you if the information is correct.

Note – If you choose to make this server NIS-compatible, you also need to edit a file and restart the `rpc.nisd` daemon before it will work. See "How to Configure a Client as an NIS+ Server (Scripts)" for more information.

```
YP compatibility (0=off, 1=on): [0]
Domainname              : Wiz.com.
NIS+ Group              : netadmin.Wiz.com.
YP compatibility        : OFF
Security level          : 2=DES

Is this information correct? (Y or N)
```

Once the information is correct, continue with Step 3 in "How to Create a Root Master Server (Scripts)." You can keep choosing n until the information is correct.

Note – This script sets machines only at security level 2. You cannot change the security level when using this script. After the script has completed, you can change the security level with the appropriate NIS+ command.

Populating NIS+ Tables with Scripts

Once the root master server has been set up, populate its standard NIS+ tables with network services information. This section shows you how to populate the root master server's tables with data from files or NIS maps, using the `nispopulate` script with default settings. The script uses:

- The domain created in the previous example (Wiz.com.)
- System information files or NIS maps as the source of network services
- The standard NIS+ tables: `auto_master`, `auto_home`, `ethers`, `group`, `hosts`, `networks`, `passwd`, `protocols`, `services`, `rpc`, `netmasks`, `bootparams`, `netgroup`, **and** `aliases`

Note – The `shadow` file contents are merged with the `passwd` file contents to create the `passwd` table when files are the tables' information source. No shadow table is created.

Prerequisites to Running nispopulate

Before you can run the script nispopulate:

- The information in the files must be formatted appropriately for the table into which it will be loaded. Appendix A, "Information in NIS+ Tables," describes the format required for a text file to be transferred into its corresponding NIS+ table. Local /etc files are usually formatted properly. NIS maps from running NIS domains are presumed to be correctly formatted.

- We recommend that, for safety, you make copies of the /etc files and use the copies to populate the tables instead of using the actual ones. (This example uses files in a directory called /nis+files, for instance.) You also may want to edit four of the copied files, passwd, shadow, aliases, and hosts, for security. For example, you may want to remove the following lines from the copy of your local passwd file so they will not be distributed across the namespace:

```
root:x:0:1:0000-Admin(0000):/:/sbin/sh
daemon:x:1:3:0000-Admin(0000):/:
bin:x:3:5:0000-Admin(0000):/usr/bin:
sys:x:3:3:0000-Admin(0000):/:
adm:x:4:4:0000-Admin(0000):/var/adm:
lp:x:78:9:0000-lp(0000):/usr/spool/lp:
smtp:x:0:0:mail daemon user:/:
uucp:x:5:5:0000-uucp(0000):/usr/lib/uucp:
nuucp:x:7:8:0000-uucp(0000):/var/spool/uucppublic:/usr/lib/
uucp/uucico
listen:x:22:6:Network Admin:/usr/net/nls:
nobody:x:60000:60000:uid no body:/:
noaccess:x:60002:60002:uid no access:/:
```

- The domain must have already been set up, and its master server must be running.

- The domain's server must have sufficient disk space to accommodate the new table information.

- You must be logged in as an NIS+ principal and have write permission to the NIS+ tables in the specified domain. In this example, you would have to be the user "root" on the machine rootmaster.

If populating from files, you need the following information:

- The new NIS+ domain name

- The path of the appropriately edited text files whose data will be transferred

- Your root password

If populating from NIS maps, you need the following information:

- The new NIS+ domain name
- The NIS domain name
- The NIS server name
- The IP address of the NIS server
- Your root password

Note – The NIS domain name is case-sensitive, while the NIS+ domain name is not.

▼ How to Populate the Root Master Server Tables (Scripts)

1. **Perform either step a or step b to populate the root master server tables; then continue with step 2.**
   Step a describes how to populate tables from files. Step b describes how to populate tables from NIS maps. Type these commands in a scrolling window, as the script's output may otherwise scroll off the screen.

Note – The `nispopulate` script may fail if there is insufficient `/tmp` space on the system. To keep this from happening, you can set the environment variable TMPDIR to a different directory. If TMPDIR is not set to a valid directory, the script uses the `/tmp` directory.

a. **Type the following to populate the tables from files.**

```
rootmaster# nispopulate -F -p /nis+files -d Wiz.com.

NIS+ Domainname           : Wiz.com.
Directory Path            : /nis+files


Is this information correct? (Y or N)
```

The -F option specifies that the tables take their data from files. The -p option specifies the directory search path for the source files. (In this case, the path is /nis+files.) The -d option specifies the NIS+ domain name. (In this case, the domain name is Wiz.com.)

The NIS+ principal user is root. You must perform this task as superuser in this instance because this is the first time that you are going to populate the root master server's tables. The nispopulate script adds credentials for all members of the NIS+ admin group.

b. **Type the following to populate the tables from NIS maps.**

```
rootmaster# nispopulate -Y -d Wiz.com. -h corporatemachine
-a 130.48.58.111 -y corporate.wiz.com.

NIS+ Domainname           : wiz.com.
YP Domain                 : corporate.wiz.com
YP Server Hostname        : corporatemachine

Is this information correct? (Y or N)
```

The -Y option specifies that the tables take their data from NIS maps. The -d option specifies the NIS+ domain name. The -h option specifies the NIS server's machine name. (In this case, the NIS server's name is corporatemachine. You would have to insert the name of a real NIS server at your site to create the sample domain.) The -a option specifies the NIS server's IP address. (In this case, the address is 130.48.58.111. You would have to insert the IP address of a real NIS server at your site to create the sample domain.) The -y option specifies the NIS domain name. (In this case, corporate.wiz.com is the domain's name. You would have to insert the NIS domain name of the real NIS domain at your site to create the sample domain. Remember that NIS domain names are case-sensitive.)

The NIS+ principal user is root. You must perform this task as superuser in this instance because this is the first time that you are going to populate the root master server's tables. The `nispopulate` script also adds credentials for all members of the NIS+ admin group.

2. **Type y (if the information returned on the screen is correct).**
   Typing n causes the script to prompt you for the correct information. (See "How to Change Incorrect Information (Scripts)" on page 180 for what you need to do if the information is incorrect.)

   a. **If you performed step 1a, you will see the following:**

   ```
   Is this information correct? (Y or N) y

   This script will populate the following NIS+ tables for domain
   Wiz.com. from the files in /nis+files:
   auto_master auto_home ethers group hosts networks passwd
   protocols services rpc netmasks bootparams netgroup aliases
   shadow

   Do you want to continue? (Y or N)
   ```

   b. **If you performed step 1b, you will see the following:**

   ```
   Is this information correct? (Y or N) y

   This script will populate the following NIS+ tables for domain
   wiz.com. from the YP maps in domain corporate:
   auto_master auto_home ethers group hosts networks passwd
   protocols services rpc netmasks bootparams netgroup aliases

   Do you want to continue? (Y or N) y
   ```

3. **Type y to continue populating the tables.**
   (Typing n safely stops the script.) If you interrupt the script after you have chosen y and while the script is running, the script stops running and may leave the tables only partially populated. The table that was currently being populated may be

only partially populated. The script does not do any automatic recovery or cleaning up. You can safely rerun the script; however, the tables will be overwritten with the latest information.

a. If you are populating tables from files, you will see the following:

```
Do you want to continue? (Y or N) y

populating auto_master table from file /nis+files/auto_master...

auto_master table done.

populating auto_home table from file /nis+files/auto_home...

auto_home table done.

populating ethers table from file /nis+files/ethers...

ethers table done.

populating group table from file /nis+files/group...

group table done.

populating hosts table from file /nis+files/hosts...

hosts table done.

Populating the NIS+ credential table for domain Wiz.com.
from hosts table. The passwd used will be nisplus.

dumping hosts table...
loading credential table...

The credential table for domain Wiz.com. has been populated.

populating networks table from file /nis+files/networks...
networks table done.

populating passwd table from file /nis+files/passwd...
passwd table done.
Populating the NIS+ credential table for domain Wiz.com.
from passwd table. The passwd used will be nisplus.

dumping passwd table...
```

```
loading credential table...
The credential table for domain Wiz.com. has been populated.

populating protocols table from file /nis+files/protocols...

protocols table done.

populating services table from file /nis+files/services...

services table done.

populating rpc table from file /nis+files/rpc...

rpc table done.

populating netmasks table from file /nis+files/netmasks...

netmasks table done.

populating bootparams table from file /nis+files/bootparams...
bootparams table done.

populating netgroup table from file /nis+files/netgroup...
netgroup table done

populating aliases table from file /nis+files/aliases...

aliases table done.

populating shadow table from file /nis+files/shadow...

shadow table done.
Done!
```

The script continues until it has searched for all the files it expects and loads all the tables it can from the available files.

b. If you are populating tables from NIS maps, you will see the following:

```
Do you want to continue? (Y or N) y

populating auto_master table from corporate.wiz.com YP domain...
auto_master table done.
```

```
populating auto_home table from file corporate.wiz.com YP
domain...
auto_home table done.

populating ethers table from corporate.wiz.com YP domain...
ethers table done.

populating group table from corporate.wiz.com YP domain...
group table done.

populating hosts table from corporate.wiz.com YP domain...
hosts table done.

Populating the NIS+ credential table for domain Wiz.com.
from hosts table. The passwd used will be nisplus.ᵃ

dumping hosts table...
loading credential table...

The credential table for domain Wiz.com. has been populated.

populating networks table from corporate.wiz.com YP domain...
networks table done.

populating passwd table from corporate.wiz.com YP domain...
passwd table done.

Populating the NIS+ credential table for domain Wiz.com.
from passwd table. The passwd used will be nisplus.ᵇ

dumping passwd table...
loading credential table...
The credential table for domain Wiz.com. has been populated.

populating protocols table from corporate.wiz.com YP domain...
protocols table done.

populating services table from corporate.wiz.com YP domain...
services table done.

populating rpc table from corporate.wiz.com YP domain...
rpc table done.
```

```
populating netmasks table from corporate.wiz.com YP domain...
parse error: no mask (key #)
netmasks table done.

populating bootparams table from corporate.wiz.com YP domain...
parse error: no value (key )
bootparams table done.

populating netgroup table from corporate.wiz.com YP domain...
netgroup table done.

populating aliases table from corporate.wiz.com YP domain...
aliases table done.

Done!
```

a. Here the script tells you that the network password will be `nisplus`. The script is using Hosts and Passwd information to create the credentials for hosts and users.
b. Here the script tells you that the network password will be `nisplus`. The script is using Hosts and Passwd information to create the credentials for hosts and users.

All the tables are now populated. You can ignore the `parse error` warnings shown above. The errors indicate that NIS+ found empty or unexpected values in a field of a particular NIS map. You may want to verify the data later after the script completes.

4. Type the following command to add yourself and other administrators to the root domain's admin group. (Optional step)

Note – This step is necessary only if you want to add additional users to the admin group now, which is a good time to add administrators to the root server. You can also add users to the admin group after you have set up NIS+.

You don't have to wait for the other administrators to change their default passwords to perform this step; however, they must already be listed in the Passwd table before you can add them to the admin group. Members of the admin group will be unable to act as NIS+ principals until they add themselves to the domain. See "How to Initialize an NIS+ User (Scripts)" for more information on initializing users. The group cache also has to expire before the new members will become active.

Use the nisgrpadm command with the -a option. The first argument is the group name, the remaining arguments are the names of the administrators. This example adds two administrators, topadmin and secondadmin, to the admin.Wiz.Com. group:

```
rootmaster# nisgrpadm -a admin.Wiz.Com.  topadmin.Wiz.Com. \
    secondadmin.Wiz.Com.
Added "topadmin.Wiz.Com." to group "admin.Wiz.Com.".
Added "secondadmin.Wiz.Com." to group "admin.Wiz.Com.".
```

5. Type the following command to checkpoint the domain.

```
rootmaster# nisping -C Wiz.Com.
Checkpointing replicas serving directory wiz.com. :
Master server is rootmaster.wiz.com.
        Last update occurred at <date>

Master server is rootmaster.wiz.com.
checkpoint scheduled on rootmaster.wiz.com..
```

This step ensures that all the servers supporting the domain transfer the new information from their initialization (.log) files to the disk-based copies of the tables. Since you have just set up the root domain, this step affects only the root master server, as the root domain does not yet have replicas.

 Caution – If you don't have enough swap or disk space, the server will be unable to checkpoint properly, but it won't notify you. One way to make sure all goes well is to list the contents of a table with the niscat command. For example, to check the contents of the rpc table, type:

```
rootmaster# niscat rpc.org_dir
rpcbind rpcbind 100000
rpcbind portmap 100000
rpcbind sunrpc 100000
```

If you don't have enough swap space, you'll see the following error message instead of the sort of output you see above:

```
can't list table: Server busy, Try Again.
```

Even though it doesn't *seem* to, this message indicates that you don't have enough swap space. Increase the swap space and checkpoint the domain again.

Setting Up Root Domain NIS+ Client Machines with Scripts

Once the root master server's tables have been populated from files or NIS maps, you can initialize an NIS+ client machine. Since the root master server is an NIS+ client of its own domain, no further steps are required to initialize it. This section shows you how to initialize an NIS+ client, using the `nisclient` script with default settings. The NIS+ client machine is a different workstation than the NIS+ root server. The script will use:

- The domain used in previous examples, Wiz.com.
- The network password created by the `nispopulate` script in the previous example (`nisplus`, the default password)

Note – The `-i` option used in "How to Initialize a New Client Machine (Scripts)" does not set up an NIS+ client to resolve hostnames requiring DNS. You need to explicitly set DNS for clients that have this option.

Prerequisites to Running `nisclient`

Before you can use the `nisclient` script:

- The domain must have already been set up, and its master server must be running.
- The master server of the domain's tables must be populated. (At a minimum, the Hosts table must have an entry for the new client machine.)
- You must be logged in as superuser on the machine that is to become an NIS+ client. In this example, the new client machine is named `wizclient1`.

You need the following information:

- The domain name
- The default network password (`nisplus`)
- The root password of the workstation that will become the client
- The IP address of the NIS+ server (in the client's home domain)

▼ How to Initialize a New Client Machine (Scripts)

1. **Type the following to initialize the new client on the new client machine.**

```
wizclient1#nisclient -i -d Wiz.com. -h rootmaster

Initializing client wizclient1 for domain "Wiz.com."...
Once initialization is done, you will need to reboot your
machine.

Do you want to continue? (Y or N)
```

The -i option initializes a client. The -d option specifies the new NIS+ domain name. (If the domain name is not specified, the default would be the current domain name.) The -h option specifies the NIS+ server's hostname.

2. **Type y.**
   Typing n exits the script. The script prompts you for the root server's IP address only if there is no entry for it in the client's /etc/hosts file.

```
Do you want to continue? (Y or N) y

Enter server rootmaster's IP address:
```

3. **Type the correct IP address, then press Return. This example uses the address 126.141.246.63.**

```
Enter server rootmaster's IP address: 126.141.246.63

setting up the name service switch information...
```

4. **Type the network password (also known as the Secure-RPC password) only if the network password differs from the root login password. In this case, use the default,** `nisplus`.

   The password does not echo on the screen. If you mistype it, you are prompted for the correct one. If you mistype it twice, the script exits and restores your previous network service. If this happens, try running the script again.

   ```
   Please enter the network password that your administrator gave
   you.
   Please enter the Secure-RPC password for root:
   ```

5. **Type the root password for this client machine.**

   The password does not echo on the screen. (If the network password and the root login password happen to be the same, you will not be prompted for the root login password.)

   Typing the root password changes the credentials for this machine. The RPC password and the root password are now the same for this machine.

   ```
   Please enter the login password for root:
   Wrote secret key into /etc/.rootkey


   Client initialization completed!!
   Please reboot your machine for changes to take effect.
   ```

6. **Reboot your new client machine.**

   Your changes will not take effect until you reboot the machine.

You can now have the users of this NIS+ client machine add themselves to the NIS+ domain.

Creating Additional Client Machines

Repeat the preceding client initiation procedure on as many machines as you like. To initiate clients for another domain, repeat the preceding procedure but change the domain and master server names to the appropriate ones.

The sample NIS+ domain described in this chapter assumes that you will initialize four clients in the domain Wiz.com. You are then going to configure two of the clients as nonroot NIS+ servers and a third client as a root replica of the root master server of the Wiz.com domain.

Note – You always have to make a system into a client of the parent domain before you can make the same system a server of any type.

Initializing NIS+ Client Users with Scripts

Once a machine has become an NIS+ client, the users of that machine must add themselves to the NIS+ domain. Adding a user to the domain means changing the network password to that user's login password. What actually happens is that the user's password and the network password are bound together. This procedure uses the `nisclient` script.

Prerequisites to Running `nisclient`

Before you can use the `nisclient` script to initialize a user:

- The domain must have already been set up and its master server must be running.
- The master server of the domain's tables must be populated. (At a minimum, the hosts table must have an entry for the new client machine.)
- You must have initialized a client machine in the domain.
- You must be logged in as a *user* on the client machine. In this example, the user is named `user1`.

You need the following information:

- A user's login name—`user1` in this example
- The default network password—`nisplus` in this example
- The login password of the user that will become the NIS+ client

▼ How to Initialize an NIS+ User (Scripts)

1. **Type the following while logged in as the user to become an NIS+ client.**

```
user1prompt% nisclient -u
Please enter the network password that your administrator gave
you.
Please enter the Secure-RPC password for user1:
```

2. **Type the network password (Secure-RPC password), which is** `nisplus` **in this case, and then press Return.**
   The password does not echo on the screen.

```
Please enter the login password for user1:
```

3. **Type the user's login password and then press Return.**
   The password does not echo on the screen.

This user is now an NIS+ client. You need to have all users make themselves NIS+ clients.

Setting Up NIS+ Servers with Scripts

Now that the clients have been initialized, you can change any of them to NIS+ servers but not into root NIS+ servers. Root NIS+ servers are a special type of NIS+ server. See "Setting Up NIS+ Root Servers with Scripts" for more information. You need NIS+ servers for three purposes:

- To be root replicas—to contain copies of the NIS+ tables that reside on the root master server

- To be master servers of subdomains of the root domain

- To be replicas of master servers of subdomains of the root domain

You can configure servers any of three different ways:

- Without NIS compatibility

- With NIS compatibility

- With NIS compatibility and DNS forwarding—you need to set DNS forwarding only if you are going to have SunOS 4.x clients in your NIS+ namespace

Servers and their replicas should have the same NIS compatibility settings. If they do not have the same setting, a client that needs NIS compatibility set to receive network information may not be able to receive it if either the server or replica it needs is unavailable.

This example shows the machine `wizclient1` being changed to a server. This procedure uses the NIS+ command `rpc.nisd` instead of an NIS+ script.

Prerequisites to Running `rpc.nisd`

Before you can run `rpc.nisd`:

- The domain must have already been set up, and its master server must be running.
- The master server of the domain's tables must be populated. (At a minimum, the Hosts table must have an entry for the new client machine.)
- You must have initialized the client machine in the domain.
- You must be logged in as root on the client machine. In this example, the client machine is named `wizclient1`.

You need the following information:

- The superuser password of the client that you will convert into a server

▼ How to Configure a Client as an NIS+ Server (Scripts)

◆ **Perform any of the following to configure a client as a server.**
  This step creates a directory with the same name as the server and creates the server's initialization files. They are placed in `/var/nis`.

Note – All servers in the same domain must have the same NIS compatibility setting. For example, if the master server is NIS-compatible, then its replicas also should be NIS-compatible.

- To configure an NIS+ server without NIS compatibility:

```
wizclient1# rpc.nisd
```

- To configure an NIS+ server *with* NIS compatibility:

  i. **Edit the** `/etc/init.d/rpc` file on the server.
     Uncomment the whole line containing the string `EMULYP="-Y"`.

ii. **Type the following as superuser:**

```
wizclient1# rpc.nisd -Y
```

- To configure an NIS+ server *with* NIS compatibility and DNS forwarding (needed for SunOS 4.x NIS clients):

   i. **Edit the** /etc/init.d/rpc file on the server.
   Uncomment the whole line (remove the # character from the beginning of the line) containing the string EMULYP="-Y".

   ii. **Add** -B **to the above line inside the quotes.**
   EMULYP="-Y -B"

   iii. **Type the following as superuser:**

```
wizclient1# rpc.nisd -Y -B
```

Now this server is ready to be designated a master or replica of a domain.

Creating Additional Servers

Repeat the preceding client-to-server conversion procedure on as many client machines as you like.

The sample NIS+ domain described in this section assumes that you will convert three clients to servers. You will then configure one of the servers to a root replica, another to a master of a new subdomain, and the third to a replica of the master of the new subdomain.

Designating Root Replicas with Scripts

To have regularly available NIS+ service, you should always create a root replica. Having a replica may also speed network request resolution because two servers are available to handle requests. The root replica server contains exact copies of the NIS+ tables on the root server. Replication of the master's database starts a few minutes after you perform this procedure and can take anywhere from a few minutes to a couple of hours to complete, depending on the size of your tables.

This example shows the machine wizclient1 being configured as a root replica. This procedure uses the NIS+ script nisserver.

Prerequisites to Running `nisserver`

Before you can run `nisserver` to create a root replica:

- The domain must have already been set up, and its master server must be running.

- The master server of the domain's tables must be populated. (At a minimum, the Hosts table must have an entry for the new client machine.)

- You must have initialized the client machine in the domain.

- You must have started `rpc.nisd` on the client.

- You must be logged in as root on the root master server. In this example, the root master machine is named `rootmaster`.

You need the following information:

- The domain name

- The client machine name; `wizclient1` in this example

- The superuser password for the root master server

▼ How to Create a Root Replica (Scripts)

1. **Type the following as superuser (root) on the NIS+ domain's root master server to create a root replica.**

```
rootmaster# nisserver -R -d Wiz.com. -h wizclient1
This script sets up a NIS+ Replica server for domain wiz.com.

Domainname : wiz.com.
NIS+ Server: rootmaster

Is this information correct? (Y or N)
```

The `-R` option indicates that a replica should be set up. The `-d` option specifies the NIS+ domain name, Wiz.com. in this instance. The `-h` option specifies the client machine, `wizclient1` in this example, that will become the root replica.

All About Administering NIS+

2. **Type** y **to continue.**

Typing n causes the script to prompt you for the correct information. (See "How to Change Incorrect Information (Scripts)" for what to do if you type n.)

```
Is this information correct? (Y or N) y

This script will set up machine "wizclient1" as a NIS+
Replica Server for domain wiz.com.
In order for wizclient1 to serve this domain, you will need
start up the NIS+ server daemon (rpc.nisd) with proper
options on wizclient1 if not already running.

Do you want to continue? (Y or N)
```

3. **Type** y **to continue.**

Typing n safely stops the script. The script will exit on its own if rpc.nisd is *not* running on the client machine.

```
Is this information correct? (Y or N) y

Added "wizclient1.wiz.com." to group "admin.wiz.com.".

The system wizclient1 is now configured as a replica server for
domain wiz.com..
In order for wizclient1 to serve this domain, you will need
start up the NIS+ server daemon (rpc.nisd) with proper
options on wizclient1 if not already running.

You should also modify the /etc/init.d/rpc file on the replica
server to set the proper options for rpc.nisd and restart
rpc.nisd with the proper options:
-Y        if you want to turn on YP compatibility mode
```

Note – The above notice refers to an optional step. Modify the /etc/init.d/rpc file only if you want the root replica to be NIS-(YP)-compatible and it is not now NIS-compatible. That is, the file needs modification only if you want the root replica to fulfill NIS client requests and it was not already configured as an NIS-compatible server. See "How to Configure a Client as an NIS+ Server (Scripts)" for more information on creating NIS-compatible servers.

The machine `wizclient1` is now an NIS+ root replica. The new root replica can handle requests from the clients of the root domain. Since there are now two servers available to the domain, information requests may be fulfilled faster.

Creating Additional Replicas

Repeat the preceding server-to-replica conversion procedure on as many server machines as you like. However, for overall performance, we recommend that you do not have more than a few replicas per domain. Do create as many replicas, though, as are necessary to serve physically distant sites. For example, it may make sense from an organizational point of view to have two physically distant sites in the same NIS+ domain. If a root replica and the master of the domain are at the first site, there will be much network traffic between the first site and the second site of the domain. Creating an additional root replica at the second site should reduce network traffic.

The sample NIS+ domain described in this chapter includes only one root replica. One of the other clients of the Wiz.com. domain will be converted to a replica of the subdomain created in the next section.

Creating a Subdomain with Scripts

This section shows you how to create the master server of a new nonroot domain. The new domain will be a subdomain of the Wiz.com. domain. The hierarchical structure of NIS+ allows you to create a domain structure that parallels your organizational structure.

This example shows the machine `wizclient2` being converted to the master server of a new domain called Subwiz.Wiz.com. This procedure uses the NIS+ script `nisserver`.

Prerequisites to Running `nisserver`

Before you can run `nisserver` to create a master server for a new nonroot domain:

- The parent domain must have already been set up, and its master server must be running.
- The parent domain's tables must be populated. (At a minimum, the Hosts table must have an entry for the new client machine.)
- You must have initialized the new client machine in the parent domain.
- You must have started `rpc.nisd` on the client.
- You must have adequate permissions to add the new domain. In this case, you must be logged in as root on the parent master server. In this example, the parent master machine is named `rootmaster`.

You need the following information:

- A name for the new nonroot domain—the name of the new domain includes the name of the parent domain, for example, newdomain.rootdomain.
- The client machine name; `wizclient2` in this example
- The superuser password for the parent master server

In the following example, the new nonroot domain is called Subwiz.Wiz.com.

Note – Any NIS+ client can be converted to an NIS+ master server as long as it is itself in a domain above the domain it will be serving. For example, an NIS+ client in domain Subwiz.Wiz.com can serve domains, such as Corp.Subwiz.Wiz.com or even East.Corp.Subwiz.Wiz.com, below it in the hierarchy. This client cannot, however, serve the domain Wiz.com because Wiz.com is above the domain Subwiz.Wiz.com in the hierarchy. Root replicas are the only exception to this rule. They are clients of the domain that they serve.

▼ How to Create a New Nonroot Domain (Scripts)

1. **Type the following as superuser (root) on the NIS+ domain's root master server to create a new nonroot domain master server.**

```
rootmaster# nisserver -M -d Subwiz.Wiz.com. -h wizclient2
This script sets up a non-Root NIS+ Master server for domain
Subwiz.wiz.com.

Domainname              : subwiz.wiz.com.
NIS+ Server             : wizclient2
NIS+ Group              : admin.subwiz.wiz.com.
YP compatibility        : OFF
Security level          : 2=DES

Is this information correct? (Y or N)
```

The `-M` option indicates that a master server for a new nonroot domain should be created. The `-d` option specifies the *new* domain name, Subwiz.Wiz.com. in this instance. The `-h` option specifies the client machine, `wizclient2` in this example, that will become the master server of the new domain.

Master servers of new nonroot domains are created with the same set of default values as root servers. See "How to Create a Root Master Server (Scripts)" for more information on NIS+ Group, YP (NIS) compatibility, and security level.

2. **Type** y **to continue.**
   Typing n causes the script to prompt you for the correct information. (See "How to Change Incorrect Information (Scripts)" for what you need to do if you type n.)

```
Is this information correct? (Y or N) y

This script sets up machine "wizclient2" as a NIS+
non-Root Master Server for domain subwiz.wiz.com.

Do you want to continue? (Y or N)
```

3. **Type** y **to continue.**
   Typing n safely exits the script. The script will exit on its own if rpc.nisd is *not* running on the client machine.

```
Do you want to continue? (Y or N) y
running nissetup ...
org_dir.subwiz.wiz.com. created
groups_dir.subwiz.wiz.com. created
passwd.org_dir.subwiz.wiz.com. created
group.org_dir.subwiz.wiz.com. created
auto_master.org_dir.subwiz.wiz.com. created
auto_home.org_dir.subwiz.wiz.com. created
bootparams.org_dir.subwiz.wiz.com. created
cred.org_dir.subwiz.wiz.com. created
ethers.org_dir.subwiz.wiz.com. created
hosts.org_dir.subwiz.wiz.com. created
mail_aliases.org_dir.subwiz.wiz.com. created
sendmailvars.org_dir.subwiz.wiz.com. created
netmasks.org_dir.subwiz.wiz.com. created
netgroup.org_dir.subwiz.wiz.com. created
networks.org_dir.subwiz.wiz.com. created
protocols.org_dir.subwiz.wiz.com. created
rpc.org_dir.subwiz.wiz.com. created
services.org_dir.subwiz.wiz.com. created
timezone.org_dir.subwiz.wiz.com. created
```

```
setting NIS+ group admin.subwiz.wiz.com. ...

The system wizclient2 is now configured as a non-root server for
domain subwiz.wiz.com.. You can now populate the standard NIS+
tables by using the nispopulate or /usr/lib/nis/nisaddent
commands
```

The machine `wizclient2` is now the master server of the Subwiz.Wiz.com. domain. The Subwiz.Wiz.com. domain is a subdomain of the Wiz.com. domain. The machine `wizclient2` is simultaneously still a client of the root domain Wiz.com. and also the master server of the Subwiz.Wiz.com. domain. See Figure 14-1.

You can now populate the standard NIS+ tables on the new master server of the Subwiz.Wiz.com. domain.

Creating Additional Domains

Repeat the preceding procedure for changing servers to master servers of new nonroot domains on as many server machines as you like. Every new master server is a new domain. Plan your domain structure before you start creating a NIS+ namespace.

Populating the New Domain's Tables with Scripts

After you have created a new domain, populate its master server's standard NIS+ tables. You use the same procedure to populate the new master server's tables as you used to populate the root master server's tables. The major difference is that the `nispopulate` script is run on the new master server instead of on the root master server. The domain names and file paths or NIS servers' names may change as well.

This example shows the tables of the new domain, Subwiz.Wiz.com., being populated.

Prerequisites to Running *nispopulate*

Before you can run the script `nispopulate` to populate the new master server's tables:

- The information in the files must be formatted appropriately for the table into which it will be loaded. Appendix A, "Information in NIS+ Tables," describes the format required for a text file to be transferred into its corresponding NIS+ table. Local `/etc` files are usually formatted properly. NIS maps from running NIS domains are presumed to be correctly formatted.

- We recommend that, for safety, you make copies of the `/etc` files and use the copies to populate the tables instead of the actual ones. (This example uses files in a directory called `/nis+files`, for instance.) You also may want to edit four of the copied files, `passwd`, `shadow`, `aliases` and `hosts`, for security. For example, you may want to remove the following lines from the copy of your local `passwd` file so they will not be distributed across the namespace:

```
root:x:0:1:0000-Admin(0000):/:/sbin/sh
daemon:x:1:3:0000-Admin(0000):/:
bin:x:3:5:0000-Admin(0000):/usr/bin:
sys:x:3:3:0000-Admin(0000):/:
adm:x:4:4:0000-Admin(0000):/var/adm:
lp:x:78:9:0000-lp(0000):/usr/spool/lp:
smtp:x:0:0:mail daemon user:/:
uucp:x:5:5:0000-uucp(0000):/usr/lib/uucp:
nuucp:x:7:8:0000-uucp(0000):/var/spool/uucppublic:/usr/lib/
uucp/uucico
listen:x:22:6:Network Admin:/usr/net/nls:
nobody:x:60000:60000:uid no body:/:
noaccess:x:60002:60002:uid no access:/:
```

- The domain must have already been set up, and its master server must be running.

- The domain's servers must have sufficient disk space to accommodate the new table information.

- You must be logged in as an NIS+ principal and have write permission to the NIS+ tables in the specified domain. In this example, you would have to be the user root on the machine `wizclient2`.

Note – The `nispopulate` script may fail if there is insufficient `/tmp` space on the system. To keep this from happening, you can set the environment variable TMPDIR to a different directory. If TMPDIR is not set to a valid directory, the script will use the `/tmp` directory instead.

If populating from files, you need the following information:
- The new NIS+ domain name
- The path of the appropriately edited text files whose data will be transferred
- The root password of the NIS+ master server

If populating from NIS maps, you need the following information:
- The new NIS+ domain name

- The NIS domain name
- The NIS server name
- The IP address of the NIS server
- The root password of the NIS+ master server

Note – The NIS domain name is case-sensitive, while the NIS+ domain name is not.

▼ How to Populate Master Server Tables (Scripts)

Since this procedure is essentially the same as the procedure shown in "How to Populate the Root Master Server Tables (Scripts)," this example only shows you what you would type to populate the tables of the new domain, Subwiz.Wiz.com. For more information about this procedure, see "How to Populate the Root Master Server Tables (Scripts)."

Note – This script should be run on the new domain's master server, not on the root master server.

◆ **Perform either step a or step b to populate the master server tables on the new master server.**
Step a describes how to populate tables from files. Step b describes how to populate tables from NIS maps. Type these commands in a scrolling window, as the script's output may otherwise scroll off the screen.

a. **Type the following to populate the tables from files.**

```
wizclient2# nispopulate -F -p /nis+files -d Subwiz.Wiz.com.

NIS+ Domainname        : Subwiz.Wiz.com.
Directory Path         : /nis+files


Is this information correct? (Y or N)
```

b. **Type the following to populate the tables from NIS maps**.

```
wizclient2# nispopulate -Y -d Subwiz.Wiz.com. -h businessmachine
-a 130.48.58.242 -y business.wiz.com

NIS+ Domainname         : subwiz.wiz.com.
YP Domain               : business.wiz.com
YP Server Hostname      : businessmachine

Is this information correct? (Y or N)
```

See "How to Populate the Root Master Server Tables (Scripts)" for the rest of the script output.

Designating Replicas with Scripts

Just as you did in the Wiz.com. domain, to have regularly available NIS+ service, you should always create a replica. Having a replica may also speed network request resolution because two servers are available to handle requests. The replica server contains exact copies of the NIS+ tables on the master server of your new domain. Replication of the master's database starts a few minutes after you perform this procedure and can take anywhere from a few minutes to a couple of hours to complete, depending on the size of your tables.

You use the same procedure to create a replica as you do to create a root replica. The major difference between creating the root replica and this replica is that the machine you are going to convert to a replica is going to remain a client of the domain above the one it will be serving as a replica. This example only shows you what you would type to create a replica for the new domain. For more information about the procedure, see "How to Create a Root Replica (Scripts)."

Prerequisites to Running nisserver

Before you can run nisserver to create a replica:

- The domain must have already been set up, and its master server must be running.
- The domain's tables must be populated. (At a minimum, the Hosts table must have an entry for the new client machine.)
- You must have initialized the client machine in the parent domain.
- You must have started rpc.nisd on the client.

- You must be logged in as root on the master server. In this example, the master machine is named `wizclient2`.

You need the following information:

- The domain name
- The client machine name; `wizclient3` in this example
- The superuser password for the root master server

▼ How to Create a Replica (Scripts)

♦ **Type the following as superuser (root) on the NIS+ domain's master server (`wizclient2`) to create a replica.**

```
wizclient2# nisserver -R -d Subwiz.Wiz.com. -h wizclient3
This script sets up a NIS+ Replica server for domain
subwiz.wiz.com.

Domainname : subwiz.wiz.com.
NIS+ Server: wizclient2

Is this information correct? (Y or N)
```

The `-R` option indicates that a replica should be set up. The `-d` option specifies the NIS+ domain name, Subwiz.Wiz.com. in this instance. The `-h` option specifies the client machine, `wizclient3` in this example, that will become the replica. Notice that this machine is still a client of the Wiz.com. domain and not a client of the Subwiz.Wiz.com. domain.

See "How to Create a Root Replica (Scripts)" for the rest of the script output.

Initializing Subdomain NIS+ Client Machines with Scripts

Once the master server's tables have been populated from files or NIS maps, you can initialize an NIS+ client machine. This section shows you how to initialize an NIS+ client in the new domain, using the `nisclient` script with default settings. The NIS+ client machine is a different workstation than the NIS+ master server.

Note – The `-i` option used in "How to Initialize a New Subdomain Client Machine (Scripts)" does not set up an NIS+ client to resolve hostnames requiring DNS. You must explicitly set DNS for clients that have this option.

You use the same procedure to initialize a client in the new domain as you do to initialize a client in the root domain. This example only shows you what you would type to initialize a client for the new domain. For more information, see "How to Initialize a New Client Machine (Scripts)."

Prerequisites to Running `nisclient`

Before you can use the `nisclient` script to initialize a user:

- The domain must have already been set up, and its master server must be running.
- The master server of the domain's tables must be populated. (At a minimum, the Hosts table must have an entry for the new client machine.)
- You must have initialized a client machine in the domain.
- You must be logged in as a *user* on the client machine. In this example, the user is named `user1`.

You need the following information:

- The domain name—Subwiz.wiz.com. in this example
- The default network password (`nisplus`)
- The root password of the workstation that will become the client
- The IP address of the NIS+ server (in the client's home domain)—in this example, the address of the master server `wizclient2`

▼ How to Initialize a New Subdomain Client Machine (Scripts)

- **Type the following as superuser to initialize the new client on the new client machine.**

```
subclient1#nisclient -i -d Subwiz.Wiz.com. -h wizclient2

Initializing client subclient1 for domain "Subwiz.Wiz.com."...
Once initialization is done, you will need to reboot your
machine.

Do you want to continue? (Y or N)
```

The -i option initializes a client. The -d option specifies the new NIS+ domain name. (If the domain name is not specified, the default would be the current domain name.) The -h option specifies the NIS+ server's hostname.

See "How to Initialize a New Client Machine (Scripts)" for the rest of the script output.

Initializing Subdomain NIS+ Client Users with Scripts

You use the same procedure (`nisclient`) to initialize a user in the new domain as you do to initialize a user in the root domain. All users must make themselves NIS+ clients. This example only shows you what you would type to initialize a user for the new domain. For more information, see "How to Initialize an NIS+ User (Scripts)."

Prerequisites to Running `nisclient`

Before you can use the `nisclient` script to initialize a user:

- The domain must have already been set up, and its master server must be running.
- The master server of the domain's tables must be populated. (At a minimum, the Hosts table must have an entry for the new client machine.)
- You must have initialized a client machine in the domain.
- You must be logged in as a *user* on the client machine. In this example, the user is named `user2`.

You need the following information:

- The user's login name—`user2` in this example
- The default network password—`nisplus` in this example
- The login password of the user that will become the NIS+ client

▼ How to Initialize an NIS+ Subdomain User (Scripts)

- ◆ **Type the following while logged in as the user to become an NIS+ client.**

```
user2prompt% nisclient -u
Please enter the network password that your administrator gave
you.
Please enter the Secure-RPC password for user1:
```

See "How to Initialize an NIS+ User (Scripts)" for the rest of the script output.

Summary of Commands for the Sample NIS+ Namespace

Table 14-2 summarizes the actual commands that you typed to create the sample namespace. The prompt preceding each command indicates on which machine the command should be typed. See Figure 14-1 on page 174 for a diagram of the sample namespace.

Table 14-2 Sample NIS+ Namespace Command Lines Summary

Command Line	Purpose
#**setenv PATH $PATH:/usr/lib/nis** or #**PATH=$PATH:/usr/lib/nis; export PATH**	Set environment path to include /usr/lib/nis—C shell or Bourne shell.
rootmaster# **nisserver -r -d Wiz.com.**	Create root master server for Wiz.com. domain.
rootmaster# **nispopulate -F -p /nis+files -d Wiz.com.** or rootmaster# **nispopulate -Y -d Wiz.com. -h corporatemachine -a 130.48.58.111 -y corporate.wiz.com**	Populate the root master server's NIS+ tables from files or from NIS maps.
rootmaster# **nisgrpadm -a admin.Wiz.Com. topadmin.Wiz.Com. \ secondadmin.Wiz.Com.**	Add additional members to the admin group (2).
rootmaster# **nisping -C Wiz.Com.**	Make a checkpoint of the NIS+ database.
wizclient1# **nisclient -i -d Wiz.com. -h rootmaster**	Initialize an NIS+ client machine in the Wiz.com. domain.
wizclient1user1prompt% **nisclient -u**	Initialize user as an NIS+ client.
wizclient1#**rpc.nisd** or wizclient1#**rpc.nisd -Y** or wizclient1#**rpc.nisd -Y -B**	Convert NIS+ client to NIS+ server, without or with NIS compatibility or with NIS and DNS.
rootmaster# **nisserver -R -d Wiz.com. -h wizclient1**	Create a root replica.
rootmaster# **nisserver -M -d Subwiz.Wiz.com. -h wizclient2**	Convert a server to a nonroot master server of the Subwiz.Wiz.com. domain.

Table 14-2 Sample NIS+ Namespace Command Lines Summary (Continued)

Command Line	Purpose
wizclient2# **nispopulate -F -p /nis+files -d** **Subwiz.Wiz.com.** or wizclient2# **nispopulate -Y -d Subwiz.Wiz.com. -h ** **businessmachine -a 130.48.58.242 -y** **business.wiz.com**	Populate the new master server's NIS+ tables from files or from NIS maps.
wizclient2# **nisserver -R -d Subwiz.Wiz.com. -h** **wizclient3**	Create a master server replica.
subclient1# **nisclient -i -d Subwiz.Wiz.com. -h** **wizclient2**	Initialize an NIS+ client in the Subwiz.Wiz.com. domain.
subclient1user2prompt% **nisclient -u**	Initialize user as an NIS+ client.

Setting Up the Root Domain   15 ≡

This chapter provides step-by-step instructions for one task:

This task sets up the root domain with DES authentication. It walks through the setup process at a leisurely pace, pointing out the effects of each step and related information that might be of interest. Once you are familiar with the setup process and prefer a quicker-paced approach, you can use the summary that is provided at the end of the chapter.

▼ How to Set Up the Root Domain

This task describes how to set up the root domain for DES operation; that is, with the root master server running at security level 2. Setting up the root domain involves three major tasks:

- Preparing the root master server
- Creating the root domain
- Creating credentials for the root domain

However, setting up the root domain is not as simple as performing these three tasks in order; they are intertwined with each other. For instance, you must specify some security parameters before you create the root directory; the rest, after. To make the root domain easier to set up, this section separates these tasks into individual steps and arranges them in their most efficient order.

Differences Between Standard and NIS-compatible Setup Procedures

The steps in this section apply to both a standard NIS+ root domain and an NIS-compatible root domain. There are, however, some important differences. The NIS+ daemon for an NIS-compatible domain must be started with the -Y option, which allows the root master server to answer requests from NIS clients. This procedure is described in Step 7. The equivalent step for standard NIS+ domains is Step 8.

An NIS-compatible domain also requires Read rights to the Passwd table for the Nobody class, which allows NIS clients to access the information stored in the table's Passwd column. This access is accomplished with the -Y option to the nissetup command, in Step 9. The standard NIS+ domain version uses the same command but without the -Y option.

Here is a summary of the entire setup process:

Step 1.   Log in as superuser to the root master server.

Step 2.   Check the root master server's domain name.

Step 3.   Check the root master server's Switch configuration file.

Step 4.   Clean out leftover NIS+ material and processes.

Step 5.   Name the root domain's admin group.

Step 6.   Create the root directory and initialize the root master server.

Step 7.   —NIS-Compatibility Only— Start the NIS+ daemon with -Y.

Step 8.   —Standard NIS+ Only—Start the NIS+ daemon.

Step 9.   Create the root domain's subdirectories and tables.

Step 10.   Create DES credentials for the root master server.

Step 11.   Create the root domain's admin group.

Step 12.   Add the root master to the root domain's admin group.

Step 13.   Update the root domain's public keys.

Step 14.   Start the NIS+ cache manager.

Step 15.   Restart the NIS+ daemon with security level 2.

Step 16.   Add your LOCAL credentials to the root domain.

Step 17.   Add your DES credentials to the root domain.

Step 18.   Add credentials for other administrators.

Step 19.   Add yourself and other administrators to the root domain's admin group.

Security Considerations

NIS+ provides preset security defaults for the root domain. As described on page 57 (Chapter 4), you can override or change these security defaults. To do this while setting up the root domain, see "How to Override Defaults" on page 328.

Prerequisites

- The /etc/passwd file on the root master server must contain an entry for you and every other administrator whose credentials will be added to the root domain in this setup process.
- If the server will operate in NIS compatibility mode and support DNS forwarding for Solaris 1.x clients, it must have a properly configured /etc/resolv.config file.

You need the following information:

- The superuser password of the workstation that will become the root master server (for Step 1)
- The name of the root domain (for Step 2)
- The name of the root domain's admin group (for Step 5)
- Your UID and password
- The UID of any administrator whose credentials you will add to the root domain

Instructions

1. **Log in as superuser to the root master server.**

    Log in as *superuser* to the workstation that will become the root master server. The examples in these steps use rootmaster as the root master server and Wiz.Com. as the root domain.

    ```
    rootmaster% su
    Password: <enter password>
    rootmaster#
    ```

2. **Check the root master server's domain name.**

    Make sure the root master server is using the correct domain name. Use the domainname command, as shown below:

    ```
    rootmaster# domainname
    domainname
    ```

    The domainname command returns a workstation's current domain name. If the name is not correct, change it.   Complete instructions are provided in Chapter 17, "Setting Up an NIS+ Client," but here is an example. It changes the domain name of the root master server from StrangeDomain to Wiz.Com:

    ```
    rootmaster# domainname
    Strange.Domain
    rootmaster# domainname Wiz.Com
    rootmaster# domainname
    Wiz.Com
    rootmaster# domainname > /etc/defaultdomain
    ```

Note – Make sure that you don't include a trailing dot with the domain name in this instance. The domainname command is not an NIS+ command, so it does not follow the NIS+ conventions of a trailing dot. Also make sure that the domain name has at least two labels; for example, Wiz.Com instead of Wiz.

3. **Check the root master server's Switch configuration file.**
   Make sure the root master server is using the NIS+ version of the `nsswitch.conf`
   file, even if it will run in NIS compatibility mode. This step ensures that the
   primary source of information for the root master will be NIS+ tables. Figure 15-1
   shows the NIS+ version of the file.

```
rootmaster# more /etc/nsswitch.conf
```

If the root master server's configuration file is different from the one in Figure 15-1,
change it to the NIS+ version. Complete instructions are provided in Chapter 20,
"Setting Up the Name Service Switch," but here is an example:

```
rootmaster# cp /etc/nsswitch.nisplus /etc/nsswitch.conf
rootmaster# ps -e | grep keyserv
    root   145    1  67  16:34:44   ?   keyserv
       .
       .
       .
rootmaster# kill -9 145
rootmaster# rm -f /etc/.rootkey
rootmaster# keyserv
```

```
rootmaster# more /etc/nsswitch.conf
#
# /etc/nsswitch.nisplus:
#
# An example file that could be copied over to /etc/nsswitch.conf; it
# uses NIS+ (NIS Version 3) in conjunction with files.
#
# "hosts:" and "services:" in this file are used only if the /etc/netconfig
# file contains "switch.so" as a nametoaddr library for "inet" transports.

# the following two lines obviate the "+" entry in /etc/passwd and
/etc/group.
passwd:       files nisplus
group:        files nisplus

# consult /etc "files" only if nisplus is down.
hosts:        nisplus [NOTFOUND=return] files
#Uncomment the following line, and comment out the above, to use both DNS and
NIS+
#hosts:        nisplus dns [NOTFOUND=return] files

services:     nisplus [NOTFOUND=return] files
networks:     nisplus [NOTFOUND=return] files
protocols:    nisplus [NOTFOUND=return] files
rpc:          nisplus [NOTFOUND=return] files
ethers:       nisplus [NOTFOUND=return] files
netmasks:     nisplus [NOTFOUND=return] files
bootparams:   nisplus [NOTFOUND=return] files

publickey:    nisplus

netgroup:     nisplus

automount:    files nisplus
aliases:      files nisplus
```

Figure 15-1 NIS+ Version of `nsswitch.conf` *File*

4. **Clean out leftover NIS+ material and processes.**
   If the workstation you are working on was previously used as an NIS+ server or client, remove any files that might exist in /var/nis and kill the cache manager, if it is still running. In this example, a coldstart file and a directory cache file still exist in /var/nis.

```
rootmaster# ls /var/nis
NIS_COLD_START      NIS_SHARED_CACHE
rootmaster# rm -rf /var/nis/*
rootmaster# ps -ef | grep nis_cachemgr
   root  295    260 10 15:26:58 pts/0  0:00 grep nis_cachemgr
   root  286      1 57 15:21:55 ?      0:01 /usr/sbin/nis_cachemgr
rootmaster# kill -9 286
```

This step makes sure that files left in /var/nis or directory objects stored by the cache manager are completely erased so they do not conflict with the new information generated during this setup process. If you have stored any admin scripts in /var/nis, you may want to consider temporarily storing them elsewhere, until you finish setting up the root domain.

5. **Name the root domain's admin group.**
   Although you won't actually create the admin group until Step 11, you need to identify it now. Identifying it now ensures that the root domain's org_dir directory object, groups_dir directory object, and all its table objects are assigned the proper default group when they are created in Step 9.

   To name the admin group, set the value of the environment variable NIS_GROUP to the name of the root domain's admin group. Here are two examples, one for csh users, and one for sh/ksh users. They both set NIS_GROUP to admin.Wiz.Com.

```
rootmaster# setenv NIS_GROUP admin.Wiz.Com.     # for csh

rootmaster# NIS_GROUP=admin.Wiz.Com.            # for sh/ksh
rootmaster# export NIS_GROUP                     # for sh/ksh
```

(To view the workstation's environment variables, use the env command.)

6. Create the root directory and initialize the root master server.

root
directory

root master
server

This step creates the first object in the namespace—the root directory—and converts the workstation into the root master server. Use the `nisinit -r` command, as shown below:[1]

```
rootmaster# nisinit -r

This machine is in the Wiz.Com. NIS+ domain
Setting up root server ...
All done.
```

A UNIX directory with the name of the server (e.g., `rootmaster`) is created under `/var/nis`. Beneath it is a file named `root.object`:

```
rootmaster# ls -l /var/nis/rootmaster
-rw-rw-rw-  1  root   other   384   <date>   root.object
```

This is not the root directory object; it is actually a file that NIS+ uses to describe the root of the namespace for internal purposes. The NIS+ root directory object will be created in the following step.

In subsequent steps, other files will be added beneath the directory created in this step. Although you can verify the existence of these files by looking directly into the UNIX directory, NIS+ provides more appropriate commands. They are called out where applicable in the following steps.

7. —NIS-Compatibility Only— Start the NIS+ daemon with `-Y`.

Namespace   Servers

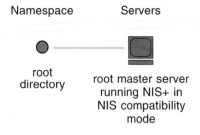

root
directory

root master server
running NIS+ in
NIS compatibility
mode

Perform this step only if you are setting up the root domain in NIS compatibility mode; if setting up a standard NIS+ domain, perform Step 8 instead. This step includes instructions for supporting the DNS-forwarding capabilities of NIS clients.

This step consists of two substeps, a and b. Step a starts the NIS+ daemon in NIS compatibility mode, and Step b makes sure that when the server is

---

1. This is the only instance in which you will create a domain's directory object and initialize its master server in one step. In fact, `nisinit -r` performs an automatic `nismkdir` for the root directory. In any case except the root master, these two processes are performed as separate tasks.

rebooted, the NIS+ daemon restarts in NIS compatibility mode. After Step b, skip to Step 9.

a. Use `rpc.nisd` **with the** `-r`, `-Y`, `-B`, **and** `-S 0` **options:**

```
rootmaster# rpc.nisd -r -Y -B -S 0
```

The `-r` option runs the root domain's version of a master server, which is slightly different from a nonroot domain's version. The `-Y` option invokes an interface that answers NIS requests in addition to NIS+ requests. The `-B` option supports DNS forwarding. The `-S 0` flag sets the server's security level to 0, which is required at this point for bootstrapping. Since no Cred table exists yet, no NIS+ principals can have credentials; if you used a higher security level, you would be locked out of the server.

b. Edit the `/etc/init.d/rpc` **file.**
Search for the string `EMULYP="Y"` in the `/etc/init.d/rpc` file. Uncomment the line and, to retain DNS forwarding capabilities, add a `-B` flag.

```
rootmaster# vi /etc/init.d/rpc
  .
  .
  .
#        EMULYP="-Y"
  .
  .

        ------uncomment and change to------

        EMULYP="-Y -B"
```

If you don't need to retain DNS forwarding capabilities, uncomment the line, but don't add the `-B` flag.

8. —Standard NIS+ Only—Start the NIS+ daemon.
Use the `rpc.nisd -r` command, but be sure to add the `-S 0` flag.

```
rootmaster# rpc.nisd -r -S 0
```

The -S 0 flag sets the server's security level to 0, which is required at this point for bootstrapping. Since no Cred table exists yet, no NIS+ principals can have credentials, and if a higher security level is used, you would be locked out of the server.

As a result of this step (or Step 7), your namespace now has:

- A root directory object (root_dir)
- A root master server (rootmaster) running the NIS+ daemon (rcp.nisd)
- A coldstart file for the master server (NIS_COLD_START)
- A transaction log file (*servername*.log)
- A table dictionary file (*servername*.dict)

The root directory object is stored in the directory created in Step 6.

```
rootmaster# ls -l /var/nis/rootmaster
-rw-rw-rw-  1  root    other    384    <date>   root.object
-rw-rw-rw-  1  root    other    124    <date>   root.dir
```

At this point, the root directory is empty; in other words, it has no subdirectories. You can verify this by using the nisls command (described on page 339).

```
rootmaster# nisls -l Wiz.Com.
Wiz.Com.:
```

However, the directory has several *object* properties, which you can examine by using niscat -o.

```
rootmaster# niscat -o Wiz.Com.
Object Name    : Wiz
Owner          : rootmaster.Wiz.Com.
Group          : admin.Wiz.Com.
Domain         : Com.
Access Rights  : r---rmcdrmcdr---
    .
    .
    .
```

Note that the root directory object provides full (Read, Modify, Create, and Destroy) permissions to both the Owner and the Group, while providing only Read access to the World and Nobody categories.[2]

You can verify that the NIS+ daemon is running by using the ps command:

```
rootmaster# ps -ef | grep rpc.nisd
root 1081      1  61  16:43:33  ?       0:01  rpc.nisd -r -S 0
root 1087   1004  11  16:44:09  pts/1   0:00  grep rpc.nisd
```

The root domain's NIS_COLD_START file, which contains the Internet address (and eventually, public keys) of the root master server, is placed in /var/nis. Although there is no NIS+ command that you can use to examine its contents, its contents are loaded into the server's directory cache (NIS_SHARED_DIRCACHE). You can examine those contents with the /usr/lib/nis/nisshowcache command, described on page 349.

Also created are a transaction log file (*servername*.log) and a dictionary file (*servername*.dict). As described in "How Servers Propagate Changes" on page 29, the transaction log of a master server stores all the transactions performed by the master server and all its replicas since the last update. You can examine its contents by using the nislog command (described on page 353). The dictionary file is used by NIS+ for internal purposes; it is of no interest to an administrator.

9. **Create the root domain's subdirectories and tables.**

groups_dir org_dir

This step adds the org_dir and groups_dir directories and the NIS+ tables beneath the root directory object. Use the nissetup utility. For an NIS-compatible domain, be sure to include the -Y flag. Here are examples for both versions:

```
rootmaster# /usr/lib/nis/nissetup -Y      # NIS-compatible only

rootmaster# /usr/lib/nis/nissetup         # Standard NIS+ only
```

---

2. If your directory object does not provide these rights, you can change them with the nischmod command.

Each object added by the utility is listed in the output:

```
rootmaster# /usr/lib/nis/nissetup
org_dir.Wiz.Com. created
groups_dir.Wiz.Com. created
auto_master.org_dir.Wiz.Com. created
auto_home.org_dir.Wiz.Com. created
bootparams.org_dir.Wiz.Com. created
cred.org_dir.Wiz.Com. created
ethers.org_dir.Wiz.Com. created
group.org_dir.Wiz.Com. created
hosts.org_dir.Wiz.Com. created
mail_aliases.org_dir.Wiz.Com. created
sendmailvars.org_dir.Wiz.Com. created
netmasks.org_dir.Wiz.Com. created
netgroup.org_dir.Wiz.Com. created
networks.org_dir.Wiz.Com. created
passwd.org_dir.Wiz.Com. created
protocols.org_dir.Wiz.Com. created
rpc.org_dir.Wiz.Com. created
services.org_dir.Wiz.Com. created
timezone.org_dir.Wiz.Com. created
```

The -Y option creates the same tables and subdirectories as for a standard NIS+ domain, but assigns Read rights to the Passwd table to the Nobody category so that requests from NIS clients, which are unauthenticated, can access the encrypted password in that column. For more information about the differences between standard and NIS-compatible treatment of the Passwd table, see"Protecting the Encrypted Password Field" on page 140.

Recall that when you examined the contents of the root directory with nisls (in Step 8), it was empty. Now, however, it has two subdirectories:

```
rootmaster# nisls Wiz.Com.
Wiz.Com.:
org_dir
groups-dir
```

You can examine the object properties of the subdirectories and tables by using the niscat -o command. You can also use the niscat option without a flag to examine the information in the tables, although at this point they are empty.

All About Administering NIS+

10. **Create DES credentials for the root master server.**

The root master server requires DES credentials so that its own requests can be authenticated. To create those credentials, use the `nisaddcred` command as shown below. When prompted, enter the server's root password.

```
rootmaster# nisaddcred des
DES principal name : unix.rootmaster@Wiz.Com
Adding key pair for unix.rootmaster@Wiz.Com
                    (rootmaster.Wiz.Com.).
Enter login password: <enter login password>
Wrote secret key into /etc/.rootkey
```

If you enter a password that is different from the server's root password, you'll get a warning message and a prompt to repeat the password:

```
Enter login password: <if you enter different password>
nisaddcred: WARNING: password differs from login password.
Retype password:
```

You can persist and retype the same password, and NIS+ will still create the credential. The new password will be stored in `/etc/.rootkey` and used by the keyserver when it starts up. To give the keyserver the new password right away, execute a `keylogin -r`, as described in Chapter 22, "Administering NIS+ Credentials."

If you decide to use your login password after all, press Control-C and start the sequence over. If you were to simply retype your login password as encouraged by the server, you would see an error message designed for another purpose, but which in this instance, given the server's instructions, could be confusing.

```
nisaddcred: WARNING: password differs from login password.
Retype password: <enter login password>
nisaddcred: password incorrect.
nisaddcred: unable to create credential.
```

If you need to change the root master's DES credential, you can remove the old credential with the `nisaddcred -r` command, as described in Chapter 22.

As a result of this step, the root server's private and public keys are stored in the root domain's Cred table (cred.org_dir.Wiz.Com.) and its secret key is stored in /etc/.rootkey. You can verify the existence of the credentials in the Cred table by using the niscat command (described in Chapter 24.) Since the default domain name is Wiz.Com., you don't have to enter the Cred table's fully qualified name; the org_dir suffix is enough. You can locate the root master's credential by looking for its secure RPC netname.

11. **Create the root domain's admin group.**

This step creates the admin group named in Step 5. Use the nisgrpadm with the -c option. The example below creates the admin.Wiz.Com. group:

```
rootmaster# nisgrpadm -c admin.Wiz.Com.
Group "admin.Wiz.Com." created.
```

This step only creates the group—it does not identify its members. That is done in Step 12. To observe the object properties of the group, use niscat -o, but be sure to use groups_dir in the group's name. For example:

```
rootmaster# niscat -o admin.groups_dir.Wiz.Com.
Object Name    : admin
Owner          : rootmaster.Wiz.Com.
Group          : admin.Wiz.Com.
Domain         : groups_dir.Wiz.Com.
Access Rights  : ----rmcdr---r---
Time to Live   : 1:0:0
Object Type    : GROUP
Group Flags    :
Group Members  :
```

12. **Add the root master to the root domain's admin group.**

Since at this point the root master server is the only NIS+ principal that has DES credentials, it is the only member you should add to the admin group. Use the nisgrpadm command again, but with the -a option. The first argument is the group name, the second is the name of the root master server. This example adds rootmaster.Wiz.Com. to the admin.Wiz.Com. group:

```
rootmaster# nisgrpadm -a admin.Wiz.Com.  rootmaster.Wiz.Com.
Added "rootmaster.Wiz.Com." to group "admin.Wiz.Com."
```

To verify that the root master is indeed a member of the group, use the `nisgrpadm` command with the `-l` option[3] (see Chapter 21, "Administering NIS+ Groups").

```
rootmaster# nisgrpadm -l admin.Wiz.Com.
Group entry for "admin.Wiz.Com." group:
    Explicit members:
        rootmaster.Wiz.Com.
    No implicit members
    No recursive members
    No explicit nonmembers
    No implicit nonmembers
    No recursive nonmembers
```

13. Update the root domain's public keys.

Normally, directory objects are created by an NIS+ principal who already has DES credentials. In this case, however, the root master server could not acquire DES credentials until *after* it created the Cred table (since there was no parent domain in which to store its credentials). As a result, three directory objects—root, org_dir, and groups_dir—do not have a copy of the root master server's public key. (You can verify this by using the `niscat -o` command with any of the directory objects. Look for the `Public Key:` field. Instructions are provided in Chapter 24, "Administering NIS+ Directories.")

To propagate the root master server's public key from the root domain's Cred table to those three directory objects, use the `/usr/lib/nis/nisupdkeys` utility for each directory object, as shown below:

```
rootmaster# /usr/lib/nis/nisupdkeys Wiz.Com.
rootmaster# /usr/lib/nis/nisupdkeys org_dir.Wiz.Com.
rootmaster# /usr/lib/nis/nisupdkeys groups_dir.Wiz.Com.
```

After each instance, you'll see a confirmation message such as this one:

```
Fetch Public key for server rootmaster.Wiz.Com.
    netname = 'unix.rootmaster@Wiz.Com.'
Updating rootmaster.Wiz.Com.'s public key.
    Public key : public-key
```

---

3. With group-related commands such as `nisgrpadm`, you don't have to include the `groups_dir` subdirectory in the name. You need to include that directory with commands like `niscat` because they are designed to work on NIS+ objects in general. The group-related commands are targeted at the `groups_dir` subdirectory.

Now, if you look in any of those directories (use `niscat -o`), you'll see this entry under the `Public Key`: field:

```
Public Key : Diffie-Hellman (196 bits)
```

14. **Start the NIS+ cache manager.**
   The cache manager maintains a local cache of location information for an NIS+ client (in this case, the root master server). It obtains its initial set of information from the client's coldstart file (created in Step 7 or Step 8), and downloads it into a file named NIS_SHARED_DIRCACHE in /var/nis.

   To start the cache manager, simply enter the nis_cachemgr command, as shown below:

```
rootmaster# nis_cachemgr
```

   Once the cache manager has been started, you only need to restart it if you have explicitly killed it. You don't need to restart it if you reboot, since the coldstart file in /var/nis starts it automatically when the client is rebooted. For more information about the NIS+ cache manager, see Chapter 24, "Administering NIS+ Directories."

15. **Restart the NIS+ daemon with security level 2.**
   Now that the root master server has DES credentials and the root directory object has a copy of the root master's public key, you can restart the root master with security level 2. First, kill the existing daemon, then restart one with security level 2. Be sure to use the -r flag and, for an NIS-compatible root domain, the -Y flag (and -B flag). Here is an example:

```
rootmaster# ps -e | grep rpc.nisd
1081   ?           0:03 rpc.nisd
rootmaster# kill 1081
rootmaster# rpc.nisd -r               # Standard NIS+ domain only
rootmaster# rpc.nisd -r -Y -B         # NIS-compatible NIS+ domain
```

   Since security level 2 is the default, you don't need to use the -S 2 flag.

16. Add your LOCAL credentials to the root domain.

Since you don't have access rights to the root domain's Cred table, you must perform this operation as superuser. In addition, as mentioned in "Prerequisites," the root master's /etc/passwd file must contain an entry for you. Use the nisaddcred command with the -p and -P flags. Here is the syntax, followed by an example:

```
nisaddcred -p uid -P principal-name local
```

The *principal-name* consists of the administrator's login name and domain name. This example adds a LOCAL credential for an administrator with a UID of 11177 and an NIS+ principal name of topadmin.Wiz.Com.

```
rootmaster# nisaddcred -p 11177 -P topadmin.Wiz.Com. local
```

For more information about the nisaddcred command, see Chapter 22.

17. Add your DES credentials to the root domain.

Use the nisaddcred command again, but with the following syntax:

```
nisaddcred -p secure-RPC-netname -P principal-name des
```

The secure RPC netname consists of the prefix "unix." followed by your UID, the symbol "@" and your domain name, but *without* a trailing dot. The principal name is the same as for LOCAL credentials: your login name followed by your domain name, *with* a trailing dot.

```
rootmaster# nisaddcred -p unix.11177@Wiz.Com \
                      -P topadmin.Wiz.Com. des
Adding key pair for unix.11177@Wiz.Com (topadmin.Wiz.Com.).
Enter login password: <enter login password>
```

If, after entering your login password, you see a warning such as this one—

```
nisaddcred: WARNING: password differs from login password.
Retype password:
```

—and yet the password you entered is your correct login password, ignore the error message. The message appears because NIS+ cannot read the protected `/etc/shadow` file that stores the password, as expected. The message would not have appeared if you had no user password information stored in the `/etc/passwd` file.

18. **Add credentials for other administrators.**
    Add the credentials, both LOCAL and DES, of the other administrators who will work in the root domain. You can do this in two different ways. One way is to ask them to add their own credentials. However, they will have to do this as superuser. Here is an example that adds credentials for an administrator with a UID of 33355 and a principal name of bobee.Wiz.Com.

```
rootmaster# nisaddcred -p 33355 -P bobee.Wiz.Com. local
rootmaster# nisaddcred -p unix.33355@Wiz.Com \
                       -P bobee.Wiz.Com. des
Adding key pair for unix.33355@Wiz.Com (bobee.Wiz.Com.).
Enter login password:  <enter bobee's login password>
```

The other way is for you to create temporary credentials for the other administrators, using dummy passwords (note that each administrator must have an entry in the NIS+ Passwd table).

```
rootmaster# /usr/lib/nis/nisaddent -a -f  \
            /etc/passwd.xfr  passwd
rootmaster# /usr/lib/nis/nisaddent -a -f \
            /etc/shadow.xfr  shadow
rootmaster# nisaddcred -p 33355 -P bobee.Wiz.Com. local
rootmaster# nisaddcred -p unix.33355@Wiz.Com \
                       -P bobee.Wiz.Com. des
Adding key pair for unix.33355@Wiz.Com (bobee.Wiz.Com.).
Enter bobee's login password: <enter dummy password>
nisaddcred: WARNING: password differs from login passwd.
Retype password: <reenter dummy password>
```

The first instance of `nisaddent` populates the Passwd table—except for the actual password column. The second instance populates the shadow column. Each administrator can later change his or her network password by using the `chkey` command. Chapter 22, "Administering NIS+ Credentials," describes how to do this.

19. Add yourself and other administrators to the root domain's admin group.
You don't have to wait for the other administrators to change their dummy passwords to perform this step. Use the `nisgrpadm` command with the `-a` option. The first argument is the group name, the remaining arguments are the names of the administrators. This example adds two administrators, topadmin and bobee, to the admin.Wiz.Com. group.

```
rootmaster# nisgrpadm -a admin.Wiz.Com.  topadmin.Wiz.Com. \
                        bobee.Wiz.Com.
Added "topadmin.Wiz.Com." to group "admin.Wiz.Com.".
Added "bobee.Wiz.Com." to group "admin.Wiz.Com.".
```

This step completes this task. A summary of the entire task is provided below.

Summary

Below is a summary of the steps required to set up the root domain. It assumes the simplest case, so be sure you are familiar with the more thorough task descriptions before you use this summary as a reference. Also, this summary does not show the server's responses to each command.

<table>
<tr><td>rootmaster% su
Password: <enter root password></td><td>1. Log in as superuser to rootmaster.</td></tr>
<tr><td># domainname</td><td>2. Check domain name.</td></tr>
<tr><td># more /etc/nsswitch.conf</td><td>3. Check Switch file.</td></tr>
<tr><td># rm -rf /var/nis*</td><td>4. Remove leftover NIS+ material.</td></tr>
<tr><td># NIS_GROUP=admin.Wiz.Com.;export NIS_GROUP</td><td>5. Name the admin group.</td></tr>
<tr><td># nisinit -r</td><td>6. Initialize the root master.</td></tr>
<tr><td></td><td>7. NIS-compat only:</td></tr>
<tr><td># rpc.nisd -r -Y -B -S 0</td><td>a. Start daemon with -Y -B, S 0.</td></tr>
<tr><td># vi /etc/inet.d/rpc</td><td>b. Change to EMULYP="-Y -B".</td></tr>
<tr><td># rpc.nisd -r -S 0</td><td>8. NIS+ Only: Start daemon with S 0.</td></tr>
<tr><td># /usr/lib/nis/nissetup [-Y]</td><td>9. Create org_dir, groups_dir tables.</td></tr>
<tr><td># nisaddcred des
Enter login password: <enter login password></td><td>10. Create DES credentials for root master.</td></tr>
<tr><td># nisgrpadm -c admin.Wiz.Com.</td><td>11. Create admin group.</td></tr>
<tr><td># nischmod g+rmcd Wiz.Com.</td><td>12. Assign full group rights to root directory.</td></tr>
<tr><td># nisgrpadm -a admin.Wiz.Com. rootmaster.Wiz.Com.</td><td>13. Add root master to admin group.</td></tr>
<tr><td># /usr/lib/nis/nisupdkeys Wiz.Com.</td><td>14. Update root directory's keys.</td></tr>
<tr><td># /usr/lib/nis/nisupdkeys org_dir.Wiz.Com.</td><td>Update org_dir's keys.</td></tr>
<tr><td># /usr/lib/nis/nisupdkeys groups_dir.Wiz.Com.</td><td>Update groups_dir's keys.</td></tr>
<tr><td># nis_cachemgr</td><td>15. Start NIS+ cache manager</td></tr>
<tr><td># ps -ef | grep rpc.nisd</td><td>16. Restart the NIS+ daemon with sec 2.</td></tr>
<tr><td># kill -9 <process-id></td><td>First kill existing daemon.</td></tr>
<tr><td># rpc.nisd -r [-Y] [-B]</td><td>Use -Y for NIS compat and -B for DNS.</td></tr>
<tr><td># nisaddcred -p 11177 -P topadmin.Wiz.Com. local</td><td>17. Add your LOCAL credentials.</td></tr>
<tr><td># nisaddcred -p unix.11177@Wiz.Com \
-P topadmin.Wiz.Com. des
Enter login password: <enter login password></td><td>18. Add your DES credentials.</td></tr>
<tr><td># nisaddcred . . .</td><td>19. Add credentials for other admins.</td></tr>
<tr><td># nisgrpadm -a admin.Wiz.Com. member...</td><td>20. Add other admins to admin group.</td></tr>
</table>

Setting Up NIS+ Tables 16 ☰

This chapter provides step-by-step instructions for populating NIS+ tables. The tables should have already been created with the `nissetup` utility in the process of setting up a domain, either root or nonroot. Although you can populate a domain's tables at any time after they are created, the Planning chapter recommends you do so immediately after setting up the domain. Doing so enables you to add clients more easily, since the required information about the clients is already available in the domain's tables. If you waited till later, you would have to add the clients' information into the master's `/etc` files.

You can populate NIS+ tables in two ways: from files or from NIS maps. This chapter provides a task for each. It also describes how to transfer information back from NIS+ tables to NIS maps, a procedure that may be required during a transition from NIS to NIS+. Finally, it includes two tasks that describe how to limit access to the passwd column of the Passwd table:

Replace vs. Append vs. Merge

When you populate a table—whether from a file or an NIS map—you can use any of three options: replace, append, or merge.

The append option simply adds the source entries to the NIS+ table.

With the replace option, NIS+ first deletes all existing entries in the table and then adds the entries from the source. In a large table, this adds a large set of entries into the table's .log file (one set for removing the existing entries, another for adding the new ones), taking up space in /var/nis and making propagation to replicas time-consuming.

The merge option produces the same result as the replace option, but uses a different process, one that can greatly reduce the number of operations that must be sent to the replicas. With the merge option, NIS+ handles three types of entries differently:

- Entries that exist only in the source are added to the table
- Entries that exist in both the source and the table are updated in the table
- Entries that exist only in the NIS+ table are deleted from the table

When updating a large table with a file or map whose contents are not vastly different from those of the table, the merge option can spare the server a great many operations. Because it deletes only the entries that are not duplicated in the source (the replace option deletes *all* entries, indiscriminately), it saves one delete and one add operation for every duplicate entry.

▼ How to Populate NIS+ Tables from Files

This task transfers the contents of an ASCII file, such as /etc/hosts, into an NIS+ table. Here is a list of the steps:

Step	1.	Log in to an NIS+ client.
Step	2.	Add /usr/lib/nis to the search path for this shell.
Step	3.	Use nisaddent to transfer any of these files, one at a time.
Step	4.	Transfer the publickey file.
Step	5.	Transfer the automounter information.
Step	6.	Checkpoint the tables.

Security Considerations

You can perform the task from any NIS+ client, including the root master server, as long as you have the proper credentials and access rights. If you are going to replace or merge the entries in the table with the entries from the text file, you must have Create and Destroy rights to the table. If you are going to append the new entries, you only need Create rights.

After you complete the operation, the table entries will be owned by the NIS+ principal that performed the operation and the group specified by the NIS_GROUP environment variable.

Prerequisites

- The domain must have already been set up, and its master server must be running.
- The domain's servers must have enough swap space to accommodate the new table information. See "Disk Space and Memory Requirements" on page 124.
- The information in the file must be formatted appropriately for the table into which it will be loaded. Chapter 3, "Understanding NIS+ Tables," describes the format a text file must have for transfer into its corresponding NIS+ table. Local /etc files are usually formatted properly, but may have several comments that you would need to remove.

You need the following information:

- The name and location of the text files that will be transferred

Instructions

1. **Log in to an NIS+ client.**
   You can perform this task from any NIS+ client—just be sure that the client belongs to the same domain as the tables into which you want to transfer the information. The examples in this task use the root master server. Since the administrator in these examples is logged in as superuser, the NIS+ principal actually performing this operation (and therefore needing the proper credentials and access rights) is the root master server.

2. **Add** /usr/lib/nis **to the search path for this shell.**
    Since you will be using the /usr/lib/nis/nisaddent command once per table, adding its prefix to the search path will save you the trouble of typing it each time. Here are two examples, one for csh users, one for sh/ksh users:

```
rootmaster# setenv $PATH:/usr/lib/nis          # csh users

rootmaster# PATH=$PATH:/usr/lib/nis            # sh/ksh users
rootmaster# export PATH
```

If you are using the Solaris 1.x distribution of NIS+, the path may be different; check the README file.

3. **Use** nisaddent **to transfer any of these files, one at a time.**

aliases	netmasks
bootparams	networks
ethers	passwd
group	protocols
hosts	rpc
netgroup	services

    The publickey and automounter files require slightly different procedures; for the publickey file, go to Step 4, and for the automounter files, go to Step 5.

    By default, nisaddent *appends* the file information to the table information. To replace or merge instead, use the -r or -m options.

```
rootmaster# nisaddent -r -f filename table [domain]    # to replace
rootmaster# nisaddent -a -f filename table [domain]    # to append
rootmaster# nisaddent -m -f filename table [domain]    # to merge
```

    The best option for populating the tables for the first time is the -a option, which is the default. The best option for synchronizing the NIS+ tables with NIS maps or /etc files is the -m (merge) option.

Filename is the name of the file. *Table* is the name of the NIS+ table. The *domain* argument is optional; use it only to populate tables in a different domain. Here are some examples, entered from the root domain's master server. The source files are simply edited versions of the /etc files.

```
rootmaster# nisaddent -m -f /etc/hosts.xfr hosts
rootmaster# nisaddent -m -f /etc/passwd.xfr passwd
rootmaster# nisaddent -m -f /etc/groups.xfr groups
```

If you perform this operation from a nonroot server, keep in mind that a nonroot server belongs to the domain above the one it supports. Therefore, it is a client of another domain. For example, the Sales.Wiz.Com. master server belongs to the Wiz.Com. domain. To populate tables in the Sales.Wiz.Com. domain from that master server, you would append the Sales.Wiz.Com. domain name to the nisaddent statement. For example:

```
salesmaster# nisaddent -f /etc/hosts.xfr hosts \
                    Sales.Wiz.Com.
```

If you performed this operation as a client of the Sales.Wiz.Com. domain, you would not need to append the domain name to the syntax. For more information about nisaddent, see Chapter 25, "Administering NIS+ Tables."

To verify that the entries were transferred into the NIS+ table, use the niscat command (described in Chapter 25). Here is an example:

```
rootmaster# niscat group.org_dir
root::0:root
other::1::
bin::2:root,bin,daemon
  .
  .
  .
```

4. **Transfer the publickey file.**
   Since the domain's Cred table already stores some credentials, make sure they are not overwritten by the contents of the publickey text file that you transfer into the Cred table. You can avoid this overwriting by removing those credentials from the publickey text file. For rootmaster, that line would be:

   > unix.rootmaster@Wiz.Com   *public-key*:*private-key*

   Then, you can transfer the contents of the publickey file into the Cred table. Use nisaddent, but with the -a (add) option.

   ```
   rootmaster# nisaddent -a -f /etc/publickey.xfr cred [domain]
   ```

   Note, however, that this operation transfers only DES credentials into the Cred table. Principals must still create their LOCAL credentials to the Cred table.

5. **Transfer the automounter information.**
   Although the nissetup utility creates Auto_Master and Auto_Home tables, they are not considered standard NIS+ tables. Therefore, transferring information into them requires a slightly different syntax; in particular, you must use the -t flag and specify that the table is of type key-value.

   ```
   rootmaster# nisaddent -f auto.master.xfr \
                         -t auto_master.org_dir key-value
   rootmaster# nisaddent -f auto.home.xfr \
                         -t auto_home.org_dir   key-value
   ```

6. **Checkpoint the tables.**

This step ensures that all the servers supporting the domain transfer the new information from their `.log` files to the disk-based copies of the tables. If you have just set up the root domain, this step affects only the root master server, since the root domain does not yet have replicas. Use the `nisping` command with the `-C` (uppercase) option.

```
rootmaster# nisping -C org_dir
Checkpointing replicas serving directory org_dir.Wiz.Com. :
Master server is rootmaster.Wiz.Com.
    Last update occurred at <date>

Master server is rootmaster.Wiz.Com.
checkpoint succeeded.
```

If you don't have enough swap space, the server will be unable to checkpoint properly, but it won't notify you. One way to make sure all went well is to list the contents of a table with the `niscat` command. If you don't have enough swap space, you'll see this error message:

```
can't list table: Server busy, Try Again.
```

Even though it doesn't *seem* to, this message indicates that you don't have enough swap space. Increase the swap space and checkpoint the domain again.

This step completes this task.

▼ How to Populate NIS+ Tables from NIS Maps

This task transfers the contents of an NIS map into an NIS+ table.   Here is a list of the steps:

Step 1.   Log in to an NIS+ client.

Step 2.   Add /usr/lib/nis to the search path for this shell.

Step 3.   Use nisaddent to transfer any of these maps, one at a time.

Step 4. Transfer the publickey map.

Step 5. Transfer the automounter information.

Step 6. Checkpoint the tables.

Security Considerations

You can perform this task from any NIS+ client as long as you (or superuser on the client) have the proper credentials and access rights. If you are going to replace or merge the entries in the table with the entries from the NIS map, you must have Create and Destroy rights to the table. If you are going to append the new entries, you need only Create rights.

After you complete this operation, the table entries will be owned by the NIS+ principal that performed the operation (either you or, if logged in as superuser, the client) and the group specified by the NIS_GROUP environment variable.

Prerequisites

- The domain must have already been set up, and its master server must be running.
- The dbm files (.pag and .dir files) for the NIS maps you are going to load into the NIS+ tables must already be in a subdirectory of /var/yp. If they are not, you can use /usr/lib/netsvc/yp/ypxfr to get the maps from an NIS server.

You need the following information:

- The name and location of the NIS maps

Instructions

1. **Log in to an NIS+ client.**
   You can perform this task from any NIS+ client—just be sure that the client belongs to the same domain as the tables into which you will transfer the information. The examples in this task use the root master server. Since the administrator in these examples is logged in as superuser, the NIS+ principal actually performing this operation (and therefore needing the proper credentials and access rights) is the root master server.

2. **Add** /usr/lib/nis **to the search path for this shell.**
   Since you will be using the /usr/lib/nis/nisaddent command once per table, adding its prefix to the search path will save you the trouble of typing it each time. Here are two examples, one for csh users, one for sh/ksh users.

   ```
   rootmaster# setenv $PATH:/usr/lib/nis          # csh users

   rootmaster# PATH=$PATH:/usr/lib/nis            # sh/ksh users
   rootmaster# export PATH
   ```

   If you are using the Solaris 1.x distribution of NIS+, the path may be different; check the README file.

3. **Use** nisaddent **to transfer any of these maps, one at a time.**

aliases	netmasks
bootparams	networks
ethers	passwd
group	protocols
hosts	rpc
netgroup	services

   The publickey and automounter maps require slightly different procedures; for the publickey file, go to Step 4, and for the automounter files, go to Step 5.

   By default, nisaddent *appends* the file information to the table information. To replace or merge instead, use the -r or -m options.

   ```
   rootmaster# nisaddent -r -y nisdomain  table     # to replace
   rootmaster# nisaddent -a -y nisdomain  table     # to append
   rootmaster# nisaddent -m -y nisdomain  table     # to merge
   ```

   The best option for populating the tables for the first time is the -a option, which is the default. The best option to synchronize the NIS+ tables with NIS maps or /etc files is the -m (merge) option.

The -y (lowercase) option indicates an NIS domain instead of a text file. The *nisdomain* argument is the name of the NIS domain whose map you are going transfer into the NIS+ table. You don't have to name the actual map; the nisaddent utility automatically selects the NIS map that corresponds to the *table* argument. Here are some examples:

```
rootmaster# nisaddent -m -y OldWiz hosts
rootmaster# nisaddent -m -y OldWiz passwd
rootmaster# nisaddent -m -y OldWiz groups
```

The first example transfers the contents of the hosts.byname and hosts.byaddr maps in the OldWiz (NIS) domain to the NIS+ Hosts table in the root domain (NIS+). The second transfers the NIS maps that store password-related information into the NIS+ Passwd table. The third does the same with group-related information. For more information about the nisaddent command, see Chapter 25, "Administering NIS+ Tables."

4. **Transfer the publickey map.**
   Since the domain's Cred table already stores some credentials, make sure they are not overwritten by the contents of the publickey map that you transfer into the Cred table. First, dump the publickey map to a file.

```
rootmaster# makedbm -u /var/yp/OldWiz/publickey.byname > \
            /etc/publickey.xfr
rootmaster# vi /tmp/publickey
```

Open the file and remove the credentials of the workstation you are logged in to from the publickey map. For rootmaster, that line is:

```
unix.rootmaster@Wiz.Com       public-key:private-key
```

Now you can transfer the contents of the *file*—not the map—into the Cred table. Use nisaddent, but with the -a (add) option.

```
rootmaster# nisaddent -a -f /etc/publickey.xfr cred
```

Note, however, that this operation transfers only DES credentials into the Cred table. Principals must still create their LOCAL credentials to the Cred table.

5. **Transfer the automounter information.**

Although the `nissetup` utility creates Auto_Master and Auto_Home tables, they are not considered standard NIS+ tables. Therefore, transferring information into them requires a slightly different syntax.

```
rootmaster# nisaddent -y OldWiz -Y auto.master \
                     -t auto_master.org_dir key-value
rootmaster# nisaddent -y OldWiz -Y auto.home \
                     -t auto_home.org_dir key-value
```

The `-m` and `-y` options are still required, as is the NIS domain name (in this instance, OldWiz). However, you must precede the name of the NIS map (e.g., `auto.master`) with a `-Y` (uppercase).   Then, as is required when transferring automounter *text files*, use the `-t` option, which indicates that this is a nonstandard NIS+ table. Its arguments are the name of the NIS+ table (auto_master.org_dir) and the type of table (`key-value`).   Be sure to append the org_dir suffixes to the NIS+ table names.

6. **Checkpoint the tables.**

This step ensures that all the servers supporting the domain transfer the new information from their `.log` files to the disk-based copies of the tables. If you just finished setting up the root domain, this step affects only the root master server, since the root domain does not yet have replicas. Use the `nisping` command with the `-C` (uppercase) option.

```
rootmaster# nisping -C org_dir
Checkpointing replicas serving directory org_dir.Wiz.Com. :
Master server is rootmaster.Wiz.Com.
     Last update occurred at <date>

Master server is rootmaster.Wiz.Com.
checkpoint succeeded.
```

If you don't have enough swap space, the server will be unable to checkpoint properly, but it won't notify you. One way to make sure all went well is to list the contents of a table with the `niscat` command. If you don't have enough swap space, you'll see this error message:

```
can't list table: Server busy, Try Again.
```

Even though it doesn't *seem* to, this message indicates that you don't have enough swap space. Increase the swap space and checkpoint the domain again.

This step completes this task.

▼ How to Transfer Information from NIS+ to NIS

This task transfers the contents of NIS+ tables into the NIS maps on a Solaris 1.x NIS master server. Here is a list of the steps:

Step 1. Log in to the NIS+ server.

Step 2. Transfer the NIS+ tables into output files.

Step 3. Transfer the contents of the output files into the NIS maps.

Security Considerations

To perform this task, you must have Read access to each table whose contents you transfer.

Prerequisites

The maps must have already been built on the NIS server.

Instructions

1. **Log in to the NIS+ server.**
    This example uses the server named `dualserver`.

2. **Transfer the NIS+ tables into output files.**
    Use the `nisaddent` command with the `-d` option, as shown below, once for each table.

    ```
    dualserver% /usr/lib/nis/nisaddent -d -t table > filename
    ```

    The `-d` option dumps the contents of *table* to *filename*, converting the contents back to standard `/etc` file format.

All About Administering NIS+

3. **Transfer the contents of the output files into the NIS maps.**
   The NIS+ output files are ASCII files that you can use as input files for the NIS maps. Copy them into the NIS master's /etc directory and then use makedbm as usual.

   ```
   dualserver# makedbm flags output-file   NIS-dbm-file
   ```

▼ How to Limit Access to the Passwd Column

This task describes how to limit Read access to the passwd column of the Passwd table only to authenticated users without affecting the Read access of unauthenticated principals (i.e., applications) to the remaining columns in the Passwd table. Use this task only for NIS+ releases prior to Solaris 2.3, since Solaris 2.3 supplies as a default the access rights provided by this task.

Security Considerations

- For an explanation of the circumstances under which you would perform this task, see "Protecting the Encrypted Password Field" on page 140
- The domain must *not* be running in NIS-compatibility mode
- All NIS+ clients of the domain must have DES credentials

Prerequisites

- The Passwd table must have already been set up. It need not have any information in it, however.
- The NIS+ principal performing this task must have Modify rights to the Passwd table.

You need the following information:

- Name of the Passwd table.

Instructions

1. **Log in to the domain's master server.**
   The examples in this task use the root master server, "rootmaster."

2. **Check the current table and column permissions.**
    Use the `niscat -o` command:

    ```
    rootmaster# niscat -o passwd.org_dir
    ```

    If the table has the permissions shown below, you don't need to perform this task; the table is already set up properly.

    ```
    rootmaster# niscat -o passwd.org_dir
    Object Name      : passwd
    .
    .
    .
    Access Rights    : ----rmcdrmcdr---
    .
    .
    .
    Columns          :
            [0]  Name          : name
                 Access Rights : r-----------r---
            [1]  Name          : passwd
                 Access Rights : -----m----------
            [2]  Name          : uid
                 Access Rights : r-----------r---
            [3]  Name          : gid
                 Access Rights : r-----------r---
            [4]  Name          : gcos
                 Access Rights : r----m------r---
            [5]  Name          : home
                 Access Rights : r-----------r---
            [6]  Name          : shell
                 Access Rights : r-----------r---
            [7]  Name          : shadow
                 Access Rights : r-----------r---
    ```

3. **Change the table permissions.**
    Use the `nischmod` command to change the table's object-level permissions to:

    ```
    ---- rmcd rmcd r---
    ```

    ```
    rootmaster# nischmod n=,og=rmcd,w=r  passwd.org_dir
    ```

4. **Change the column permissions.**

Use the `nistbladm` command with the `-u` option to change the column permissions to:

```
name     r---  ----  ----  r---
passwd   ----  -m--  ----  ----
uid      r---  ----  ----  r---
gid      r---  ----  ----  r---
gcos     r---  ----  ----  r---
home     r---  ----  ----  r---
shell    r---  ----  ----  r---
shadow   r---  ----  ----  r---
```

You could use `nistbladm` once—

```
rootmaster# nistbladm -u [name=n+r,uid=n+r,gid=n+r,gcos=n+r, \
            home=n+r,shell=n+r,shadow=n+r],passwd.org_dir
```

— but if you made a typing error, you'd have to retype the whole line, possibly several times over. You might prefer to use the command once for each column.

```
rootmaster# nistbladm -u [name=n+r],passwd.org_dir
rootmaster# nistbladm -u [uid=n+r],passwd.org_dir
rootmaster# nistbladm -u [gid=n+r],passwd.org_dir
rootmaster# nistbladm -u [gcos=n+r],passwd.org_dir
rootmaster# nistbladm -u [home=n+r],passwd.org_dir
rootmaster# nistbladm -u [shell=n+r],passwd.org_dir
rootmaster# nistbladm -u [shadow=n+r],passwd.org_dir
```

This example assumes the columns had no previous Read permissions assigned to the Nobody class. Notice that no Read permissions are added to the passwd column. If your table provided different permissions, you would use a different syntax; for details, see the description of the `nistbladm -u` command on page 331.

5. **Verify the new permissions.**

Use the `niscat -o` command as you did in Step 2. The permissions should look the same as they do in that step's output.

▼ How to Further Limit Access to the Passwd Column

This task describes how to limit Read access to the passwd column of the Passwd table only to the entry owner and table administrator without affecting the Read access of other authenticated or unauthenticated principals (i.e., applications) to the remaining columns in the Passwd table. Here is the difference between the permissions provided by this task and those provided by the previous task:

This task:

```
                             Nobody    Owner    Group    World
     Table Level Rights   :  ----      rmcd     rmcd     ----
     Passwd Column Rights :  ----      rm--     ----     ----
     Shadow Column Rights :  ----      rm--     ----     ----
```

Previous task:

```
                             Nobody    Owner    Group    World
     Table Level Rights   :  ----      rmcd     rmcd     r---
     Passwd Column Rights :  ----      -m--     ----     ----
     Shadow Column Rights :  r---      ----     ----     ----
```

Security Considerations

- For an explanation of the circumstances under which you would perform this task, see "Protecting the Encrypted Password Field" on page 140.
- The domain must *not* be running in NIS compatibility mode.
- All clients of the domain must have DES credentials.
- All clients of the domain must be running Solaris 2.3 or a later release.
- Users' network passwords (used to encrypt their DES credentials) must be the same as their login passwords.

Prerequisites

- The Passwd table must have already been set up. It need not have any information in it, however.
- The NIS+ principal performing this task must have Modify rights to the Passwd table.
- The previous task, "How to Limit Access to the Passwd Column," must have already been performed.

You need the following information:

* Name of the Passwd table.

Instructions

1. **Log in to the domain's master server.**
   The examples in this task use the root master server, rootmaster.

2. **Check the current table and column permissions.**
   Use the niscat -o command.

```
rootmaster# niscat -o passwd.org_dir
```

This task assumes the existing permissions are:

```
Access Rights     : ----rmcdrmcdr---
Columns           :
        [0]  Name            : name
             Access Rights : r-----------r---
        [1]  Name            : passwd
             Access Rights : -----m----------
        [2]  Name            : uid
             Access Rights : r-----------r---
        [3]  Name            : gid
             Access Rights : r-----------r---
        [4]  Name            : gcos
             Access Rights : r----m------r---
        [5]  Name            : home
             Access Rights : r-----------r---
        [6]  Name            : shell
             Access Rights : r-----------r---
        [7]  Name            : shadow
             Access Rights : r-----------r---
```

If your permissions are different, you may need to use a different syntax. For instructions, see Chapter 23, "Administering NIS+ Access Rights."

3. **Change the table permissions.**
   Use the `nischmod` command to change the table's object-level permissions to:

   ```
   ---- rmcd rmcd ----
   ```

   ```
   rootmaster# nischmod og=rmcd,nw=  passwd.org_dir
   ```

4. **Change the column permissions.**
   Use the `nistbladm` command with the `-u` option to change the permissions of the passwd and shadow columns to:

   ```
   passwd      ---- rm-- ---- ----
   shadow      ---- r--- ---- ----
   ```

   ```
   rootmaster# nistbladm -u [passwd=o+r,
   shadow=o+r],passwd.org_dir
   ```

5. **Verify the new permissions.**
   Use the `niscat -o` command as you did in Step 2. The permissions should look the same as they do in that step's output.

Summary

Following is a summary of the steps required to populate NIS+ tables. It assumes the simplest case, so be sure you are familiar with the more thorough task descriptions before you use this summary as a reference. For brevity, this summary does not show the server's responses to each command.

To Transfer Files Into NIS+ Tables:

```rootmaster%```
 ``` % PATH=$PATH:/usr/lib/nis; export PATH```
 	
 ``` % nisaddent -m -f /etc/hosts.xfr hosts```
 ``` % .```
 ``` % .```
 ``` % .```
 ``` % vi /etc/publickey.xfer```
 	
 ``` % nisaddent -a -f /etc/publickey.xfr cred```
 ``` % nisaddent -f auto.master.xfr \```
 ```   -t auto_master.org_dir key-value```
 ``` % nisaddent -f auto.home.xfr \```
 ```   -t auto_home.org_dir key-value```
 ``` % nisping -C org_dir```
	1. Log in to an NIS+ client.
	 2. Add /usr/lib/nis to search path.
	 3. Transfer each file, one at a time.
	
	 4. Transfer publickey file. First remove new credentials from the file. Then transfer it.
	 5. Transfer the automounter files.
	
	 6. Checkpoint the table directory.

To Transfer Maps into NIS+ Tables:

```rootmaster%```
 ``` % PATH=$PATH:/usr/lib/nis; export PATH```
 	
 ``` $ nisaddent -m -y OldWiz hosts```
 ``` % .```
 ``` % .```
 ``` % .```
 ``` % makedbm -u /var/yp/OldWiz/publickey.byname > \```
 ```   /etc/publickey.xfr```
 ``` % vi /etc/publickey.xfr```
 ``` % nisaddent -a -f /etc/publickey.xfr cred```
 ``` % nisaddent -y OldWiz -Y auto.master \```
 ```   -t auto_master.org_dir key-value```
 ``` % nisaddent -y OldWiz -Y auto.home \```
 ```   -t auto_home.org_dir key-value```
 ``` % nisping -C org_dir```
	1. Log in to an NIS+ client.
	 2. Add /usr/lib/nis to search path.
	 3. Transfer each map, one at a time.
	
	 4. Transfer publickey file. First dump the publickey map to a file. Then remove new credentials. Then transfer the file.
	 5. Transfer the automounter maps.
	
	 6. Checkpoint the table directory.

To Transfer NIS+ Tables into NIS Maps:

``` dualserver% % /usr/lib/nis/nisaddent -d -t table > filename % . % . % . % makedbm flags output-file NIS-dbm-file ```	1. Log in to NIS+ server. 2. Transfer NIS+ tables to files. 3. Transfer files to NIS maps.

To Limit Access to the Passwd Column:

``
rootmaster#
 	
# niscat -o passwd.org_dir 	
# nischmod n=,og=rmcd,w=r passwd.org_dir 	
# nistbladm -u [name=n+r,uid=n+r,gid=n+r, \ 	
                gcos=n+r,home=n+r,shell=n+r, \
                shadow=n+r], passwd.org_dir
# niscat -o passwd.org_dir 	
``
	1. Log in to the domain's master server.
	2. Check the table's existing rights.
	3. Assign the table new rights.
	4. Assign the columns new rights.
	
	5. Verify the new rights.

To Further Limit Access to the Passwd Column:

``` rootmaster# # niscat -o passwd.org_dir # nischmod og=rmcd,nw= passwd.org_dir # nistbladm -u [passwd=o+r, shadow=n+r], \ passwd.org_dir # niscat -o passwd.org_dir ```	1. Log in to the domain's master server. 2. Check the table's existing rights. 3. Assign the table new rights. 4. Assign the columns new rights. 5. Verify the new rights.

Setting Up an NIS+ Client   17 ☰

This chapter provides step-by-step instructions for one major task and four related subtasks:

The central task in this chapter, "How to Set Up an NIS+ Client," applies to clients in a standard NIS+ domain and in an NIS-compatible domain. In this task, Step 7 instructs you to initialize the client by one of three methods: broadcast, hostname, or coldstart file. Since each method is implemented differently, each has its own task description. After initializing a client by one of these methods, you can continue setting up the client by returning to Step 8.

The last task in the chapter describes how to change a workstation's domain name. This task is referenced by several different setup procedures in Part 3 and is closely related to setting up a client, so it seems fitting to include it here.

This chapter walks through the client setup process at the same leisurely pace as the task for setting up the root domain. For a quicker pace, see the summary at the end of the chapter.

▼ How to Set Up an NIS+ Client

This task describes how to set up a typical NIS+ client, whether in the root domain or in a nonroot domain. It applies to regular NIS+ clients and to those clients that will later become NIS+ servers. It applies, as well, to clients in a standard NIS+ domain and those in an NIS-compatible domain. Setting up an NIS+ client involves the following tasks:

- Creating credentials for the client
- Preparing the workstation
- Initializing the workstation as an NIS+ client

However, as with setting up the root domain, setting up a client is not as simple as carrying out these three tasks in order. To make the setup process easier to execute, these tasks have been broken down into individual steps, and the steps have been arranged in the most efficient order. They are:

Step	1.	Log in to the domain's master server.
Step	2.	Create DES credentials for the new client workstation.
Step	3.	Log in as superuser to the client.
Step	4.	Assign the client its new domain name.
Step	5.	Check the client's Switch configuration file.
Step	6.	Clean out leftover NIS+ material and processes.
Step	7.	Initialize the client.
Step	8.	Kill and restart the keyserv daemon.
Step	9.	Run keylogin.
Step	10.	Reboot the client.

Security Considerations

Setting up a client has two main security requirements: both the administrator and the client must have the proper credentials and access rights. If you are setting up the client according to the sequence recommended in the Planning chapter, you already have the proper credentials and access rights.

Otherwise, the only way for a client to obtain credentials in a domain running at security level 2 is for the credentials to be created by an administrator who has valid DES credentials and Modify rights to the Cred table in the client's home domain. The administrator can either have DES credentials in the client's home domain or in his or her own home domain.

Once an administrator creates the client's credentials, the client can complete the setup process. However, the client still needs Read access to the directory object of its home domain. If you set up the client's home domain according to the instructions in either Chapter 15 or Chapter 19, Read access was provided to the World category by the NIS+ commands used to create the directory objects (`nisinit` and `nismkdir`, respectively).

You can check the directory object's access rights by using the `niscat -o` command. It displays the properties of the directory, including its access rights. Here is an example:

```
rootmaster# niscat -o Wiz.Com.
ObjectName    : Wiz
Owner         : rootmaster.Wiz.Com.
Group         : admin.Wiz.Com.
Domain        : Com.
Access Rights : r---rmcdr---r---
   .
   .
   .
```

You can change the directory object's access rights, provided you have Modify rights to it yourself, by using the `nischmod` command, described in Chapter 23, "Administering NIS+ Access Rights."

Prerequisites

- The administrator setting up the client's credentials must have valid DES credentials and Modify rights to the Cred table in the client's home domain
- The client must have Read rights to the directory object of its home domain
- The client's home domain must already be set up and running NIS+
- The client must have an entry either in the master server's `/etc/hosts` file or in its domain's Hosts table

You need the following information:

- The name of the client's home domain
- The superuser password of the workstation that will become the client

- The IP address of an NIS+ server in the client's home domain

Instructions

1. **Log in to the domain's master server.**
   You can log in as superuser or as yourself, depending on which NIS+ principal has the proper access rights to add credentials to the domain's Cred table.

2. **Create DES credentials for the new client workstation.**
   Use the `nisaddcred` command with the `-p` and `-P` arguments. Here is the syntax, followed by an example:

       nisaddcred -p *secure-RPC-netname* -P *principal-name* des [*domain*]

   The secure RPC netname consists of the prefix "unix." followed by the client's hostname, the symbol "@" and the client's domain name, but without a trailing dot. The principal name consists of the client's hostname and domain name, with a trailing dot. If the client belongs to a domain different the server from which you enter the command, append the client's domain name after the second argument.

   This example adds a DES credential for a client workstation named "client1" in the Wiz.Com. domain.

   ```
   rootmaster% nisaddcred -p unix.client1@Wiz.Com \
                          -P client1.Wiz.Com. des
   Adding key pair for unix.client1@Wiz.Com (client1.Wiz.Com.).
   Enter client1.Wiz.Com.'s root login passwd:   <enter password>
   Retype password: <enter password>
   ```

   For more information about the `nisaddcred` command, see Chapter 22, "Administering NIS+ Credentials."

3. **Log in as superuser to the client.**
   Now that the client workstation has credentials, you can log out of the master server and begin working from the client itself. You can do this locally or remotely.

4. **Assign the client its new domain name.**
   Assign the client its new domain name, using the task listed below. Then return to Step 5.

   ▼ Changing a Workstation's Domain Name   Page 259

5. **Check the client's Switch configuration file.**

Make sure the client is using the NIS+ version of the `nsswitch.conf` file. This version ensures that the primary source of information for the client will be NIS+ tables. Figure 17-1 shows the correct version of the file.

```
client1# more /etc/nsswitch.conf
#
# /etc/nsswitch.nisplus:
#
# An example file that could be copied over to /etc/nsswitch.conf; it
# uses NIS+ (NIS Version 3) in conjunction with files.
#
# "hosts:" and "services:" in this file are used only if the /etc/netconfig
# file contains "switch.so" as a nametoaddr library for "inet" transports.

# the following two lines obviate the "+" entry in /etc/passwd and /etc/group.
passwd:     files nisplus
group:      files nisplus

# consult /etc "files" only if nisplus is down.
hosts:        nisplus [NOTFOUND=return] files
#Uncomment the following line, and comment out the above, to use both DNS and NIS+
#hosts:        nisplus dns [NOTFOUND=return] files

services:     nisplus [NOTFOUND=return] files
networks:     nisplus [NOTFOUND=return] files
protocols:    nisplus [NOTFOUND=return] files
rpc:          nisplus [NOTFOUND=return] files
ethers:       nisplus [NOTFOUND=return] files
netmasks:     nisplus [NOTFOUND=return] files
bootparams:   nisplus [NOTFOUND=return] files

publickey:    nisplus

netgroup:     nisplus

automount:    files nisplus
aliases:      files nisplus
```

Figure 17-1 NIS+ Version of `nsswitch.conf` File

If the file does not look like the one above, change it to the version recommended for NIS+. Complete instructions are provided in Chapter 20, "Setting Up the Name Service Switch," but here is an example.

```
client1# cp /etc/nsswitch.nisplus /etc/nsswitch.conf
```

Although the instructions in Chapter 20 tell you to kill and restart the keyserver, you don't need to do so at this point, since you'll do so in Step 8.

6. **Clean out leftover NIS+ material and processes.**
   If the workstation you are working on was previously used as an NIS+ server or client and you no longer want to retain those bindings, remove any files that might exist in /var/nis and kill the cache manager, if it is still running. In this example, a coldstart file and a directory cache file still exist in /var/nis.

```
client1# ls /var/nis
NIS_COLD_START      NIS_SHARED_CACHE
client1# rm -rf /var/nis/*
client1# ps -ef | grep nis_cachemgr
    root   295   260 10 15:26:58 pts/0  0:00 grep nis_cachemgr
    root   286     1 57 15:21:55 ?      0:01 /usr/sbin/nis_cachemgr
client1# kill -9 286
```

This step makes sure that files left in /var/nis or directory objects stored by the cache manager are completely erased so they do not conflict with the new information generated during this setup process. If you have stored any admin scripts in /var/nis, you may want to consider temporarily storing them elsewhere until you finish setting up the root domain.

7. **Initialize the client.**
   You can initialize a client in three different ways: by hostname, by coldstart file, or by broadcast. Select a method and follow the instructions, which begin on the pages listed below. Then proceed with Step 8.

▼ Initializing an NIS+ Client by Broadcast	Page 262
▼ Initializing an NIS+ Client by Hostname	Page 263
▼ Initializing an NIS+ Client by Coldstart File	Page 264

8. **Kill and restart the keyserv daemon.**

   The following step stores the client's secret key on the keyserver. Before that can be done, you must kill and restart the keyserv daemon. This also has the side effect of updating the key server's Switch information about the client.

   First kill the keyserv daemon, then remove the /etc/.rootkey file, then restart the keyserver. Here is an example:

   ```
   client1# ps -e | grep keyserv
   root   145    1   67  16:34:44   ?    keyserv
        .
        .
        .
   client1# kill 145
   client1# rm -f /etc/.rootkey
   client1# keyserv
   ```

9. **Run keylogin.**

   This step stores the client's secret key with the keyserver. It also saves a copy in /etc/.rootkey, so that the superuser on the client does not have to do a keylogin to use NIS+. Use keylogin with the -r option. When prompted for a password, enter the client's superuser password. It must be the same as the password supplied to create the client's DES credentials.

   ```
   client1# keylogin -r
   Password: <enter-superuser-password>
   Wrote secret key into /etc/.rootkey
   ```

10. **Reboot the client.**

    This step completes this task.

▼ Changing a Workstation's Domain Name

This task changes a workstation's domain name. Since a workstation's domain name is usually set during installation, you should check it (just enter domainname without an argument) before you decide to use this task.

A Note About Specifying a Domain Name After Installation

A workstation is usually assigned to its domain during installation. On an operating network, the installation script usually obtains the domain name automatically and simply asks the installer to confirm it. During the installation proper, the workstation's domain name is assigned to a variable called `domainname` and stored in the kernel. There, it is made available to any program that needs it.

However, when a workstation is rebooted, the setting of the `domainname` variable is lost. As a result, unless the domain name is saved somewhere, the operating system no longer knows which domain the workstation belongs to. To solve this problem, the domain name is stored in a file called `/etc/defaultdomain`.

When the workstation is rebooted, the kernel automatically obtains the domain name from this file and resets the `domainname` variable. However, only at reboot is the variable updated automatically. If you change a workstation's domain name sometime after installation, you must also edit the `/etc/defaultdomain` file; if you don't, after the next reboot, the workstation will revert to its previous domain name.

Security Considerations

You must perform this task as superuser on the workstation whose domain name you will change.

You need the following information:

- The workstation's superuser password
- The new domain name

Instructions

1. **Log in to the workstation and become superuser.**
   The examples in this task use `client1` as the workstation and Wiz.Com. as the new domain name.

   ```
   client1% su
   Password: <enter password>
   ```

All About Administering NIS+

2. **Change the workstation's domain name.**
   Enter the new name with the domainname command, as shown below. Do not use a trailing dot.

   ```
   client1# domainname Wiz.Com
   ```

   If the workstation was an NIS client, it may no longer be able to get NIS service.

3. **Verify the result.**
   Use the domainname command again, this time without an argument, to display the server's current domain.

   ```
   client1# domainname
   Wiz.Com
   ```

4. **Save the new domain name.**
   Redirect the output of the domainname command into the /etc/defaultdomain file.

   ```
   client1# domainname > /etc/defaultdomain
   ```

5. **At a convenient time, reboot the workstation.**
   Even after entering the new domain name into the /etc/defaultdomain file, some processes may still operate with the old domain name. To ensure that all processes are using the new domain name, reboot the workstation.

   Since you may be performing this task in a sequence of many other tasks, examine the work remaining to be done on the workstation before rebooting. Otherwise, you might find yourself rebooting several times instead of just once.

   This step completes this task.

To Return to . . .

▼ Initializing an NIS+ Client by Broadcast

This method *initializes* an NIS+ client by sending an IP broadcast on the client's subnet.

This is the simplest way to set up a client, but also the least secure. The NIS+ server that responds to the broadcast sends the client all the information that the client needs in its coldstart file, including the server's public key. Presumably, only an NIS+ server will respond to the broadcast. However, since the client has no way of knowing whether the workstation that responded to the broadcast is indeed a trusted server, this is the least secure method of setting up a client. As a result, this method is only recommended for sites with small, secure networks.

Security Considerations

You must perform this task as superuser on the client.

Prerequisites

At least one NIS+ server must exist on the same subnet as the client.

You need the following information:

- The superuser password to the client

Instructions

1. **Initialize the client.**
   This step initializes the client and creates an NIS_COLD_START file in its /var/nis directory. Use the nisinit command with the -c and -B options.

   ```
   Client1# nisinit -c -B
   This machine is in the Wiz.Com. NIS+ domain.
   Setting up NIS+ client ...
   All done.
   ```

An NIS+ server on the same subnet will reply to the broadcast and add its location information into the client's coldstart file.

This step completes this task.

To Return to . . .

Where You Left Off in:	Go to:
▼ How to Set Up an NIS+ Client	Page 259

▼ Initializing an NIS+ Client by Hostname

Initializing a client by hostname consists of explicitly identifying the IP address of its trusted server. This server's name, location information, and public keys are then placed in the client's coldstart file.

This method is more secure than the broadcast method because it actually specifies the IP address of the trusted server, rather than relying on a server to identify itself. However, if a router exists between the client and the trusted server, it could intercept messages to the trusted IP address and route them to an untrusted server.

Security Considerations

You must perform this operation as superuser on the client.

Prerequisites

- The NIS+ service must be running in the client's domain
- The client must have an entry in its /etc/hosts file for the trusted server

You need the following information:

- The name and IP address of the trusted server

Instructions

1. **Check the client's** /etc/hosts **file.**
   Make sure the client has an entry for the trusted server.

2. **Initialize the client.**
    This step initializes the client and creates an NIS_COLD_START file in its
    /var/nis directory. Use the nisinit command with the -c and -H options. This
    example uses rootmaster as the trusted server.

```
Client1# nisinit -c -H rootmaster
This machine is in the Wiz.Com. NIS+ domain.
Setting up NIS+ client ...
All done.
```

The nisinit utility looks for the server's address in the client's /etc/hosts file,
so don't append a domain name to the server. If you do, the utility won't be able to
find its address.

This step completes this task.

To Return to . . .

Where You Left Off in:	*Go to:*
▼ How to Set Up an NIS+ Client	Page 259

▼ Initializing an NIS+ Client by Coldstart File

This task initializes an NIS+ client by using the coldstart file of another NIS+ client—
preferably from the same domain. This is the most secure method of setting up an NIS+
client. It ensures that the client obtains its NIS+ information from a trusted server—
something that cannot be guaranteed by the hostname or broadcast method.

Security Considerations

You must perform this task as superuser on the client.

Prerequisites

The servers specified in the coldstart file must already be set up and running NIS+.

You need the following information:

*   The name and location of the coldstart file you will copy

Instructions

1. **Copy the other client's coldstart file.**
   Copy the other client's coldstart file into a directory in the new client. This may be easier to do while logged on as yourself rather than as superuser on the client. Be sure to switch back to superuser before initializing the client.

   Don't copy the NIS_COLD_START file into /var/nis though, because during initialization that file gets overwritten. This example copies the coldstart file of client1 into the /tmp directory of client2.

   ```
   client2# exit
   client2% rcp client1:/var/nis/NIS_COLD_START /tmp
   client2% su
   ```

2. **Initialize the client from the coldstart file.**
   Use the nisinit command with the -c and -C options, as shown below.

   ```
   client2# nisinit -c -C /tmp/NIS_COLD_START
   This machine is in the Wiz.Com. NIS+ domain.
   Setting up NIS+ client ...
   All done.
   ```

   This step completes this task.

To Return to . . .

Where You Left Off in:	*Go to:*
▼ How to Set Up an NIS+ Client	Page 259

17

Summary

This is a summary of the steps required to set up a client. It assumes the simplest case, so be sure you are familiar with the more thorough task descriptions before you use this summary as a reference. For brevity, this summary does not show the responses to each command.

```rootmaster%```
```rootmaster% nisaddcred -p unix.client1.Wiz.Com \```
```   -P client1.Wiz.Com. des```
	1. Log in to domain's master.
	2. Create DES credentials for client.

```client1% su``` ```Password: <enter password>```	3. Log in, as superuser, to the client.
```client1# domainname Wiz.Com``` ```client1# domainname > /etc/defaultdomain```	4. Assign the client a domain name.
```client1# more /etc/nsswitch.conf```	5. Check the switch configuration file.
```client1# rm -rf /var/nis/*```	6. Clean out /var/nis.
```client1# nisinit -c -H rootmaster```	7. Initialize the client.
``client1# ps -ef	grep keyserv```	8. Kill and restart the keyserver.
```client1# kill -9 <process-id>``` ```client1# keyserv```	
```client1# keylogin -r```	9. Keylogin the client.
```Password: <enter superuser password>```	
```client1# init 6```	10. Reboot the client.

Setting Up NIS+ Servers 18 ≡

This chapter provides step-by-step procedures for three server-related tasks:

The first task describes how to set up an NIS+ server. The second describes how to add a server to an existing domain, whether root or nonroot. The third describes how to change a server's security level, whether to upgrade it for normal DES operation or to downgrade it for debugging. A summary of each task is provided at the end of the chapter.

▼ How to Set Up an NIS+ Server

This task applies to any NIS+ server except the root master; that is, to a root replica, a nonroot master, or a nonroot replica, whether running in NIS compatibility mode or not.

Differences Between Standard and NIS-Compatible Setup Procedures

The differences between an NIS-compatible and a standard NIS+ server are the same as for the root master server. The NIS+ daemon for an NIS-compatible server must be started with the -Y option (and the -B option for DNS forwarding), which allows the server to answer requests from NIS clients. This is described in Step 2. The equivalent step for standard NIS+ servers is Step 3.

As you may recall, the instructions for setting up the root master server in NIS compatibility mode (Chapter 15) also required a -Y flag with the nissetup utility, which creates the NIS+ tables with the proper permissions for an NIS-compatible domain. That step is not included in this task because with every server other than the root master, the nissetup utility is not used until the server is associated with a domain (as described in Chapter 19, "Setting Up a Nonroot Domain").

Here is a summary of the entire setup process:

Step 1. Log in as superuser to the new replica server.

Step 2. —NIS-Compatibility Only—Start the NIS+ daemon with -Y.

Step 3. —Standard NIS+ Only—Start the NIS+ daemon.

Security Considerations

You must perform this operation as superuser on the server. The security level at which you start the server (Step 4) determines the credentials that its clients must have. For instance, if the server is set up with security level 2, the clients in the domain it supports must have DES credentials. If you have set up the client according to the instructions in this book, the client has DES credentials in the proper domain, and you can start the server with security level 2.

Prerequisites

- The root domain must already be set up—see Chapter 15, "Setting Up the Root Domain"
- The server must have already been initialized as an NIS+ client—see Chapter 17, "Setting Up an NIS+ Client"
- If the server will run in NIS compatibility mode and support DNS forwarding, it must have a properly configured /etc/resolv.config file (described in Chapter 17, "Setting Up an NIS+ Client")

You need the following information:

- The superuser password of the client that you will convert into a server.

Instructions

1. **Log in as superuser to the new replica server.**
   The following steps assume you rebooted the workstation after you set it up as an NIS+ client, as instructed in *"How to Set Up an NIS+ Client,"* in Chapter 17. Rebooting, among other things, starts the cache manager, which is a recommended prerequisite to the following step. If you did not reboot the workstation, restart the cache manager now, using `nis_cachemgr`.

2. **—NIS-Compatibility Only—Start the NIS+ daemon with** `-Y`.
   Perform this step only if you are setting up the server in NIS compatibility mode; if setting up a standard NIS+ server, perform Step 3 instead. This step includes instructions for supporting the DNS forwarding capabilities of NIS clients.

   This step consists of two substeps, a and b. Step a starts the NIS+ daemon in NIS compatibility mode and Step b makes sure that when the server is rebooted, the NIS+ daemon restarts in NIS compatibility mode.

   a. **Use** `rpc.nisd` **with the** `-Y` **and** `-B` **flags.**

   ```
   compatserver# rpc.nisd -Y -B
   ```

   The `-Y` option invokes an interface that answers NIS requests in addition to NIS+ requests. The `-B` option supports DNS forwarding.

   b. **Edit the** `/etc/init.d/rpc` **file.**
   Search for the string `EMULYP="-Y"` in the `/etc/init.d/rpc` file.
   Uncomment the line and, to retain DNS-forwarding capabilities, add a `-B` flag.

   ```
   compatserver# vi /etc/init.d/rpc
   .
   .
   .
   #        EMULYP="-Y"
   .
   .
                 -------uncomment and change to------

            EMULYP="-Y  -B"
   ```

If you don't need to retain DNS forwarding capabilities, uncomment the line, but don't add the -B flag.

This step creates a directory with the same name as the server and the server's .log file, which are located in /var/nis.

```
compatserver# ls -F /var/nis
NIS_COLD_START   compatserver/  compatserver.log
```

The compatserver.log file is the transaction log (described in Chapter 2). You can examine the contents of the transaction log by using the nislog command, described in Chapter 24, "Administering NIS+ Directories."

3. **—Standard NIS+ Only—Start the NIS+ daemon.**
Use the rpc.nisd command.

```
server# rpc.nisd
```

To verify that the NIS+ daemon is indeed running, use the ps command.

```
server# ps -ef | grep rpc.nisd
root 1081     1 61  16:43:33  ?       0:01  rpc.nisd
root 1087  1004 11  16:44:09  pts/1  0:00  grep rpc.nisd
```

This step creates a directory with the same name as the server and the server's .log file, which are placed in /var/nis.

```
server# ls -F /var/nis
NIS_COLD_START   server/  server.log
```

The compatserver.log file is the transaction log (described in Chapter 2). You can examine the contents of the transaction log by using the nislog command, described in Chapter 24, "Administering NIS+ Directories."

Now this server is ready to be designated a master or replica of a domain, as described in Chapter 19, "Setting Up a Nonroot Domain." This step completes this task. A task summary is provided at the end of the chapter.

▼ How to Add a Replica to an Existing Domain

This task describes how to add a replica server to an existing domain, whether root or nonroot. Here is a list of the steps:

Step 1. Log in to the domain's master server.

Step 2. Add the replica to the domain.

Step 3. Ping the replica.

Security Considerations

The NIS+ principal performing this operation must have Modify rights to the domain's directory object.

Prerequisites

- The server that will be designated a replica must have already been set up
- The domain must have already been set up and assigned a master server

You need the following information:

- The name of the server
- The name of the domain

Instructions

1. **Log in to the domain's master server.**

2. **Add the replica to the domain.**

Namespace   Servers

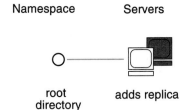

root
directory   adds replica

Use the `nismkdir` command with the `-s` option, as shown in the example below. The example adds the replica "rootreplica" to the Wiz.Com. domain.

```
rootmaster# nismkdir -s rootreplica  Wiz.Com.
```

When you use the `nismkdir` command on a directory object that already exists, it does not recreate the directory, it simply modifies it according to the flags you provide. In this case, the `-s` flag assigns the domain an additional replica server. You can verify that the replica was added by examining the directory object's definition, using the `niscat -o` command.

3. **Ping the replica.**

This step sends a message (a "ping") to the new replica, telling it to ask the master server for an update. If the replica does not belong to the root domain, be sure to specify its domain name. (The example below includes the domain name only for completeness; since the example used throughout this task adds a replica to the root domain, the Wiz.Com. domain name in the example below is not necessary.)

```
rootmaster# /usr/lib/nis/nisping Wiz.Com.
Pinging replicas servering directory Wiz.Com. :
Master server is rootmaster.Wiz.Com.
        Last update occurred at Wed Nov 25 10:53:37 1992

Replica server is rootreplica.Wiz.Com.
        Last update seen was Wed Nov 18 11:24:32 1992

        Pinging ... rootreplica.Wiz.Com.
```

If you have followed the suggestions in the Planning chapter and set up the domain's tables immediately after completing the domain setup, this step propagates the tables down to the replica. For more information about `nisping`, see Chapter 24, "Administering NIS+ Directories."

This step completes this task. A summary is provided at the end of this chapter.

▼ How to Change a Server's Security Level

This task changes the security level of a previously set up NIS+ server. You can assign it security level 0 (lowest), 1, or 2 (highest). The default is 2.   Here is a list of the steps:

Step 1. Log in as superuser to the server.

Step 2. Kill the NIS+ daemon.

Step 3. Restart the NIS+ daemon with the desired security level.

Security Considerations

You must perform this task as superuser on the server. If changing to security level 1, at least one NIS+ principal must have LOCAL credentials in the Cred table of the server's home domain. Otherwise, the server will be unable to authenticate anyone, and no one will be able to operate on that domain. If changing to security level 2, at least one NIS+ principal must have DES credentials in the domain's Cred table. Security level 0 requires no credentials.

Instructions

1. **Log in as superuser to the server.**

2. **Kill the NIS+ daemon.**
   Find the daemon's process ID and then kill it, using the `kill` command as shown below. Note that this command interrupts NIS+ service.

   ```
   server# ps -e | grep rpc.nisd
   root 1081      1  61  16:43:33  ?       0:01  rpc.nisd
   root 1386  1004  11  16:44:09  pts/1  0:00  grep rpc.nisd
   server# kill 1081
   ```

   If you reinvoke the `ps` command, it should no longer list the daemon process.

   ```
   server# ps -ef | grep rpc.nisd
   root  1094  1004  11  16:54:28  pts/1  0:00  grep rpc.nisd
   ```

3. **Restart the NIS+ daemon with the desired security level.**
   Use the `rpc.nisd` command, as shown below.

   ```
   server# rpc.nisd -r -S security-level     # for server in root domain
   server# rpc.nisd -S security-level        # for server in nonroot domain
   ```

   Note the use of the `-r` flag for a root replica. This flag is not required for normal root replica setup; however, it is required when the server is killed and restarted.

   Security-level can be 0 (lowest), 1, or 2 (highest). Security level 2 is the default; to select it, you don't have to use the `-S` option. If the server is running in NIS compatibility mode, make sure you use the `-Y` (and `-B` for DNS forwarding) options.

To verify that the NIS+ daemon is indeed running, use the ps command, as shown below.

```
server# ps -ef | grep rpc.nisd
root 1081      1  61  16:43:33  ?      0:01  rpc.nisd -S 0
root 1087  1004  11  16:44:09  pts/1  0:00  grep rpc.nisd
```

This step completes this task. A summary is provided below.

Summary

Below is a summary of the tasks described in this chapter. It assumes the simplest case, so be sure you are familiar with the more thorough task descriptions before you use this summary as a reference. Also, this summary does not show the server's responses to each command.

To Set up an NIS+ Server:

`server% su`	1. Log in to the server.
	2. NIS-compat only:
`compatserver#      rpc.nisd  -Y - B`	a. Start daemon with `-Y  -B`
`compatserver#      vi /etc/inet.d/rpc`	b. Change to `EMULYP="-Y  -B"`
`server# rpc.nisd`	3. NIS+-Only: Start daemon.

To Add a Replica to an Existing Domain:

`rootmaster% su`	1. Log in as superuser to domain master.
`# nismkdir -s rootreplica Wiz.Com.`	2. Designate the new replica.
`# /usr/lib/nis/nisping`	3. Ping the replica.

To Change a Server's Security Level:

`server% su`	1. Log in as superuser to the server.
`server# ps -ef	grep rpc.nisd`	2. Kill the daemon.
`server# kill <process-id>`	
`server# rpc.nisd [ -r ] -S <security-level>`	3. Restart the NIS+ daemon. Use `-r` for root domain servers. Use `-Y` and `-B` as appropriate.

Setting Up a Nonroot Domain 19 ≡

This chapter provides step-by-step instructions for setting up a nonroot domain. If you follow the guidelines in the Planning chapter, you'll start setting up a nonroot domain *after* you have set up its servers.

A summary of the task is provided at the end of the chapter.

▼ How to Set Up a Nonroot Domain

This task describes how to set up a nonroot domain, whether in NIS compatibility mode or in standard NIS+ mode. Setting up a nonroot domain involves the following tasks:

- Establishing security for the domain
- Creating the domain's directories
- Creating the domain's tables
- Designating the domain's servers

However, as with setting up the root domain, these tasks cannot be performed sequentially. To make the setup process easier to execute, they have been broken down into individual steps, and the steps have been arranged in the most efficient order.

Differences Between Standard and NIS-compatible Setup Procedures

The differences between an NIS-compatible and a standard NIS+ server are the same as for the root domain. The NIS+ daemon for each server in an NIS-compatible domain should have been started with the -Y option, as instructed in Chapter 18.

An NIS-compatible domain also requires its tables to provide Read rights for the Nobody category, which allows NIS clients to access the information stored in them. This is accomplished with the -Y option to the `nissetup` command, in Step 4. The standard NIS+ domain version uses the same command but without the -Y option, so it is described in the same step.

Here is a summary of the entire setup process:

Step	1.	Log in to the domain's master server.
Step	2.	Name the domain's administrative group.
Step	3.	Create the domain's directory and designate its servers.
Step	4.	Create the domain's subdirectories and tables.
Step	5.	Create the domain's admin group.
Step	6.	Assign full group access rights to the directory object.
Step	7.	Add the servers to the domain's admin group.
Step	8.	Add credentials for other administrators.
Step	9.	Add the administrators to the domain's admin group.

Security Considerations

In most sites, to preserve the security of the parent domain, only the parent domain's master server or an administrator who belongs to the parent domain's admin group is allowed to create a domain beneath it. Although this is a policy decision and not a requirement of NIS+, the instructions in this chapter assume that you are following that policy. Of course, the parent domain's admin group must have Create rights to the parent directory object. To verify this, use the `niscat -o` command.

```
rootmaster# niscat -o Wiz.Com.
Object Name    : Wiz
Owner          : rootmaster
Group          : admin.Wiz.Com.
Domain         : Com.
Access Rights  : r---rmcdrmcdr---
   .
   .
   .
```

If you are more concerned about convenience than security, you could simply make the new domain's master server a member of its parent domain's admin group and then perform the entire procedure from the server. Use the `nisgrpadm` command, described in Chapter 21, "Administering NIS+ Groups."

Prerequisites

- The parent domain must be set up and running
- The server that will be designated as this domain's master must be initialized and running NIS+
- If you will designate a replica server, the master server must be able to obtain the replica's IP address through its `/etc/hosts` file or from its NIS+ Hosts table

You need the following information:

- The name of the new domain (for Step 3)
- The name of the new domain's master and replica servers
- The name of the new domain's admin group (for Step 2)
- Userids (UID) of the administrators who will belong to the new domain's admin group (for Step 8)

Instructions

1. **Log in to the domain's master server.**
   Log in to the server that you will designate as the new domain's master. The steps in this task use the server named `salesmaster`, which belongs to the Wiz.Com. domain and will become the master server of the Sales.Wiz.Com. domain. The

administrator performing this task is "topadmin.Wiz.Com.," a member of the admin.Wiz.Com. group. That group has full access rights to the Wiz.Com. directory object.

2. **Name the domain's administrative group.**

   Although you won't actually create the admin group until Step 5, you need to identify it now. This identification enables the `nismkdir` command used in the following step to create the directory object with the proper access rights for the group. It does the same for the `nissetup` utility used in Step 4.

   Set the value of the environment variable NIS_GROUP to the name of the domain's admin group. Here are two examples, one for `csh` users, and one for `sh/ksh` users. They both set NIS_GROUP to admin.Sales.Wiz.Com.

   ```
   salesmaster# setenv NIS_GROUP admin.Sales.Wiz.Com.     # for csh

   salesmaster# NIS_GROUP=admin.Sales.Wiz.Com.            # for sh/ksh
   salesmaster# export NIS_GROUP                          # for sh/ksh
   ```

3. **Create the domain's directory and designate its servers.**

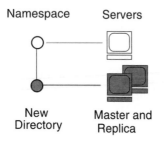

Namespace   Servers

New Directory   Master and Replica

The `nismkdir` command, in one step, creates the new domain's directory and designates its supporting servers. It has the following syntax:

   nismkdir -m *master* -s *replica domain*

The `-m` flag designates its master server, and the `-s` flag designates its replica. Here is an example:

   ```
   salesmaster# nismkdir -m salesmaster -s salesreplica \
                Sales.Wiz.Com.
   ```

The directory is loaded into `/var/nis`, but to view it, use the `niscat -o` command.

```
salesmaster# niscat -o Sales.Wiz.Com.
Object Name    : Sales
Owner          : topadmin.Wiz.Com.
Group          : admin.Sales.Wiz.Com.
Domain         : Wiz.Com.
Access Rights  : ----rmcdr---r---
     .
     .
     .
```

Unlike the root directory, this directory object *does* have the proper group assignment. As a result, you won't have to use `nischgrp`.

4. **Create the domain's subdirectories and tables.**

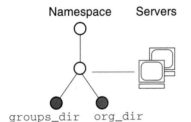

Namespace   Servers

groups_dir   org_dir

This step adds the `org_dir` and `groups_dir` directories, and the NIS+ tables, beneath the new directory object. Use the `nissetup` utility, but be sure to add the new domain name. And, for an NIS-compatible domain, include the `-Y` flag. Here are examples of both versions:

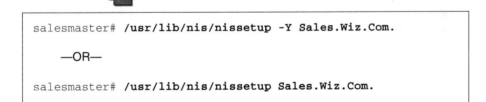

```
salesmaster# /usr/lib/nis/nissetup -Y Sales.Wiz.Com.

   —OR—

salesmaster# /usr/lib/nis/nissetup Sales.Wiz.Com.
```

The `-Y` option creates the same tables and subdirectories as for a standard NIS+ domain, but assigns Read rights to the Nobody category so that requests from NIS clients, which are unauthenticated, can access information in the NIS+ tables.

Each object added by the utility is listed in the output.

```
salesmaster# /usr/lib/nis/nissetup
org_dir.Sales.Wiz.Com. created
groups_dir.Sales.Wiz.Com. created
auto_master.org_dir.Sales.Wiz.Com. created
auto_home.org_dir.Sales.Wiz.Com. created
bootparams.org_dir.Sales.Wiz.Com. created
cred.org_dir.Sales.Wiz.Com. created
ethers.org_dir.Sales.Wiz.Com. created
group.org_dir.Sales.Wiz.Com. created
hosts.org_dir.Sales.Wiz.Com. created
mail_aliases.org_dir.Sales.Wiz.Com. created
sendmailvars.org_dir.Sales.Wiz.Com. created
netmasks.org_dir.Sales.Wiz.Com. created
netgroup.org_dir.Sales.Wiz.Com. created
networks.org_dir.Sales.Wiz.Com. created
passwd.org_dir.Sales.Wiz.Com. created
protocols.org_dir.Sales.Wiz.Com. created
rpc.org_dir.Sales.Wiz.Com. created
services.org_dir.Sales.Wiz.Com. created
timezone.org_dir.Sales.Wiz.Com. created
```

If you are curious, you can verify the existence of the `org_dir` and `groups_dir` directories by looking in your master's equivalent of `/var/nis/salesmaster`. They are listed along with the root object and other NIS+ files. The tables are listed under the `org_dir` directory. You can examine the contents of any table by using the `niscat` command, described in Chapter 25 (although at this point the tables are empty).

5. **Create the domain's admin group.**
   This step creates the admin group named in Step 2. Use the `nisgrpadm` command with the `-c` option. The example below creates the "admin.Sales.Wiz.Com." group.

```
salesmaster# nisgrpadm -c admin.Sales.Wiz.Com.
Group "admin.Sales.Wiz.Com." created.
```

This step only creates the group—it does not identify its members. That is done in Step 9.

6. **Assign full group access rights to the directory object.**
By default, the directory object only grants its group Read access, which makes the group no more useful than the World category. To make the setup of clients and subdomains easier, change the access rights that the directory object grants its group from Read to Read, Modify, Create, and Destroy. Use the `nischmod` command.

```
salesmaster# nischmod g+rmcd Sales.Wiz.Com.
```

Complete instructions for using the `nischmod` command are provided in Chapter 23, "Administering NIS+ Access Rights."

7. **Add the servers to the domain's admin group.**
At this point, the domain's group has no members. Add the master and replica servers, using the `nisgrpadm` command with the `-a` option. The first argument is the group name; the rest are the names of the new members. This example adds "salesmaster.Wiz.Com." and "salesreplica.Wiz.Com." to the admin.Sales.Wiz.Com. group.

```
salesmaster# nisgrpadm -a admin.Sales.Wiz.Com. \
           salesmaster.Wiz.Com. salesreplica.Wiz.Com.
Added "salesmaster.Wiz.Com." to group "admin.Sales.Wiz.Com."
Added "salesreplica.Wiz.Com." to group "admin.Sales.Wiz.Com."
```

To verify that the servers are indeed members of the group, use the `nisgrpadm` command with the `-l` option (see Chapter 21, "Administering NIS+ Groups").

```
salesmaster# nisgrpadm -l admin.Sales.Wiz.Com.
Group entry for "admin.Sales.Wiz.Com." group:
    Explicit members:
        salesmaster.Wiz.Com.
        salesreplica.Wiz.Com.
    No implicit members
    No recursive members
    No explicit nonmembers
    No implicit nonmembers
    No recursive nonmembers
```

8. **Add credentials for other administrators.**
Add the credentials of the other administrators who will work in the domain.

For administrators who already have DES credentials in another domain, simply add LOCAL credentials. Use the `nisaddcred` command with both the `-p` and the `-P` flags. For example:

```
salesmaster# nisaddcred -p 33355 -P topadmin.Wiz.Com. local
```

For administrators who do not yet have credentials, you can proceed in two different ways. One way is to ask them to add their own credentials. However, they will have to do this as superuser. Here is an example in which an administrator with a UID of 22244 and a principal name of moe.Sales.Wiz.Com. adds his own credentials to the Sales.Wiz.Com. domain.

```
salesmaster# nisaddcred -p 22244 -P moe.Sales.Wiz.Com. local
salesmaster# nisaddcred -p unix.22244@Sales.Wiz.Com \
                        -P moe.Sales.Wiz.Com. des
Adding key pair for unix.22244@Sales.Wiz.Com.
Enter login password:    <enter moe's login password>
```

The other way is for you to create temporary credentials for the other administrators, using dummy passwords (note that each administrator must have an entry in the NIS+ Passwd table).

```
salesmaster# nisaddcred -p 22244 -P moe.Sales.Wiz.Com. local
salesmaster# nisaddcred -p unix.22244@Sales.Wiz.Com \
                        -P moe.Sales.Wiz.Com. des
Adding key pair for unix.22244@Sales.Wiz.Com.
Enter moe's login password: <enter dummy password>
nisaddcred: WARNING: password differs from login passwd.
Retype password: <reenter dummy password>
```

Each administrator can later change his or her network password using the `chkey` command. Chapter 22, "Administering NIS+ Credentials," describes how to do this.

9. **Add the administrators to the domain's admin group.**
   You don't have to wait for the other administrators to change their dummy passwords to perform this step. Use the `nisgrpadm` command with the `-a` option. The first argument is the group name; the remaining arguments are the names of the administrators. This example adds the administrator "moe" to the admin.Sales.Wiz.Com. group:

```
salesmaster# nisgrpadm -a admin.Sales.Wiz.Com. \
                   moe.Sales.Wiz.Com.
Added "moe.Sales.Wiz.Com." to group "admin.Sales.Wiz.Com.".
```

This step completes this task. A summary of this task is provided below.

Summary

This is a summary of the steps required to set up a nonroot domain. It assumes the simplest case, so be sure you are familiar with the more thorough task descriptions before you use this summary as a reference. Also, this summary does not show the server's responses to each command.

How to Set Up a Nonroot Domain

```salesmaster% su```	1. Log in as superuser to domain master.
```# NIS_GROUP=admin.Sales.Wiz.Com.``` ```# export NIS_GROUP```	2. Name the domain's admin group.
```# nismkdir -m salesmaster -s salesreplica \``` ``` Sales.Wiz.Com.```	3. Create the domain's directory and designate its servers.
```# /usr/lib/nis/nissetup Sales.Wiz.Com.```	4. Create `org_dir`, `groups_dir`, and tables.
	For NIS compatibility, use `-Y`.
```# nisgrpadm -c admin.Sales.Wiz.Com.```	5. Create the admin group.
```# nischmod g+rmcd Sales.Wiz.Com.```	6. Assign full group rights to the domain's directory.

```# nisgrpadm -a admin.Sales.Wiz.Com. \```
```   salesmaster.Wiz.Com. \```
```   salesreplica.Wiz.Com.```
	7. Add servers to admin group.

```# nisaddcred -p 22244 -P moe.Sales.Wiz.Com. local```	8. Add credentials for other admins.
```# nisaddcred -p unix.22244@Sales.Wiz.Com. \``` ``` -P moe.Sales.Wiz.Com. des```	
```# nisgrpadm -a admin.Sales.Wiz.Com. \``` ``` moe.Sales.Wiz.Com.```	9. Add admins to domain's admin group.

Setting Up the Name Service Switch

20 ≣

This section provides the following step-by-step instructions for using the Name Service Switch:

These tasks are so brief that no summary is provided at the end of the chapter.

▼ How to Select an Alternate Configuration File

This task describes how to select an alternate Switch configuration file for an NIS+ client. Make sure the sources listed in the file are properly set up. In other words, if you are going to select the NIS+ version, the client must eventually have access to NIS+ service; if you are going to select the local files version, those files must be properly set up on the client.

Here is a list of the steps:

Step 1. Log in as superuser to the client.

Step 2.	Copy the alternate file over the nsswitch.conf file.
Step 3.	Kill and restart the key server at an appropriate time.
Step 4.	Reboot the workstation at an appropriate time.

Security Considerations

You must perform this operation as superuser.

Instructions

1. **Log in as superuser to the client.**

2. **Copy the alternate file over the** nsswitch.conf **file.**
   The /etc/nsswitch.conf file is the "working" configuration file used by the Name Service Switch. Also in the /etc directory are three alternate versions of the file: one for NIS+, one for NIS, and one for local files. To select one, simply copy it over the working file. Of course, you can create additional alternates. Here are four examples:

   ```
   client1# cd /etc
   client1# cp nsswitch.nisplus nsswitch.conf      # NIS+ version
   client1# cp nsswitch.nis nsswitch.conf          # NIS version
   client1# cp nsswitch.files nsswitch.conf        # local files version
   client1# cp nsswitch.custom  nsswitch.conf      # custom version
   ```

3. **Kill and restart the key server at an appropriate time.**
   The key server reads the publickey entry in the Name Service Switch configuration file only when the key server is started. As a result, if you change the switch configuration file, the key server does not become aware of changes to the publickey entry until it is restarted.   If you are performing this task as part of the task called "How to Set Up an NIS+ Client" in Chapter 17, you don't need to kill and restart the keyserver now, since you'll do that as part of the overall client setup procedure.

If you are performing this task independently, or as part of the task called "How to Set Up the Root Domain" in Chapter 15, you can kill and restart the keyserver now. Here is an example:

```
client1# ps -e | grep keyserv
root   145    1  67  16:34:44   ?    keyserv
client1# kill 145
client1# rm -f /etc/.rootkey
client1# keyserv
client1# keylogin -r
```

4. **Reboot the workstation at an appropriate time.**
    Because some library routines do not periodically check the `nsswitch.conf` file to see whether it has been changed, you must reboot the workstation to make sure those routines have the latest information in the file. If selecting a different configuration file as part of a setup procedure, wait until an appropriate time to reboot.

    This step completes this task.

To Return to ...

Where You Left Off in:	Go to:
▼ How to Set Up an NIS+ Client	Page 257
▼ How to Set Up the Root Domain	Page 217

▼ How to Enable an NIS+ Client to Use DNS

This task describes how to set up the Name Service Switch configuration file so that an NIS+ client can also use the DNS service. Here is a list of the steps:

Step	1.	Log in as superuser.
Step	2.	Open the /etc/nsswitch.conf file.
Step	3.	Specify DNS as a source of hosts information.
Step	4.	Save the file and reboot the workstation.

Prerequisites

The NIS+ client must have a properly configured `/etc/resolv.config` file (as described in Chapter 17, "Setting Up an NIS+ Client").

Security Considerations

You must perform this operation as superuser.

Instructions

1. **Log in as superuser.**

2. **Open the** `/etc/nsswitch.conf` **file.**

3. **Specify DNS as a source of hosts information.**
   DNS can be the only source or an additional source for the hosts information. Locate the hosts line and use "dns" in one of the ways shown below:

   ```
   hosts:    nisplus dns [NOTFOUND=return] files

   hosts:    files dns
   ```

   Do *not* use the above syntax for NIS clients, since it will make them look for unresolved names twice in DNS.

4. **Save the file and reboot the workstation.**
   Because some library routines do not periodically check the `nsswitch.conf` file to see whether it has been changed, you must reboot the workstation to make sure those routines have the latest information in the file.

   This step completes this task.

▼ How to Add Compatibility with +/- Syntax

This task describes how to add compatibility with the +/- syntax used in /etc/passwd, /etc/shadow,[1] and /etc/group files. Here is a list of the steps:

Step	1.	Log in as superuser.
Step	2.	Open the /etc/nsswitch.conf file.
Step	3.	Change the passwd and groups sources to compat.
Step	4.	Save the file and reboot the workstation.

Security Considerations

You must perform this operation as superuser.

Instructions

1. **Log in as superuser.**

2. **Open the** /etc/nsswitch.conf **file.**

3. **Change the passwd and groups sources to** compat.

```
passwd:    compat
group:     compat
```

This designation provides the same semantics as in SunOS 4.1: it looks up /etc files and NIS maps as indicated by the +/- entries in the files.

To use the +/- semantics with NIS+ instead of NIS, add the following two entries to the nsswitch.conf file:

```
passwd_compat:    nisplus
group_compat:     nisplus
```

---

1. This file is consulted to verify a user's login password.

4. **Save the file and reboot the workstation.**

   Because some library routines do not periodically check the `nsswitch.conf` file to see whether it has been changed, you must reboot the workstation to make sure those routines have the latest information in the file.

   This step completes this task.

Part 4—Administering NIS+

21 *Administering NIS+ Groups*

This chapter describes how to use the `nisgrpadm` command to perform a variety of group administration tasks, from creating an NIS+ group to testing for membership in one.

22 *Administering NIS+ Credentials*

This chapter describes how to use the commands that administer NIS+ credentials—`nisaddcred` and `nispasswd`—and other commands related to credential administration, `nisupdkeys` and `keylogin`.

23 *Administering NIS+ Access Rights*

This chapter describes how to use the commands that administer access rights to NIS+ objects and entries, such as `nisaddcred`, `nischmod`, `nischown`, `nischgrp`, and the `-c` and `-a` options of `nistbladm`.

24 *Administering NIS+Directories*

This chapter describes how to use the commands that administer NIS+ directories, `nismkdir` and `nisrmdir`; the related commands `nisls`, `nis_cachemgr`, `nisshowcache`, and `nischttl`; and the utilities `rpc.nisd` and `nisinit`.

25 *Administering NIS+ Tables*

This chapter describes how to use the commands that administer NIS+ tables and the information in them, `nistbladm`, `niscat`, `nismatch`, `nisgrep`, `nisln`, and `nisaddent`, including the `nissetup` utility.

Administering NIS+ Groups 21 ☰

This chapter describes how to use NIS+ group administration commands to perform the following tasks:

Related Commands

The `nisgrpadm` command performs most group administration tasks, but several other commands affect groups as well:

Command	Description	See
`nissetup`	Creates, among other things, the directory in which a domain's groups are stored: `groups_dir`.	Chapter 25
`nisls`	Lists the contents of the `groups_dir` directory; in other words, all the groups in a domain.	Chapter 24
`nischgrp`	Assigns a group to any NIS+ object.	Chapter 23
`nisdefaults`	Lists, among other things, the group that will be assigned to any new NIS+ object.	Chapter 23
`NIS_GROUP`	An environment variable that overrides the value of `nisdefaults` for the shell in which it is set.	Chapter 23

▼ How to Specify Group Members in All Commands

NIS+ groups can have three types of members: explicit, implicit, and recursive:

> *member*   : : =*explicit-member*
>   *implicit-member*
>   *recursive-member*

> *explicit-member*   : =   *principal-name*
> *implicit-member*   : =   * . *domain-name*
> *recursive-member*   : =   @*group-name.domain-name*

Explicit members are individual NIS+ principals. They are identified in all group administration commands by their principal name. The name does not have to be fully qualified if entered from its default domain.

Implicit members are all the NIS+ principals who belong to an NIS+ domain. They are identified by their domain name, preceded by the * symbol and a dot. The operation you select applies to all the members in the group.

Recursive members are all the NIS+ principals that are members of another NIS+ group. They are identified by their NIS+ group name, preceded by the @ symbol. The operation you select applies to all the members in the group.

Nonmembers

NIS+ groups also accept nonmembers in all three categories, explicit, implicit, and recursive. Nonmembers are identified by a minus sign in front of their name:

```
explicit-non-member    := -principal-name
implicit-non-member    := -*.domain-name
recursive-non-member   := -@group-name.domain-name
```

niscat -o

The `niscat -o` command can be used to list the object properties of an NIS+ group.

▼ How to List the Object Properties of a Group

To list the object properties of a group, you must have Read access to the `groups_dir` directory in which the group is stored. Use `niscat-o` and the group's fully qualified name, which must include its groups_dir subdirectory:

```
niscat -o group-name.groups_dir.domain-name
```

For example:

```
rootmaster# niscat -o misc.groups_dir.Wiz.Com.
Object Name    : misc
Owner          : rootmaster.Wiz.Com.
Group          : admin.Wiz.Com.
Domain         : groups_dir.Wiz.Com.
Access Rights  : ----rmcdr---r---
Time to Live   : 1:0:0
Object Type    : GROUP
Group Flags    :
Group Members  : rootmaster.Wiz.Com.
                 topadmin.Wiz.Com.
                 @.admin.Wiz.Com.
                 *.Eng.Wiz.Com.
```

Several of the group's properties are inherited from the NIS_DEFAULTS environment variable, unless they were overridden when the group was created. The `Group Flags` field is currently unused. In the list of group members, the * symbol identifies member domains, and the @ symbol identifies member groups. See the syntax below for an explanation. A better-arranged list of members is provided by the `nisgrpadm -l` command, on page 299.

`nisgrpadm`

The `nisgrpadm` command creates, deletes, and performs miscellaneous administration operations on NIS+ groups. To use `nisgrpadm`, you must have access rights appropriate for the operation.

This Operation	Requires This Access Right	To This Object
Create a group	Create	`groups_dir` directory
Destroy a group	Destroy	`groups_dir` directory
List the members	Read	the group object
Add members	Modify	the group object
Remove members	Modify	the group object

Syntax

The `nisgrpadm` has two main forms, one for working with groups, one for working with group members.

—*To create or delete a group or to list its members:*

    nisgrpadm -c group-name.domain-name
    nisgrpadm -d group-name
    nisgrpadm -l group-name

—*To add or remove members or to determine if they belong to the group:*

    nisgrpadm -a group-name member...
    nisgrpadm -r group-name member...
    nisgrpadm -t group-name member...

All operations except create (`-c`) accept a partially qualified *group-name*. However, even for the `-c` option, `nisgrpadm` does not require the use of "groups_dir" in the *group-name* argument. In fact, it won't accept it.

▼ How to Create an NIS+ Group

To create an NIS+ group, you must have Create rights to the `groups_dir` directory of the group's domain. Use the `-c` option and a fully qualified group name:

    nisgrpadm -c group-name . domain-name

The example below creates three groups named admin. The first is in the Wiz.Com. domain, the second in Sales.Wiz.Com., and the third in Eng.Wiz.Com. All three are created from the master server of their respective domains.

```
rootmaster# nisgrpadm -c admin.Wiz.Com.
Group "admin.Wiz.Com." created.
salesmaster# nisgrpadm -c admin.Sales.Wiz.Com.
Group "admin.Sales.Wiz.Com." created.
engmaser# nisgrpadm -c admin.Eng.Wiz.Com.
Group "admin.Eng.Wiz.Com." created.
```

The group you create will inherit all the object properties specified in the NIS_DEFAULTS variable; that is, its owner, owning group, access rights, time to live, and search path. You can view these defaults by using the nisdefaults command (described in Chapter 23). Used without options, it provides this output:

```
rootmaster# nisdefaults
Principal Name : rootmaster.Wiz.Com.
Domain Name    : Wiz.Com.
Host Name      : rootmaster.WIz.Com.
Group Name     :
Access Rights  : ----rmcdr---r---
Time to live   : 12:0:0
Search Path    : Wiz.Com.
```

The owner is listed in the Principal Name: field. The owning group is listed only if you have set the NIS_GROUP environment variable.

Of course, you can override any of these defaults at the time you create the group by using the -D option:

```
salesmaster# nisgrpadm -D group=special.Sales.Wiz.Com. \
             -c admin.Sales.Wiz.Com.
Group "admin.Sales.Wiz.Com." created.
```

▼ How to Delete an NIS+ Group

To delete an NIS+ group, you must have Destroy rights to the `groups_dir` directory in the group's domain. Use the `-d` option:

```
nisgrpadm -d group-name
```

If the default domain is set properly, you don't have to fully qualify the group name. However, you should check first (use `nisdefaults`), because you could unintentionally delete a group in another domain. The example below deletes the test.Sales.Wiz.Com. group.

```
salesmaster% nisgrpadm -d test.Sales.Wiz.Com.
Group "test.Sales.Wiz.Com." destroyed.
```

▼ How to Add Members to an NIS+ Group

To add members to an NIS+ group, you must have modify rights to the group object. Use the `-a` option:

```
nisgrpadm -a group-name  members ...
```

As described earlier, you can add principals (explicit members), domains (implicit members), and groups (recursive members). You don't have to fully qualify the name of the group or the name of the members who belong to the default domain. This example adds the NIS+ principals "grace" and "beth," both from the default domain, Alma.Com., and the principals "nahny" and "umpa," from the Villas.Com. domain, to the group "diapers.Alma.Com."

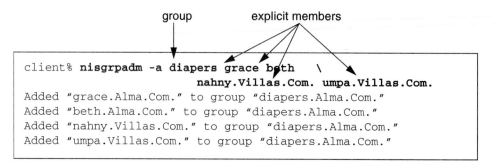

```
client% nisgrpadm -a diapers grace beth     \
                           nahny.Villas.Com. umpa.Villas.Com.
Added "grace.Alma.Com." to group "diapers.Alma.Com."
Added "beth.Alma.Com." to group "diapers.Alma.Com."
Added "nahny.Villas.Com." to group "diapers.Alma.Com."
Added "umpa.Villas.Com." to group "diapers.Alma.Com."
```

To verify the operation, use the `nisgrpadm -l` option. Look for the members under the "Explicit members" category.

This example adds all the NIS+ principals in the Wiz.Com. domain to the "all.Wiz.Com." group. It is entered from a client in the Wiz.Com. domain. Note the * symbol *and the dot* in front of the domain name.

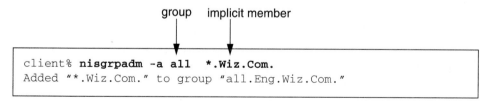

```
client% nisgrpadm -a all  *.Wiz.Com.
Added "*.Wiz.Com." to group "all.Eng.Wiz.Com."
```

This example adds the NIS+ group "admin.Wiz.Com." to the "admin.Eng.Wiz.Com." group. It is entered from a client of the "Eng.Wiz.Com." domain. Note the @ symbol in front of the group name.

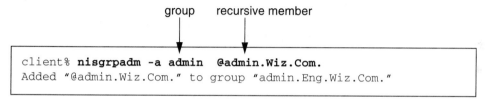

```
client% nisgrpadm -a admin  @admin.Wiz.Com.
Added "@admin.Wiz.Com." to group "admin.Eng.Wiz.Com."
```

▼ How to List the Members of an NIS+ Group

To list the members of an NIS+ group, you must have Read rights to the group object. Use the -l option:

```
nisgrpadm -l group-name
```

This example lists the members of the "admin.Eng.Wiz.Com." group. It is entered from a client in the Eng.Wiz.Com. group:

```
client% nisgrpadm -l admin
Group entry for "admin.Eng.Wiz.Com." group:
    No explicit members
    No implicit members:
    Recursive members:
        @admin.Wiz.Com.
    No explicit non-members
    No implicit non-members
    No recursive non-members
```

▼ How to Remove Members from an NIS+ Group

To remove members from an NIS+ group, you must have Modify rights to the group object. Use the -r option:

    nisgrpadm -r *group-name* *members* . . .

This example removes the NIS+ principals "grace" and "nahny.Villas.Home.Com." from the "diapers.Alma.Home.Com." group. It is entered from a client in the Alma.Home.Com. domain.

```
client% nisgrpadm -r diapers grace nahny.Villas.Home.Com.
Removed "grace.Alma.Home.Com." from group
    "diapers.Alma.Home.Com.".
```

This example removes the "admin.Wiz.Com." group from the "admin.Eng.Wiz.Com." group. It is entered from a client in the Eng.Wiz.Com. domain.

```
client% nisgrpadm -r admin @admin.Wiz.Com.
Removed "@admin.Wiz.Com." from group "admin.Eng.Wiz.Com.".
```

▼ How to Test for Membership in an NIS+ Group

To find out whether an NIS+ principal is a member of a particular NIS+ group, you must have Read access to the group object. Use the -t option:

    nisgrpadm -t *group-name* *members* . . .

This example tests whether the NIS+ principal "topadmin" belongs to the "admin.Wiz.Com." group. It is entered from a client in the Wiz.Com. domain.

```
client% nisgrpadm -t admin topadmin
"topadmin.Wiz.Com." is a member of group "admin.Wiz.Com.".
```

This example tests whether the NIS+ principal "joe," from the Sales.Wiz.Com. domain, belongs to the "admin.SalesWiz.Com." group. It is entered from a client in the Wiz.Com. domain.

```
client% nisgrpadm -t admin.Sales.Wiz.Com. joe.Sales.Wiz.Com.
"joe.Sales.Wiz.Com." is a member of group "admin.Sales.Wiz.Com.".
```

Administering NIS+ Credentials   22 ≡

This chapter describes how to use the NIS+ credential administration commands to perform the following tasks.

Related Commands

The commands listed above handle most credential-related administration tasks, but two other commands can provide marginally useful information about credentials.

Command	Description	See
niscat -o	Lists an object's properties. By looking in the Public Key field of the object's server, you can tell whether the object definition is storing a public key.	Chapter 24
niscat	Lists the contents of the Cred table. By looking through the entries, you can tell whether a principal has LOCAL and DES credentials.	Chapter 25

Where Credential-Related Information is Stored

Credential-related information, such as public keys, is stored in many locations throughout the namespace. NIS+ updates this information periodically, depending on the time-to-live values of the objects that store it, but sometimes, between updates, it gets out of sync. As a result, you may find that operations that should work, don't work. Table 22-1 lists all the objects, tables, and files that store credential-related information and describes how to reset it. Although this book does not have a troubleshooting chapter, you may find this table very helpful.

Table 22-1 Where Credential-Related Information Is Stored

Item	Stores	To Reset or Change
Cred table	NIS+ principal's secret key and public key. These are the master copies of these keys.	Use nisaddcred to create new credentials; it updates existing credentials. An alternative is chkey.
Directory object	A copy of the public key of each server that supports it.	Run the /usr/lib/nis/ nisupdkeys command on the directory object.

Table 22-1   Where Credential-Related Information Is Stored (Continued)

Item	Stores	To Reset or Change
Keyserver	The secret key of the NIS+ principal who is currently logged in.	Run `keylogin` for a client user or `keylogin -r` for a client workstation.
NIS+ daemon	Copies of directory objects, which in turn contain copies of their servers' public keys.	Kill the daemon and the cache manager. Then restart both.
Directory cache	A copy of directory objects, which in turn contain copies of their servers' public keys.	Kill the NIS+ cache manager and restart it with the `nis_cachemgr -i` command. The `-i` option resets the directory cache from the coldstart file and restarts the cache manager.
Coldstart file	A copy of a directory object, which in turn contains copies of its servers' public keys.	In the root master, kill the NIS+ daemon and restart it. The daemon reloads new information into the existing `NIS_COLD_START` file. In a client, first remove the coldstart and shared directory files from `/var/nis` and kill the cache manager. Then reinitialize the client with `nisinit -c`. The client's trusted server reloads new information into the client's existing coldstart file.
Passwd table	A user's password or a workstation's superuser password.	Use the `nispasswd` command. It changes the password in the NIS+ Passwd table and updates it in the Cred table.
Passwd file	A user's password or a workstation's superuser password.	Use the `passwd` command, whether logged in as superuser or as yourself, whichever is appropriate.
Passwd map (NIS)	A user's password or a workstation's superuser password.	Use `yppasswd`.

nisaddcred

The `nisaddcred` command creates, updates, and removes LOCAL and DES credentials. To create a credential, you must have Create rights to the proper domain's Cred table. To update a credential, you must have Modify rights to the Cred table or, at least, to that particular entry in the Cred table. To delete a credential, you must have Destroy rights to the Cred table or the entry in the Cred table.

Syntax

—To create or update credentials for another NIS+ principal:

```
nisaddcred -p uid -P principal-name local
nisaddcred -p rpc-netname -P principal-name des
```

—To update your own credentials:

```
nisaddcred des
nisaddcred local
```

—To remove credentials:

```
nisaddcred -r principal-name
```

Secure RPC Netname vs. NIS+ Principal Name

When creating credentials, you will often have to enter a principal's *rpc-netname* and *principal-name*. It is easy to confuse their syntaxes, so here is an explanation of each.

A secure RPC netname is a name whose syntax is determined by the Secure RPC protocol. Therefore, it does not follow NIS+ naming conventions:

rpc-netname`::=unix.`*uid@domain* |
`unix.`*hostname@domain*

It always begins with the `unix.` prefix and ends with a domain name. However, the domain name *does not* contain a trailing dot. If it identifies a user, it requires the user's UID. If it identifies a workstation, it requires the workstation's hostname. It is always preceded by the `-p` (lowercase) flag.

An NIS+ principal follows the normal NIS+ naming conventions, but it must always be fully qualified:

principal-name`::=`*principal*`.`*domain*`.`

Whether it identifies a client user or a client workstation, it begins with the principal's *name*, followed by a dot and the complete domain name, ending in a dot. When used to create credentials, it is always preceded by the -P (uppercase) flag. When used to remove credentials, it does not use the -P flag.

A Note About Creating Your Own Credentials

When you try to create your own credentials, you run into a problem of circularity: you cannot create your own credentials unless you have Create rights to your domain's Cred table, but you cannot have such rights until you have credentials. You can step out of the loop in two ways:

- By creating your credentials while logged in as superuser to your domain's master server

- By having another administrator create your credentials by using a dummy password, then changing your password with the chkey command

In either case, you are creating credentials for "another" NIS+ principal. Therefore, to create your own credentials, follow the instructions in the task titled *"How to Create Credentials for an NIS+ Principal."*

▼ How to Create Credentials for an NIS+ Principal

To create credentials for an NIS+ principal, you must have Create rights to the Cred table of the principal's home domain. In addition, that principal must be recognized by the server. That is, if the principal is a user, he or she must have an entry either in the domain's NIS+ Passwd table or in the server's /etc/passwd file. If the principal is a workstation, it must have an entry either in the domain's NIS+ Hosts table or in the server's /etc/hosts file.   Once those conditions are met, you can use the nisaddcred command with both the -p and -P options.

```
nisaddcred -p uid -P principal-name local
nisaddcred -p rpc.netname -P principal-name des
```

Remember that, although you can create both LOCAL and DES credentials for a client user, you can only create DES credentials for a client workstation. Also, you can create DES credentials only in the client's home domain, but you can create LOCAL credentials for a client user in other domains, in addition to those of his or her home domain. Following are several examples.

This example creates both LOCAL and DES credentials for an NIS+ principal who is a
client user named "topadmin" and has a UID of 11177. This principal belongs to the
Sales.Wiz.Com. domain, so this example enters her credentials from another client of that
domain.

```
salesclient# nisaddcred -p 11177 -P topadmin.Sales.Wiz.Com. local
salesclient# nisaddcred -p unix.11177@Sales.Wiz.Com \
                        -P topadmin.Sales.Wiz.Com. des
Adding  key pair for unix.11177@Sales.Wiz.Com
        (topadmin.Sales.Wiz.Com.).
Enter login password:  <enter login password>
```

The proper response to the login prompt is topadmin's login password or a dummy
password that she can later change.

This is a similar example, but it is more thoroughly commented and shows how another
administrator, whose credentials you create, can then use chkey to change his own
password. In this example, you create credentials for an administrator named "Bob," who
has a UID of 11199. Bob belongs to the root domain, so you would enter his credentials
from the root master server.

```
rootmaster# nisaddcred -p 11199 -P bob.Wiz.Com. local# Create LOCAL
                                                          credential for Bob.
rootmaster# nisaddcred -p unix.11199@Wiz.Com \        # Create DES credential
                                                         for Bob.
                    -P bob.Wiz.Com. des               #
Adding key pair for unix.11199@Wiz.Com                #
(bob.Wiz.Com.).
Enter bob's login password: <enter dummy password>    # Enter dummy password
                                                         for Bob.
nisaddcred: WARNING: password differs from login      #
passwd.
Retype password: <reenter dummy password>             # Reenter dummy
                                                          password.
```

```
% rlogin rootmaster -l bob              # Bob logs into
                                        #   rootmaster.
Password: <enter login password>        # Bob enters real login
                                        #   password.
Password does not decrypt secret key for # Bob gets error
  unix.11199@Wiz.Com.                   #   message but is
                                        #   allowed to login
                                        #   anyway.
$ keylogin                              # Bob does keylogin.
Password: <enter dummy password>        # Bob enters dummy
                                        #   password.
$ chkey                                 # Bob does chkey.
Updating nisplus publickey database     #
Generating new key for 'unix.11199@Wiz.Com'. #
Enter login password: <enter login password> # Bob enters real login
                                        #   password.
Retype password: <reenter login password> # Bob reenters real
Done.                                   #   login password.
```

First, you would create Bob's credentials in the usual way, but using a dummy login password. NIS+ would warn you and ask you to reenter it. When you did, the operation would be complete. The domain's Cred table would contain Bob's credential information based on the dummy password. The domain's Passwd table (or /etc/passwd file), however, would still have the "correct" entry.

Then, Bob would log into the domain's master server, entering his *correct* login password (since the login operation checks the password entry in the Passwd table or /etc/passwd file). From there, Bob would first use keylogin with the dummy password (since keylogin checks the Cred table), and then use the chkey command to change the Cred entry to the real thing.

The two previous examples created credentials for a client user while you were logged in to the master server of the client user's home domain. However, if you have the proper access rights, you can create credentials in another domain. Simply append the domain name to syntax.

```
nisaddcred -p uid -P principal-name local domain-name
nisaddcred -p rpc-netname -P principal-name des domain-name
```

This example first creates LOCAL and DES credentials for an administrator named "Betty" in her home domain, which happens to be the root domain, then adds her LOCAL credentials to the Sales.Wiz.Com. domain. Betty's UID is 11155. This command is entered from the root master server. For simplicity, the example assumes you are entering Betty's correct login password.

```
rootmaster# nisaddcred -p 11155 -P betty.Wiz.Com. local

rootmaster# nisaddcred -p unix.11155@Wiz.Com \
                       -P betty.Wiz.Com. des
Adding key pair for unix.11155@Wiz.Com (betty.Wiz.Com.).
Enter login password:  <enter login password>

rootmaster# nisaddcred -p 11155 -P betty.Wiz.Com. local \
                       Sales.Wiz.Com.
```

LOCAL credentials map a UID to an NIS+ principal name. Although an NIS+ principal who is a client user can have different UIDs in different domains, it can have only one NIS+ principal name. So, if an NIS+ principal such as "betty" will be logging in from a domain other than her home domain, not only should she have a password entry in that domain, but also a LOCAL credential in that domain's Cred table.

Here is an example that creates credentials for a client *workstation*. Its hostname is "rootclient1" and it belongs to the root domain. Therefore, its credentials are created from the root master server. In this example, you create them while logged in as root to the root master; however, if you already have valid credentials and the proper access rights, you could create them while logged in as yourself.

```
rootmaster# nisaddcred -p unix.rootclient1@Wiz.Com \
                       -P rootclient1.Wiz.Com.  des
Adding key pair for unix.rootclient1@.Wiz.Com
        (rootclient1.Wiz.Com.).
Enter rootclient1.Wiz.Com.'s root login password: <enter password>
Retype password: <reenter password>
```

The proper response to the password prompt is the client workstation's superuser password. Of course, you could use a dummy password that would later be changed by someone logged in as superuser to that client workstation.

▼ How to Update Your Own Credentials

Updating your own credentials is considerably simpler than creating them. Simply enter the simple versions of the `nisaddcred` command while logged in as yourself:

```
nisaddcred des
nisaddcred local
```

▼ How to Remove Credentials

The `nisaddcred` command removes a principal's credentials, but both at a time and only from the local domain. To use it, you must have Modify rights to the local domain's Cred table. Use the `-r` option and specify the principal with its NIS+ principal name:

```
nisaddcred -r principal-name
```

The following two examples remove the LOCAL and DES credentials of the administrator "topadmin.Wiz.Com." The first example removes both types of credentials from her home domain (Wiz.Com.), the second removes her LOCAL credentials from the Sales.Wiz.Com. domain. Note how they are each entered from the appropriate domain's master servers.

```
rootmaster#  nisaddcred -r topadmin.Wiz.Com.

salesmaster#  nisaddcred -r topadmin.Wiz.Com.
```

To verify that the credential was indeed removed, run `nismatch` on the Cred table, as shown below. For more information about `nismatch`, see Chapter 25, "Administering NIS+ Tables."

```
rootmaster#  nismatch topadmin.Wiz.Com. cred.org_dir
salesmaster#  nismatch topadmin.Wiz.Com. cred.org_dir
```

chkey

The `chkey` command changes an NIS+ principal's public and secret keys stored in the Cred table. It does not affect the principal's entry either in the Passwd table or in the `/etc/passwd` file. In fact, this command is often used to make a principal's entry in the Cred table correspond to its entry in the Passwd table.

The chkey command interacts with the keyserver, the Cred table, and the Passwd table. When you invoke it, it tries to identify you with the keyserver. Therefore, you must use the keylogin command before using chkey. However, the keyserver needs the password that was used to generate your keys in the Cred table. That password may be different from your normal login password, depending on how your credentials were created.

For all this to work, you must also have an entry in the Passwd table. If you don't have an entry, or if you forget to enter keylogin, chkey will give you the following error message:

```
chkey: unable to locate password record for uid uid
```

Once chkey identifies you, it prompts you for a new password, which it then uses to generate a new set of public and private keys. It stores those keys in the Cred table, provided you have Modify rights to it.

▼ How to Change Your DES Keys

To change your DES keys with the chkey command, you need:

- Modify rights to your domain's Cred table
- The password from which your entry in the Cred table was formed
- An entry in the domain's Passwd table
- Your login password

First, enter keylogin, using your current password, then use chkey. Here is an example:

```
rootmaster% keylogin
Password: < enter current password >
rootmaster% chkey
Updating nisplus publickey database
Generating new key for 'unix.11199@Wiz.Com'.
Enter login password: <enter new password>
Retype password: <reenter new password>
Done.
```

If you want to use chkey again before you logout, you don't have to enter keylogin again.

nispasswd

The nispasswd command changes or displays information stored in the NIS+ Passwd table. If you use it to change a principal's actual password, it tries to update the principal's secret key in the Cred table. If you have Modify rights to the Cred table and if the principal's login and network passwords are the same, it will update the keys in the Cred table. Otherwise, it changes the password, but does not change the secret keys. This means that the secret keys in the Cred table will have been formed with a password that is now different from the one stored in the Passwd table. In that case, you'll either have to change the keys with the chkey command or use keylogin after each login.

The Name Service Switch determines which processes obtain the new password. If the source for Password information in the Switch is nisplus, all processes will use the new password. However, if the source is nis or files, processes that use the standard getpwnam and getspnam interfaces (such as rlogin and ftp) will look elsewhere for the password information, and so will not get the new password stored in the NIS+ table. For more information about the Name Service Switch, see Chapter 5, "Understanding the Name Service Switch."

If you are the owner of the Password table and have the proper credentials, you can change password information at any time and without constraints. However, if you are not the owner, you must comply with aging and construction constraints.

When you attempt to change a password, if the old password has not aged sufficiently (i.e., number of days since last change is less than *min*), NIS+ will terminate and not carry out the change.

The new password must have at least six characters, but no more than eight. It must contain at least two letters and at least one number or special character. Make sure that the password is not derived in any way from the user's login name. Also, make sure that the new password has at least three characters that are different from the old password.

To use the nispasswd command, you must have the access rights appropriate for the operation.

This Operation	Requires These Rights	To This Object
Displaying information	Read	The Passwd entry
Changing information	Modify	The Passwd entry
Adding new information	Modify	The Passwd table

Related Commands

The nispasswd command provides capabilities that are similar to those offered by other commands. The table below summarizes their differences.

Command	Description
passwd	Changes information in the workstation's /etc/passwd and /etc/shadow files.
yppasswd	Changes information in the NIS password map. Has no effect on the NIS+ Passwd table.
nispasswd	Changes and displays information in the NIS+ Passwd table. When a principal's password is changed, nispasswd tries to update principal's secret key in the Cred table. Its options are customized for the Passwd tables, making the command easier to use for that table than the nistbladm command. It also allows an administrator to lock and force passwords, tasks that nistbladm doesn't allow.
nistbladm	Creates, changes, and displays information about any NIS+ table, including the Passwd table. Although the nispasswd command is easier to use for the Passwd table, nistbladm allows you to: - Create new entries - Delete an existing entry - Change the UID and GID fields in the Passwd table - Change the LastChanged, Inactive, and Expired fields in the Shadow table - Change access rights and other security-related attributes of the Passwd table
niscat	Displays the contents of the Passwd table.

Syntax

—*To display information from the Passwd table:*

```
nispasswd -a
nispasswd -d username
```

—*To change a password:*

```
nispasswd [ username ]
```

—To operate on the Passwd table of another domain:

```
nispasswd [options] -D domainname
```

▼ How to Display Password Information

You can use the `nispasswd` command to display password information about all users in a domain or about one particular user. To display information about all users, use the `-a` option:

```
nispasswd -a
```

Only the entries and columns for which you have Read permission will be displayed. To display the entry for a particular user, use the `-d` option. Without a username, it displays your password entry:

```
nispasswd -d
nispasswd -d username
```

Entries are displayed with the following format:

```
username    status    mm/dd/yy    min    max    warn
```

Field	Description
username	The user's login name..
status	The user's password status. "PS" indicates the account has a password. "LK" indicates the account is locked. "NP" indicates the account has no password.
mm/dd/yy	The date, in Greenwich Mean Time, when the user's password was last changed.
min	The minimum number of days since the last change that must pass before the password can be changed again.
max	The maximum number of days since the last change that can pass before the password must be changed.
warn	The number of days' notice that a user is given before his or her password expires.

To display entries from a Password table in another domain, use the `-D` option:

```
nispasswd -a -D domainname
nispasswd -d username -D domainname
```

▼ How to Change Passwords

To change your own password, enter the `nispasswd` command without any arguments:

    nispasswd

To change the password of another user in the local domain, add a *username*:

    nispasswd *username*

To change the password of another user in a remote domain, also add the `-D` flag:

    nispasswd *username* -D *domainname*

NIS+ prompts you once for the old password and twice for the new one. If you are the owner of the Passwd table, NIS+ does not prompt you for the old password. If you make a mistake and the two entries for the new password don't match, NIS+ will ask you again for the new password.

nisupdkeys

The public keys of NIS+ servers are stored in several locations throughout the namespace, as listed in Table 22-1 on page 304. When new credentials are created for the server, a new public key is generated and stored in the Cred table. However, the directory object still has a copy of the old public key. The `nisupdkeys` command is used to update that copy.

The `nisupdkeys` command can update the key of one particular server or of all the servers that support a directory. It can also update the server's IP address, if that has changed, and it can remove the server's public key from the directory object. However, it cannot update the `NIS_COLD_START` files on the client workstations. To update their copy, the clients should invoke the `nisinit` command. Or, if the NIS+ cache manager is running and more than one server is available in the coldstart file, they can wait until the time to live expires on the directory object. When that happens, the cache manager automatically updates the coldstart file. The default time to live is 12 hours.

To use the `nisupdkeys` command, you must have Modify rights to the directory object.

Syntax

Note that the `nisupdkeys` command is located in `/usr/lib/nis`.

—To update keys:

    /usr/lib/nis/nisupdkeys [*directory*]
    /usr/lib/nis/nisupdkeys -H *server-name*

All About Administering NIS+

—To update IP addresses:

```
/usr/lib/nis/nisupdkeys -a [ directory ]
/usr/lib/nis/nisupdkeys -a -H server-name
```

—To clear keys:

```
/usr/lib/nis/nisupdkeys -C [ directory ]
/usr/lib/nis/nisupdkeys -C -H server-name
```

When a directory name is supplied, `nisupdkeys` updates the public keys of all the servers that support that directory. If the name of a server is supplied instead, it updates the public keys of that server only. If no directory name is supplied, it updates the public keys of the local directory.

▼ How to Update All Public Keys in a Directory

To update the public keys of all servers that support a particular directory, simply provide the directory name:

```
nisupdkeys directory
```

If you don't supply a directory name, `nisupdkeys` uses the local directory. These two examples update the public keys of the root directory and a directory beneath it. They are both entered from the root master.

```
rootmaster# /usr/lib/nis/nisupdkeys
Fetch Public key for server rootmaster.Wiz.Com.
  netname= 'unix.rootmaster@Wiz.Com'
Updating rootmaster.Wiz.Com.'s public key.
   Public key : public-key
rootmaster# /usr/lib/nis/nisupdkeys Sales.Wiz.Com.
```

▼ How to Update the Keys of a Particular Server

To update the public keys of a particular server in all the directories that store them, use the `-H` option and provide the server name.

```
nisupdkeys -H server-name
```

▼ How to Clear Public Keys

To clear all the public keys stored by a directory, use the -C option and specify the directory. To clear the public keys of only one server supporting that directory, use the -C and -H options.

```
nisupdkeys -C directory
nisupdkeys -C -H server-name
```

▼ How to Update IP Addresses

To update the IP addresses of one or more servers, use the -a option.

```
nisupdkeys -a directory
nisupdkeys -a -H server-name
```

keylogin

The keylogin command helps authenticate an NIS+ principal. When a principal logs in, the login process prompts for a password, which is used to authenticate the principal. Normally, this is the only time the principal is asked to provide a password. However, if the principal's DES credentials were created with a password that is different from the login password, the login password will no longer be able to authenticate the principal.

To remedy this problem, the principal must perform a keylogin, using the keylogin command, after every login. The keylogin command prompts the principal for its network password and stores it in the key server. From there, it is used by all NIS+ processes to authenticate the principal.

Syntax

```
keylogin
keylogin -r
```

The -r flag is used to perform a keylogin for a client workstation and to store the superuser's key in /etc/.rootkey.

▼ How to Use the Keylogin Command

To log in with the `keylogin` command, simply enter it and, when prompted, supply your network password; that is, the password used to create your DES credentials. Before logging out, use the `keylogout` command. This example shows how to perform a keylogin for a client user and a client workstation:

```
Client1% login: <login name>
Password: <login password>
Client1% keylogin
Password: <network password>
Client1% su
Password: <superuser password>
Client1# keylogin -r
Password: <superuser network password>
Wrote secret key into /etc/.rootkey
```

Administering NIS+ Access Rights

23 ≡

This chapter describes how to use the NIS+ access rights administration commands to perform the following tasks:

23

▼ How to Specify Access Rights in All Commands

This section describes how to specify access rights, as well as owner, group owner, and object, when using any of the commands described in this chapter.

Syntax for Access Rights

Access rights, whether specified in an environment variable or a command, are identified with three types of arguments: *category*, *operator*, and *right*.

```
category ::= n | o | g | w | a
operator ::= + | - | =
right ::=   r | m | c | d
```

All About Administering NIS+

The *category* refers to the category of NIS+ principal to which the *rights* will apply. The *operator* indicates the operation that will be performed with the *rights*. The *rights* are the access rights themselves. The accepted values for each are listed in Table 23-1.

Table 23-1   NIS+ Access Rights

Category	Description
n	Nobody: all unauthenticated requests.
o	Owner of the object or table entry.
g	Group owner of the object or table entry.
w	World: all authenticated principals.
a	All: shorthand for Owner, Group, and World. This is the default.
Operator	**Description**
+	Adds the access rights specified by *right*.
-	Revokes the access rights specified by *right*.
=	Explicitly sets the access rights specified by *right*; that is, revokes all existing rights and replaces them with the new access rights.
Right	**Description**
r	Reads the object definition or table entry.
m	Modifies the object definition or table entry.
c	Creates a table entry or column.
d	Destroys a table entry or column.

This example *adds* the *Read* access right to the *Owner*.

    o+r

This example *adds* the *Modify* access right to the *Owner, Group*, and *World*.

    a+m

This example *sets* the rights of the *Owner, Group*, and *World* to *Read*. This means that all three categories of principal now have only Read access, regardless of what access rights they had before.

    a=r

This example *adds* the *Create* and *Destroy* rights to the *Owner*.

```
o+cd
```

This example *adds* the *Read* and *Modify* rights to the *World* and *Nobody*.

```
wn+rm
```

This example *removes* all four rights from the *Group, World,* and *Nobody*.

```
gwn-rmcd
```

This example combines the first two operations.

```
o+cd,wn+rm
```

Syntax for Owner and Group

To specify an owner, use an NIS+ principal name. To specify an NIS+ group, use an NIS+ group name with the domain name appended.

owner::= *principal-name*.*domain-name*.
group::= *group-name*.*domain-name*.

Syntax for Objects and Entries

Objects and entries use different syntaxes. Objects use simple object names, while table entries use indexed names.

object::= *object-name*
entry::= [*column-name=value*, . . .] , *table-name*

For example:

```
hosts.org_dir.Sales.Wiz.Com.
[name=butler],hosts.org_dir.Eng.Wiz.Com.
[uid=33555],passwd.org_dir.Eng.Wiz.Com.
```

Note – In this case the brackets are part of the syntax, not just the "optional" symbol of the grammar.

Indexed names can specify more than one column-value pair. If so, the operation applies only to the entries that match *all* the column-value pairs. The more column-value pairs you provide, the more stringent the search. This example uses two pairs to specify the entry:

```
[winner=yoyoma,year=1992],races.org_dir.Wiz.Com.
```

Columns use a special version of indexed names. Because you can work only on columns with the `nistbladm` command, go to page 358 for more information.

nisdefaults

The `nisdefaults` command displays the seven defaults currently active in the namespace: domain, group, host, principal, access rights, directory search path, and time to live. NIS+ supplies preset values for these defaults. They are listed under *"Options,"* below. In addition, you can specify your own security-related defaults (owner, group, access rights, and time to live) with the `NIS_DEFAULTS` environment variable. Once you set the value of `NIS_DEFAULTS`, every object you create from that shell will acquire those defaults, unless you override them by using the `-D` option when you invoke a command. This section describes how to perform tasks related to the `nisdefaults` command, the `NIS_DEFAULTS` environment variable, and the `-D` option.

Syntax

—To display individual defaults:

```
nisdefaults [ -dghprst ]
nisdefaults [ -dghprst ] [ -v ]
```

—To display all defaults:

```
nisdefaults [ -a ]
```

— Options:

-d	Domain. Display the home domain of the workstation from which the command was entered.
-g	Group. Display the group that would be assigned to the next object created from this shell. The group is taken from the NIS_GROUP environment variable.
-h	Hostname. Display the workstation's hostname.
-p	Principal. Display the userid or hostname of the NIS+ principal who entered the `nisdefaults` command.

-r   Rights. Display the access rights that will be assigned to the next object or entry created from this shell. They are:

         `----rmcdr---r---`

-s   Search Path. Display the syntax of the search path, which indicates the domains that NIS+ will search through when looking for information. By default, the search path is $.

-t   Time to live. Display the time to live that will be assigned to the next object created from this shell. The default is 12 hours.

▼ How to Display Default Values

You can display all default values or any subset of them. To display all values, enter the nisdefaults command without arguments. The values are displayed in verbose format. To use terse format, add the -a option. Here is an example:

```
rootmaster% nisdefaults
Principal Name : topadmin.Wiz.Com.
Domain Name    : Wiz.Com.
Host Name      : rootmaster.Wiz.Com.
Group Name     :
Access Rights  : ----rmcdr---r---
Time to live   : 12:0:0
Search Path    : $Wiz.Com.
```

To display a subset of the values, use the appropriate options. The values are displayed in terse mode. To display them in verbose mode, add the -v flag.

```
rootmaster% nisdefaults -rs
----rmcdr---r---
$Wiz.Com.
```

▼ How to Change Defaults

You can change the default access rights, owner, and group by changing the value of the NIS_DEFAULTS environment variable. Use the command that is appropriate for your shell with the access=, owner=, and group= arguments.

```
access=right ...
owner=principal-name
group=group-name
```

You can combine two or more arguments into one line.

```
owner=principal-name:group=group-name
```

Here are some examples:

```
client% setenv NIS_DEFAULTS access=o+r
client% setenv NIS_DEFAULTS owner=abe.Wiz.Com.
client% setenv NIS_DEFAULTS access=o+r:owner=abe.Wiz.Com.
```

All objects and entries created from the shell in which you changed the defaults will have the new values you specified. You cannot specify default settings for a table column; the column simply inherits the defaults of the table.

▼ How to Display the Value of NIS_DEFAULTS

You can check the setting of an environment variable by using the echo command.

```
client% echo $NIS_DEFAULTS
owner=butler:group=gamblers:access=o+rmcd
```

▼ How to Reset the Value of NIS_DEFAULTS

You can reset the NIS_DEFAULTS variable back to its original values (listed on page page 325) by entering the name of the variable without arguments, using the format appropriate to your shell.

```
client# unsetenv NIS_DEFAULTS                    # for csh

client# NIS_DEFAULTS=; export NIS_DEFAULTS       # for sh/ksh
```

▼ How to Override Defaults

You can override default access rights, owner, and group when you create an NIS+ object or table entry with any of these NIS+ commands.

- `nismkdir`—creates NIS+ directory objects
- `nisaddent`—transfers entries into an NIS+ table
- `nistbladm`—creates entries in an NIS+ table

Insert the `-D` option into the syntax of those commands.

> *command* `-D` `access=`*right* . . . *command-arguments*
> *command* `-D` `owner=`*principal-name* *command-arguments*
> *command* `-D` `group=`*group-name* *command-arguments*

As when setting defaults, you can combine two or more arguments into one line.

> *command* `-D` `owner=`*principal-name*`:group=`*group-name* \
> *command-arguments*

Remember that a column's owner and group are always the same as its table, so you cannot override them.

These two examples override the default access rights:

```
client% nistbladm -D access=o+d  -a  name=derby  \
                                     year=1992   \
                                     winner=yoyoma \
                                     races.org_dir.Wiz.Com.

client% nismkdir -D access=o+r  Sales.Wiz.Com.
```

                    access rights   command arguments

These two examples override the default owner:

```
Client% nistbladm -D owner=abe.Wiz.Com.  -a  name=derby  \
                                            year=1992   \
                                            winner=yoyoma \
                                            races.org_dir.Wiz.Com.

client% nismkdir -D owner=abe.Wiz.Com.  Sales.Wiz.Com.
```

All About Administering NIS+

These two examples override the default group:

```
client% nisaddent -D group=admin.Wiz.Com.  -a -f h-file hosts
client% nismkdir -D group=admin.Wiz.Com.   Sales.Wiz.Com.
```

group

command arguments

This example overrides the default owner and group:

```
client% nismkdir -D owner=abe.Wiz.Com.:group=admin.Wiz.Com. \
                Sales.Wiz.Com.
```

nischmod

The `nischmod` command operates on the access rights of an NIS+ object or table entry. It does not operate on the access rights of a table column; for columns, use the `nistbladm` command with the `-D` option. For all `nischmod` operations, you must already have Modify rights to the object or entry.

Syntax

—*To add rights for an object or entry:*

> nischmod *category*...+*right*... *object-name.*
> nischmod *category*...+*right*... [*column-name=value*] , *table-name*

—*To remove rights for an object or entry:*

> nischmod *category*...-*right*... *object-name.*
> nischmod *category*...-*right*... [*column-name=value*] , *table-name*

▼ How to Add Rights to an Object

To add access rights to an NIS+ object, use the + operator.

> nischmod *category*...+*right*... *object-name.*

This example adds Read and Modify rights to the Group of the Sales.Wiz.Com. directory object.

```
client% nischmod  g+rm    Sales.Wiz.Com.
```

▼ How to Remove Rights to an Object

To remove access rights to an NIS+ object, use the - operator.

```
nischmod category...-right... object-name
```

This example removes Create and Destroy rights from the Group of the Sales.Wiz.Com. directory object.

```
client% nischmod g-cd    Sales.Wiz.Com.
```

▼ How to Add Rights to a Table Entry

To add access rights to an entry in an NIS+ table, use the + operator and an indexed name.

```
nischmod category...+right...   [column-name=value],table-name
```

This example adds Read and Modify rights to Group for an entry in the hosts.org_dir.Wiz.Com. table. The entry is the one whose hostname column has the value of abe:

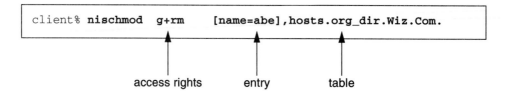

▼ How to Remove Rights to a Table Entry

To remove access rights to an entry in an NIS+ table, use the – operator and an indexed name.

> nischmod *category...-right...*   [*column-name=value*] , *table-name*

This example removes Destroy rights from Group for an entry in the hosts.org_dir.Wiz.Com. table. The entry is the one whose hostname column has the value of abe.

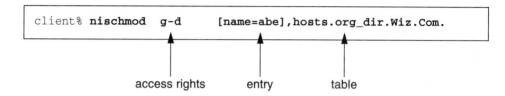

nistbladm -c,-u

The nistbladm command performs a variety of operations on NIS+ tables, as described in Chapter 25, "Administering NIS+ Tables." However, two of its options, -c and -u, enable you to perform several security-related tasks. To use the -c option, you must have Create rights to the directory under which you will create the table. To use the -u option, you must have Modify rights to the table column.

Syntax

—*To set column rights when creating a table:*

> nistbladm -c *type column=access-rights... table-name*

—*To change rights to a particular column:*

> nistbladm -u [*column=access-rights,...*] , *table-name*

▼ How to Set Column Rights When Creating a Table

When a table is created, its columns are assigned the same rights as the table object. To assign a column its own set of rights, append *access-rights* to each column's equal sign and separate the columns with a space.

> *column=access-rights*   *column=access-rights*   *column=access-rights*

Here is the full syntax:

```
nistbladm -c type column=access-rights...    table-name
```

This example creates a table with three columns and adds Modify rights for the World to the second and third columns:

```
client% nistbladm -c races.org_dir.Wiz.Com. \
                  name=S year=S,w+m winner=S,w+m races
```

For more information about the `nistbladm -c` option, see Chapter 25, "Administering NIS+ Tables."

▼ How to Add Rights to an Existing Table Column

To add access rights to a column in an existing NIS+ table, use the u option (its full syntax is described in Chapter 25, "Administering NIS+ Tables"). Use one *column=access-rights* pair for each column whose rights you want to update. To update multiple columns, separate them with commas and enclose the entire set with square brackets.

```
[column=access-rights]
[column=access-rights,column=access-rights]
```

Here is the full syntax:

```
nistbladm -u [column=category...+right...],table-name
```

This example adds Read and Modify rights to Group for the hostname column in the hosts.org_dir.Wiz.Com. table.

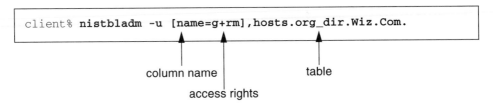

This example adds Read and Modify rights to Group for two columns in the Hosts table of the Wiz.Com. domain:

```
client% nistbladm -u \
        [name=g+rm,addr=g+rm],hosts.org_dir.Wiz.Com.
```

▼ How to Remove Rights to a Table Column

To remove access rights to a column in an NIS+ table, use the u option, the - operator, and an indexed name.

```
nistbladm -u [column=category...-access-rights...],table-name
```

This example removes Group's Read and Modify rights to the "hostname" column in the hosts.org_dir.Wiz.Com. table.

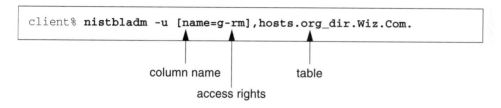

nischown

The nischown command changes the owner of one or more objects or entries. To use it, you must have Modify rights to the object or entry. The nischown command cannot change the owner of a column, since a table's columns belong to the table's owner. To change a column's owner, you must change the table's owner.

Syntax

—*To change an object's owner:*

```
nischown  new-owner object-name...
```

—*To change an entry's owner:*

```
nischown  new-owner [column=value,...],table-name...
```

▼ How to Change an Object's Owner

To change an object's owner, use the following syntax:

```
nischown new-owner object-name
```

Be sure to append the domain name to both the object name and new owner name. This example changes the owner of the Hosts table in the Wiz.Com. domain to grant.Wiz.Com. :

```
client% nischown  grant.Wiz.Com.  hosts.org_dir.Wiz.Com.
```

▼ How to Change a Table Entry's Owner

To change a table entry's owner, use an indexed name for the entry (the syntax is fully described on page 324).

```
nischown new-owner [column=value,...],table-name
```

Be sure to append the domain name to both the new owner name and the table name. This example changes the owner of an entry in the Hosts table of the Wiz.Com. domain to lee.Eng.Wiz. The entry is the one whose value in the hostname column is virginia.

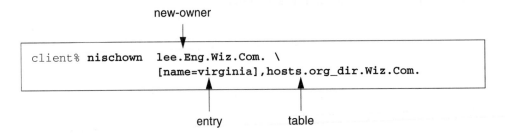

```
            new-owner
                │
                ▼
client% nischown  lee.Eng.Wiz.Com. \
                  [name=virginia],hosts.org_dir.Wiz.Com.
                        ▲                 ▲
                      entry             table
```

nischgrp

The nischgrp command changes the group owner of one or more objects or table entries. To use it, you must have Modify rights to the object or entry. The nischgrp command cannot change the group of a column, since the group assigned to a table's columns is the same as the group assigned to the table. To change a column's group owner, you must change the table's group owner.

All About Administering NIS+

Syntax

—To change an object's group:

```
nischgrp new-group object-name...
```

—To change an entry's group:

```
nischgrp new-group [column=value, ...] ,table-name...
```

▼ How to Change an Object's Group

To change an object's group, use the following syntax:

```
nischgrp new-group object-name
```

Be sure to append the domain name to both the object name and new group name. This example changes the group of the Hosts table in the Wiz.Com. domain to admins.Wiz.Com.:

```
client% nischown  admins.Wiz.Com.  hosts.org_dir.Wiz.Com.
```

▼ How to Change a Table Entry's Group

To change a table entry's group, use an indexed name for the entry (the syntax is fully described on page 324):

```
nischgrp new-group [column=value,...] ,table-name
```

Be sure to append the domain name to both the new group name and the table name. This example changes the group of an entry in the Hosts table of the Wiz.Com. domain to admins.Eng.Wiz.Com. The entry is the one whose value in the hostname column is virginia.

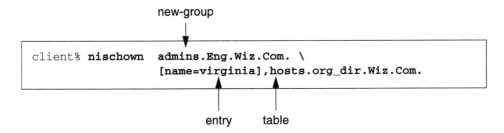

```
                        new-group
                           │
                           ▼
client% nischown   admins.Eng.Wiz.Com. \
                   [name=virginia],hosts.org_dir.Wiz.Com.
                           ▲            ▲
                           │            │
                         entry        table
```

Administering NIS+ Directories   24 ≡

This chapter describes how to use the NIS+ directory administration commands to perform the following tasks:

24

niscat -o

The `niscat -o` command can be used to list the object properties of an NIS+ directory. To use it, you must have Read access to the directory object itself.

▼ How to List the Object Properties of a Directory

To list the object properties of a directory, use `niscat-o` and the directory's name:

```
niscat -o directory-name
```

For example:

```
rootmaster# niscat -o Wiz.Com.
Object Name    : Wiz
Owner          : rootmaster.Wiz.Com.
Group          :
Domain         : Com.
Access Rights  : r---rmcdr---r---
Time to Live   : 24:0:0
Object Type    : DIRECTORY
.
.
.
```

nisls

The `nisls` command lists the contents of an NIS+ directory. To use it, you must have Read rights to the directory object.

Syntax

—To display in terse format:

```
nisls
nisls [ -dLMR ] directory-name
```

—To display in verbose format:

```
nisls -l [ -gm ] [ -dLMR ] directory-name
```

— Options:

-d   Directory Object. Instead of listing a directory's contents, treat it like another object.

-L   Links. If the directory name is actually a link, follow the link and display information about the linked directory.

-M   Master. Get the information from the Master server only. Although this option provides the most up-to-date information, it may take longer if the master server is busy.

-R   Recursive. List directories recursively. That is, if a directory contains other directories, display their contents as well.

-l   Long. Display information in long format; that is, display an object's type, creation time, owner, and access rights.

-g   Group. When displaying information in long format, display the directory's group owner instead of its owner.

-m   Modification time. When displaying information in long format, display the directory's modification time instead of its creation time.

▼ How to List the Contents of a Directory—Terse

To list the contents of a directory in the default short format, use one or more of the options listed below and a directory name. If you don't supply a directory name, NIS+ uses the default directory.

```
nisls [ -dLMR ]
nisls [ -dLMR ] directory-name
```

For example, this instance of `nisls` is entered from the root master server of the root domain Wiz.Com.:

```
rootmaster% nisls
Wiz.Com.:
org_dir
groups_dir
```

Here is another example entered from the root master server:

```
rootmaster% nisls -R Sales.Wiz.Com.
Sales.Wiz.Com.:
org_dir
groups_dir

groups_dir.Sales.Wiz.Com.:
admin

org_dir.Sales.Wiz.Com.:
auto_master
auto_home
bootparams
cred
.
.
.
```

▼ How to List the Contents of a Directory—Verbose

To list the contents of a directory in the verbose format, use the -l option and one or more of the options listed below. The -g and -m options modify the attributes that are displayed. If you don't supply a directory name, NIS+ will use the default directory.

```
nisls -l [ -gm ] [ -dLMR ]
nisls -l [ -gm ] [ -dLMR ] directory-name
```

Here is an example, entered from the master server of the root domain Wiz.Com.:

```
rootmaster% nisls -l
Wiz.Com.:
D r---rmcdr---r--- rootmaster.Wiz.Com. <date> org_dir
D r---rmcdr---r--- rootmaster.Wiz.Com. <date> groups_dir
```

nismkdir

The nismkdir command creates a nonroot NIS+ directory and associates it with a master server. (To create a root directory, use the nisinit -r command, described on page 347.) The nismkdir command can also be used to add a replica to an existing directory.

There are several prerequisites to creating an NIS+ directory, as well as several related tasks. For a complete description, see Chapter 19, "Setting Up a Nonroot Domain."

Syntax

—To create a directory:

       nismkdir [-m *master-server*] *directory-name*

— To add a replica to an existing directory:

       nismkdir -s *replica-server* *directory-name*

▼ How to Create a Directory

To create a directory, you must have Create rights to its parent directory. First use the -m option to identify the master server and then the -s option to identify the replica:

       nismkdir -m *master* *directory*
       nismkdir -s *replica* *directory*

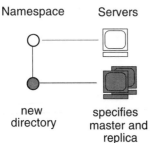

Namespace   Servers

new
directory

specifies
master and
replica

This example, entered from the root master server, creates the Sales.Wiz.Com. directory and specifies its master server, salesmaster.Wiz.Com., and its replica, salesreplica1.Wiz.Com.

```
rootmaster% nismkdir -m salesmaster.Wiz.Com. Sales.Wiz.Com.
rootmaster% nismkdir -s salesreplica1.Wiz.Com. Sales.Wiz.Com.
```

Although we don't advise it except for small or test-oriented namespaces, the nismkdir command does allow you to use the parent directory's servers for the new directory, instead of specifying its own. Here are two examples:

```
rootmaster% nismkdir Sales.Wiz.Com.
```

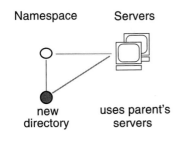

Namespace   Servers

new   uses parent's
directory   servers

The first example creates the Sales.Wiz.Com.
directory and associates it with its parent directory's
master and replica servers.

```
rootmaster% nismkdir -m salesmaster.Wiz.Com. Sales.Wiz.Com.
```

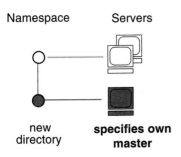

Namespace   Servers

new   specifies own
directory   master

The second example creates the Sales.Wiz.Com.
directory and specifies its own master server,
salesmaster.Wiz.Com. Since no replica server is
specified, the new directory will have only a master
server until you use nismkdir again to assign it a
replica. If the Sales.Wiz.Com. domain already
existed, the nismkdir command as shown above
would have made salesmaster.Wiz.Com. its
new master server and would have relegated its old
master server to a replica.

▼ How to Add a Replica to an Existing Directory

To assign a new replica server to an existing directory, use the -s option and the name of
the existing directory:

nismkdir -s *replica-server* *existing-directory-name*

The nismkdir command realizes that the directory already exists, so it does not re-create
it. It only assigns it the additional replica. Here is an example:

```
rootmaster% nismkdir -s rootreplica1.Wiz.Com. Wiz.Com.
```

Note that you cannot assign a server to support its parent domain—unless, of course, it
belongs to the root domain.

nisrmdir

The `nisrmdir` command can remove a directory or simply dissociate a replica server from a directory. When it removes a directory, NIS+ first dissociates the master and replica servers from the directory, and then removes the directory. To remove the directory, you must have Destroy rights to its parent directory. To dissociate a replica server from a directory, you must have Modify rights to the directory.

▼ How to Remove a Directory

To remove an entire directory and dissociate its master and replica servers, use the `nisrmdir` command without any options.

> nisrmdir *directory-name*

This example removes the `Eng.Wiz.Com.` directory from beneath the `Wiz.Com.` directory:

```
rootmaster% nisrmdir Eng.Wiz.Com.
```

▼ How to Dissociate a Replica from a Directory

To dissociate a replica server from a directory, use the `nisrmdir` command with the `-s` option.

> nisrmdir -s *server-name* *directory*

This example dissociates the engreplica1 server from the `Eng.Wiz.Com.` directory:

```
rootmaster% nisrmdir -s engreplica1 Eng.Wiz.Com.
```

nisrm

The `nisrm` command is similar to the standard `rm` system command. It removes any NIS+ object from the namespace, except directories and nonempty tables. To use the `nisrm` command, you must have Destroy rights to the object. However, if you don't, you can use the `-f` option, which tries to force the operation in spite of permissions.

You can remove group objects with the `nisgrpadm -d` command (see page 298), and you can empty tables with `nistbladm -r` or `nistbladm -R` (see page 364).

Syntax

— *To remove a nondirectory object:*

> nisrmdir [-if] *object-name*

— *Options:*

> -i   Inquire. Ask for confirmation prior to removing an object. If the *object-name* the user provides is not fully qualified, this option is used automatically.
>
> -f   Force. Attempt to force a removal even if the user does not have the proper permissions. The option attempts to change the permission by using the nischmod command and then tries to remove the object again.

▼ How to Remove Nondirectory Objects

To remove nondirectory objects, use the nisrm command and provide the object names.

> nisrm *object-name*...

This example removes a group and a table from the namespace:

```
rootmaster% nisrm -i admins.Wiz.Com. groups.org_dir.Wiz.Com.
Remove admins.Wiz.Com.? y
Remove groups.org_dir.Wiz.Com.? y
```

rpc.nisd

The rpc.nisd command starts the NIS+ daemon. The daemon can run in NIS compatibility mode, which enables it to answer requests from NIS clients as well. You don't need any access rights to start the NIS+ daemon, but you should be aware of all its prerequisites and related tasks. They are described in Chapter 15, "Setting Up the Root Domain," and Chapter 18, "Setting Up NIS+ Servers."

By default, the NIS+ daemon starts with security level 2.

Syntax

— *To start the daemon:*

> rpc.nisd [-r]

— *To start the daemon in NIS compatibility mode:*

```
rpc.nisd [ -r ] -Y [ -B ]
```

— *To start an NIS-compatible daemon with DNS-forwarding capabilities:*

```
rpc.nisd [ -r ] -Y -B
```

— *Options:*

-S *security-level*	Specify a security level.
-f	Force a checkpoint of the directory served by the daemon. This option has the side effect of emptying the directory's transaction log and freeing disk space.

▼ How to Start the NIS+ Daemon

To start the NIS+ daemon on any server except the root master, use the command without options.

```
rpc.nisd
```

The daemon starts with security level 2, which is the default. To start the daemon on the root master, use the -r option.

```
rpc.nisd -r
```

To start the daemon with security level 0 or 1, use the -S flag.

```
rpc.nisd -S level
rpc.nisd -r -S level
```

▼ How to Start an NIS-compatible NIS+ Daemon

You can start the NIS+ daemon in NIS compatibility mode in any server, including the root master. Use the -Y (uppercase) option.

```
rpc.nisd -Y
rpc.nisd -r -Y
```

If the server is rebooted, the daemon will not restart in NIS compatibility mode unless you also uncomment the line that contains 'EMULYP="Y"' in the server's /etc/init.d/rpc file.

To start the daemon with a security level 0 or 1, use the -S flag.

```
rpc.nisd -Y -S level
rpc.nisd -r -Y -S level
```

▼ How to Start a DNS-forwarding, NIS-compatible Daemon

You can add DNS forwarding capabilities to an NIS+ daemon running in NIS-compatibility mode by adding the -B option to rpc.nisd.

```
rpc.nisd -Y -B
rpc.nisd -r -Y -B
```

If the server is rebooted, the daemon will not restart in DNS-forwarding, NIS compatibility mode unless you also uncomment the line that contains 'EMULYP="-Y"' in the server's /etc/init.d/rpc file and change it to:

```
EMULYP="-Y -B"
```

▼ How to Stop the NIS+ Daemon

To stop the NIS+ daemon, whether it is running in normal or NIS compatibility mode, kill it as you would any other daemon. First, find its process ID, then kill it. Here is an example:

```
rootmaster# ps -e | grep rpc.nisd
root 1081     1 61  16:43:33  ?      0:01  rpc.nisd -r -S 0
root 1087  1004 11  16:44:09  pts/1  0:00  grep rpc.nisd
rootmaster# kill 1081
```

nisinit

The nisinit command initializes a workstation to be an NIS+ client. As with the rpc.nisd command, you don't need any access rights to use the nisinit command, but you should be aware of its prerequisites and related tasks. They are described in Chapter 15, "Setting Up the Root Domain," and Chapter 17, "Setting Up an NIS+ Client."

Syntax

—To initialize a client:

```
nisinit -c -B
nisinit -c -H hostname
nisinit -c -C filename
```

—To initialize a root master server:

```
nisinit -r
```

▼ How to Initialize a Client

You can initialize a client in three different ways:

- By hostname
- By broadcast
- By coldstart file

Each way has different prerequisites and associated tasks. For instance, before you can initialize a client by hostname, the client's /etc/hosts file must list the hostname you will use. Complete instructions for each method, including prerequisites and associated tasks, are provided in Chapter 17, "Setting Up an NIS+ Client." Following is a summary of the steps that use the nisinit command.

To initialize a client by hostname, use the -c and -H options and include the name of the server from which the client will obtain its coldstart file.

```
nisinit -c -H hostname
```

To initialize a client by coldstart file, use the -c and -C options, and provide the name of the coldstart file.

```
nisinit -c -C filename
```

To initialize a client by broadcast, use the -c and -B options.

```
nisinit -c -B
```

▼ How to Initialize the Root Master Server

To initialize the root master server, use the nisinit -r command.

```
nisinit -r
```

nis_cachemgr

The `nis_cachemgr` command starts the NIS+ cache manager program, which should run on all NIS+ clients. The cache manager maintains a cache of location information about the NIS+ servers that support the most frequently used directories in the namespace, including transport addresses, authentication information, and a time-to-live value.

When started, the cache manager obtains its initial information from the client's coldstart file, and downloads it into the `/var/nis/NIS_SHARED_DIRCACHE` file.

The cache manager makes requests as a client workstation. Make sure the client workstation has the proper credentials, or instead of improving performance, the cache manager will degrade it.

▼ How to Start the Cache Manager

To start the cache manager, simply enter the `nis_cachemgr` command.

```
client% nis_cachemgr
client% nis_cachemgr -i
```

Without the `-i` option, the cache manager is restarted, but it retains the information in the `/var/nis/NIS_SHARED_DIRCACHE` file. The information in the coldstart file is simply appended to the existing information in the file. The `-i` option clears the cache file and reinitializes it from the contents of the client's coldstart file.

To stop the cache manager, kill it as you would any other process.

nisshowcache

The `nisshowcache` command displays the contents of a client's directory cache.

▼ How to Display the Contents of the NIS+ Cache

The nisshowcache command is located in /usr/lib/nis. It displays only the cache header and the directory names. Here is an example entered from the root master server:

```
rootmaster# /usr/lib/nis/nisshowcache

Cold Start directory:
Name : 'Wiz.Com.'
Type : NIS
Master Server :
        Name        : rootmaster.Wiz.Com.
        Public Key : Diffie-Hellman (196 bits)
        Universal addresses (6)

         .

         .

         .
Replicate:
        Name        : rootreplica1.Wiz.Com.
        Public Key : Diffie-Hellman (196 bits)
        Universal addresses (6)

         .

         .

         .
Time to live : 12:0:0
Default Access Rights :
```

nisping

The nisping command sends a "ping" to replica servers, telling them to ask the master server for updates immediately.[1] Before pinging, the command checks the time of the last update received by each replica. If it is the same as the last update sent by the master, it does not send the ping to the replica.

The nisping command can also checkpoint a directory. This procedure consists of telling each server in the directory, including the master, to update its information on disk from the domain's transaction log.

Syntax

To display the time of the last update:

---

1. Actually, the replicas wait a couple of minutes.

```
/usr/lib/nis/nisping -u [ domain ]
```

To ping replicas:

```
/usr/lib/nis/nisping [ domain ]
/usr/lib/nis/nisping -H hostname [ domain ]
```

To checkpoint a directory:

```
/usr/lib/nis/nisping -C hostname [ domain ]
```

▼ How to Display the Time of the Last Update

Use the -u option to display the time of the last update. It displays the update times for the master and replicas of the local domain, unless you specify a different domain name.

```
/usr/lib/nis/nisping -u [ domain ]
```

Here is an example:

```
rootmaster# /usr/lib/nisping -u
Last updates for directory Wiz.Com.:
Master server is rootmaster.Wiz.Com.
        Last update occurred at Wed Nov 25 10:53:37 1992

Replica server is rootreplica1.Wiz.Com.
        Last update seen was Wed Nov 18 11:24:32 1992
```

▼ How to Ping Replicas

You can ping all the replicas in a domain or one in particular. To ping all the replicas, use the command without options.

```
/usr/lib/nis/nisping
```

To ping all the replicas in a domain other than the local domain, append a domain name.

```
/usr/lib/nis/nisping domain-name
```

Here is an example that pings all the replicas of the local domain, Wiz.Com.:

```
rootmaster# /usr/lib/nis/nisping
Pinging replicas servering directory Wiz.Com. :
Master server is rootmaster.Wiz.Com.
        Last update occurred at Wed Nov 25 10:53:37 1992

Replica server is rootreplica1.Wiz.Com.
        Last update seen was Wed Nov 18 11:24:32 1992

        Pinging ... rootreplica1.Wiz.Com.
```

Since the update times were different, the command proceeds with the ping. If the times had been identical, it would not have sent a ping.

▼ How to Checkpoint a Directory

To checkpoint a directory, use the -C option.

    /usr/lib/nis/nisping -C *directory-name*

All the servers that support a domain, including the master, transfer their information from their .log files to disk. This action erases the log files and frees more disk space. While a server is checkpointing, it still answers requests for service but is unavailable for updates. Here is an example of the output:

```
rootmaster# /usr/lib/nis/nisping -C
Checkpointing replicas serving directory Wiz.Com. :
Master server is rootmaster.Wiz.Com.
        Last update occurred at Wed Nov 25 10:53:37 1992

Master server is rootmaster.Wiz.Com.
checkpoint has been scheduled with rootmaster.Wiz.Com.
Replica server is rootreplica1.Wiz.Com.
        Last update seen was Wed Nov 18 11:24:32 1992

Replica server is rootreplica1.Wiz.Com.
checkpoint has been scheduled with rootmaster.Wiz.Com.
```

`nislog`

The `nislog` command displays the contents of the transaction log.

Syntax

```
/usr/sbin/nislog
/usr/sbin/nislog -h [ number ]
/usr/sbin/nislog -t [ number ]
```

▼ How to Display the Contents of the Transaction Log

To display the entire contents of the transaction log, use the `nislog` command without options.

```
/usr/sbin/nislog
```

To display the first (head) or last (tail) entry in the log, use the `-h` or `-t` options.

```
/usr/sbin/nislog -h
/usr/sbin/nislog -t
```

To display the first or last *n* entries, use the `-h` and `-t` options, but specify a *number*.

```
/usr/sbin/nislog -h number
/usr/sbin/nislog -t number
```

Each transaction consists of two parts: the particulars of the transaction and a copy of an object definition. Here is an example that shows the transaction log entry that was made when the Wiz.Com. directory was first created. "XID" refers to the transaction ID.

```
rootmaster# /usr/sbin/nislog -h 2
NIS Log printing facility.
NIS Log dump:
        Log state : STABLE
Number of updates    : 48
Current XID          : 39
Size of log in bytes : 18432
***UPDATES***
@@@@@@@@@@@@@@TRANSACTION@@@@@@@@@@@@@@@
#00000, XID : 1
Time         : Wed Nov 25 10:50:59 1992

Directory    : Wiz.Com.
Etry type    : ADD Name
Entry timestamp : Wed Nov 25 10:50:59 1992
Principal       : rootmaster.Wiz.Com.
Object name     : org_dir.Wiz.Com.
..................Object....................
Object Name    : org_dir
Owner          : rootmaster.Wiz.Com.
Group          : admin.Wiz.Com.
Domain         : Wiz.Com.
Access Rights  : r---rmcdr---r---
Time to Live   : 24:0:0
Object Type    : DIRECTORY
Name : 'org_dir.Wiz.Com.'
Type: NIS
Master Server : rootmaster.Wiz.Com.
    .
    .
    .
.............................................
@@@@@@@@@@@@@@TRANSACTION@@@@@@@@@@@@@@@
#00000, XID : 2
```

nischttl

The nischttl command changes the time-to-live value of objects or entries in the namespace. This time-to-live value is used by the Cache Manager (described in Chapter 2, "Understanding the NIS+ Namespace") to determine when to expire a cache entry. You can specify the time to live in total number of seconds or in a combination of days, hours, minutes, and seconds.

The time-to-live values you assign objects or entries should depend on the stability of the object. If an object is prone to frequent change, give it a low time-to-live value. If it is steady, give it a high one. A high time to live is a week. A low one is less than a minute. Password entries should have time-to-live values of about 12 hours to accommodate one password change per day. Entries in tables that don't change much, such as those in the RPC table, can have values of several weeks.

To change the time to live of an object, you must have Modify rights to that object. To change the time to live of a table entry, you must have Modify rights to the table; failing that, to the entry; failing that, to the columns you wish to modify.

To display the current time-to-live value of an object or table entry, use the nisdefaults -t command, described in Chapter 23, "Administering NIS+ Access Rights."

Syntax

— *To change the time-to-live value of objects:*

    nischttl *time-to-live object-name*
    nischttl [-L] *time-to-live object-name*

— *To change the time-to-live value of entries:*

    nischttl *time-to-live* [*column=value*, . . .] , *table-name*
    nischttl [-ALP] *time-to-live* [*column=value*, . . .] , *table-name*

    time-to-live ::=   *seconds* | *days* d *hours* h *minutes* m *seconds* s

— *Options:*

-A	All. Apply the change to all the entries that match the [*column=value*] specifications that the user supplies.
-L	Links. Follow links and apply the change to the linked object or entry rather than to the link itself.
-P	Path. Follow the path until there is one entry that satisfies the condition.

▼ How to Change the Time to Live of an Object

To change the time to live of an object, enter the nischttl command with the *time-to-live* value and the *object-name*. You can add the -L command to extend the change to linked objects.

```
nischttl -L  time-to-live  object-name
```

You can specify *time-to-live* in seconds or as a combination of days, hours, minutes, and seconds. For the former, just enter the number of seconds. For the latter, add the suffixes "d, h, m, and s" to the number of days, hours, minutes, and seconds. Here are two pairs of examples that accomplish the same thing:

```
client% nischttl 86400 Sales.Wiz.Com.
client% nischttl 24h Sales.Wiz.Com.

client% nischttl 176461 hosts.org_dir.Sales.Wiz.Com.
client% nischttl 2d1h1m1s hosts.org_dir.Sales.Wiz.Com.
```

The first pair changes the time to live of the Sales.Wiz.Com. directory to 86,400 seconds, or 24 hours. The second pair changes the time to live of all the entries in a Hosts table to 176,461 seconds, or 2 days, 1 hour, 1 minute, and 1 second.

▼ How to Change the Time to Live of a Table Entry

To change the time to live of entries, use the indexed entry format. You can use any of the options, -A, -L, or -P.

```
nischttl [-ALP]  time-to-live  [column=value, . . .] , table-name
```

These examples are similar to those above, but they change the value of table entries instead of objects.

```
client% nischttl 86400 [uid=99],passwd.org_dir.Wiz.Com.
client% nischttl 24h [uid=99],passwd.org_dir.Wiz.Com.

client% nischttl 176461 [name=fred],hosts.org_dir.Wiz.Com.
client% nischttl 2d1h1m1s [name=fred],hosts.org_dir.Wiz.Com.
```

Administering NIS+ Tables   25 ≡

This chapter describes how to use the NIS+ table administration commands to perform the following tasks:

nistbladm

The `nistbladm` command is the primary NIS+ table administration command. With it, you can create, modify, and delete NIS+ tables and entries. Before a table can be created, its directory must already exist. Before entries can be added to a table, the table and columns must already be defined.

To create a table, you must have Create rights to the directory under which you will create it. To delete a table, you must have Destroy rights to the directory. To modify the contents of a table, whether to add, change, or delete entries, you must have Modify rights to the table or the entries.

Syntax

— *To create or delete a table:*

```
nistbladm -c table-type column-spec... table-name
nistbladm -d table-name

    column-spec ::=  column=[CSI,rights]
```

— To add, modify, or remove entries:

```
nistbladm -a
nistbladm -A entry
nistbladm -m new-entry old-entry
nistbladm -r
nistbladm -R entry
```

      entry ::=   *column=value* . . . *table-name* |
                 [*column=value*, . . .] , *table-name*

The *column-spec* syntax is explained under the task "How to Create a Table" on page 359. The *entry* syntax is explained under the task "How to Add an Entry to a Table" on page 361. An additional option, -u, for updating a table's defaults is described in Chapter 23, "Administering NIS+ Access Rights."

▼ How to Create a Table

An NIS+ table must have at least one column, and at least one of its columns must be searchable.   To create an NIS+ table, use the nistbladm command with the -c option.

    nistbladm -c *table-type column-spec... table-name*

The *table-type* is simply a string that identifies the table as belonging to a class of tables. It can be any string you choose.

The *column-spec* argument describes how to specify the characteristics of each column. To use the default column characteristics, simply provide the column names followed by equal signs and separate the columns with spaces.

    column= column=

To assign the column some nondefault characteristics, such as access rights that are different from those of the table as a whole, append each column's characteristics to the equal sign.

    column= [CSI, *rights*] *column=* [CSI, *rights*]

A column can have any of the following characteristics:

    S   Searchable. The nismatch command can search through the column.

I	Case insensitive. When `nismatch` searches through the column, it will ignore case.
C	Encrypted.
rights	Access Rights. These access rights are beyond those granted to the table as a whole or to specific entries.

If you specify only access rights, you don't need to use a comma. If you include one or more of the S, I, or C flags, add a comma before the access rights. The syntax for access rights is described in Chapter 23, "Administering NIS+ Access Rights."

This example creates a table named "Races" in the `Wiz.Com.` directory (the `org_dir` directory is reserved for system tables). The table has three searchable columns, Name, Year, and Winner. (Within any table there should be no two entries with the same values for all searchable columns.)

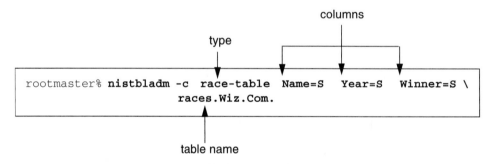

Name	Year	Winner

This is the same example as above, but access rights are added to each column:

```
rootmaster% nistbladm -c  race-table  Name=S,w+m  Year=S,w+m \
                        Winner=S,w+m   races.Wiz.Com.
```

For more information about specifying column access rights when creating a table, see "How to Set Column Rights When Creating a Table" on page 331.

▼ How to Delete a Table

To delete a table, simply use the -d option and enter the table name.

```
nistbladm -d table-name
```

The table must be empty before you can delete it (see "How to Remove a Single Entry from a Table" on page 364). This example deletes the Races table from the Wiz.Com. directory:

```
rootmaster% nistbladm -d  races.Wiz.Com.
```

▼ How to Add an Entry to a Table

You can add an entry to a table in two ways:

- With the -a option
- With the -A option

The -a option is recommended for administrators. It adds an entry to a table unless the entry already exists, in which case it returns an error. To use it, you must specify a value for every column in the table.

```
nistbladm -a entry
```

To find the name of a particular column, use the niscat -o command. You can use two different syntaxes to specify an entry:

```
entry  ::=column=value  ...  table-name  |
       [column=value, ...] , table-name
```

The first syntax consists of one or more *column=value* pairs, separated by spaces and followed by the table name. The second consists of one or more *column=value* pairs, separated by commas and enclosed in square brackets, followed by a comma and the table name. The second syntax is referred to as an *indexed-name*.

These two examples add the same entry to the Races table, but they each use a different form:

```
rootmaster% nistbladm -a Name=derby  Year=1992  Winner=yoyoma \
                      races.Wiz.Com.
```

```
rootmaster% nistbladm -a [Name=derby,Year=1992,Winner=yoyoma],\
                   races.Wiz.Com.
```

Name	Year	Winner
derby	1992	yoyoma

You can add only one entry with each instance of the `nistbladm` command. This example adds three more entries to the Races table:

```
rootmaster% nistbladm -a [Name=derby,Year=1991,\
                        Winner=elvis],  races.Wiz.Com.
rootmaster% nistbladm -a [Name=derby,Year=1990,\
                        Winner=LittleFeat], races.Wiz.Com.
rootmaster% nistbladm -a [Name=derby,Year=1989, \
                        Winner=bocefus], races.Wiz.Com.
```

Name	Year	Winner
derby	1992	yoyoma
derby	1991	elvis
derby	1990	LittleFeat
derby	1989	bocefus

The `-A` option is designed for applications. Like the `-a` option, it adds a new entry to a table. However, if the entry already exists, instead of exiting with an error, it changes the operation to "modify," as if the `-m` option had been used instead. Unlike the `-m` option, however, with the `-A` option, you must specify all columns in the entry.

This example demonstrates how `-A` overwrites an existing entry:

Name	Year	Winner
derby	1992	yoyoma
derby	1991	elvis

```
rootmaster% nistbladm -A Name=derby  Year=1992  \
                   Winner=chilipepper  races.Wiz.Com.
```

Name	Year	Winner
derby	1992	chilipepper
derby	1991	elvis

The -a option would have returned an error, since the entry specified by Name=derby Year=1992 already exists.

▼ How to Modify a Table Entry

To modify a table entry, use the -m option:

```
nistbladm -m new-entry old-entry
```

Specify the *new-entry* with a set of *column=value* pairs. Use an indexed name to specify the *old-entry* and the table name. This example modifies an entry in the Races table:

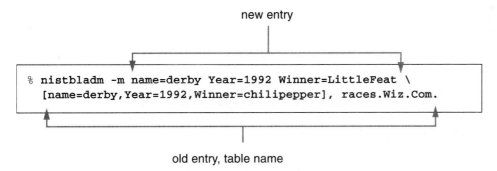

new entry

```
% nistbladm -m name=derby Year=1992 Winner=LittleFeat \
    [name=derby,Year=1992,Winner=chilipepper], races.Wiz.Com.
```

old entry, table name

Name	Year	Winner
derby	1992	LittleFeat
derby	1991	elvis
derby	1990	LittleFeat
derby	1989	bocefus

▼ How to Remove a Single Entry from a Table

To remove a single entry from a table, use the -r option:

```
nistbladm -r  indexed-name
```

You can specify as few column values as you wish. If NIS+ finds duplicates, it does not remove any entry and returns an error message instead. This example removes the Year 1990 entry from the Races table:

```
rootmaster% nistbladm -r \
        [Name=derby,Year=1990,Winner=LittleFeat],races.Wiz.Com.
```

You could have removed the same entry by specifying only the Year column value, as in this example:

```
rootmaster% nistbladm -r [Year=1990],races.Wiz.Com.
```

However, you could *not* have removed the 1990 entry by specifying only the Winner column value (LittleFeat), because two entries have that same value (1992 and 1990):

Name	Year	Winner
derby	1992	LittleFeat
derby	1991	elvis
derby	1990	LittleFeat
derby	1989	bocefus

▼ How to Remove Multiple Entries from a Table

To remove multiple entries from a table, use the -R option:

```
nistbladm -R  indexed-name
```

As with the `-r` option, you can specify as few column values as you wish. Unlike the `-r` option, however, if NIS+ finds duplicates, it removes all of them. You can find the name of a table's column by using the `niscat -o` command. This example removes all entries in which the Winner is LittleFeat:

```
rootmaster% nistbladm -R [Winner=littlefeat],races.Wiz.Com.
```

Name	Year	Winner
derby	1992	LittleFeat
derby	1991	elvis
derby	1990	LittleFeat
derby	1989	bocefus

You can use the `-R` option to remove all the entries from a table. Simply do not specify any column values, as in this example:

```
rootmaster% nistbladm -R [],races.Wiz.Com.
```

niscat

The `niscat` command displays the contents of an NIS+ table. However, you can also use it to display the object properties of the table. You must have Read rights to the table, entries, or columns that you wish to display.

Syntax

— *To display the contents of a table:*

> niscat [-hM] *table-name*

— *To display the object properties of a table:*

> niscat -o *table-name*
> niscat -o *entry*

— *Options:*

-h   Header. Display a header line above the table entries, listing the name of each column.

-M   Master. Display only the entries of the table stored on the Master server. This option ensures the most up-to-date information and should be used only for debugging.

-o   Object. Display object information about the table, such as column names, properties, and servers.

▼ How to Display the Contents of a Table

To display the contents of a table, use `niscat` with a *table-name*.

      `niscat` *table-name*

This example displays the contents of the table named Races.

```
rootmaster% niscat -h races.Wiz.Com.
#Name:Year:Winner
Derby:1992:LittleFeat
Derby:1991:Elvis
Derby:1990:LittleFeat
Stakes:1992:DaBulls
Stakes:1991:DaBulls
Stakes:1990:LittleFeat
AlmadenOpen:1992:LittleFeat
AlmadenOpen:1991:Buckaroo
AlmadenOpen:1990:Trigger
```

▼ How to Display the Object Properties of a Table or Entry

To list the object properties of a table, use `niscat-o` and the table's name.

      `niscat -o` *table-name*`.org_dir`

To display the object properties of a table entry, use `niscat -o` and specify the entry with an indexed name.

      entry `::=`*column=value* `...` *table-name* `|`
          `[`*column=value*`,...]`,*table-name*

Here are two examples, one for a table and one for a table entry:

```
rootmaster# niscat -o hosts.org_dir.Wiz.Com.
Object Name    : hosts
Owner          : rootmaster.Wiz.Com.
Group          : admin.Wiz.Com.
Domain         : org_dir.Wiz.Com.
Access Rights  : ----rmcdr---r---
Time to Live   : 12:0:0
Object Type    : TABLE
Table Type         : hosts_tbl
Number of Columns  : 4
Character Separator :
Search Path        :
Columns            :
     [0]       Name       : cname
               Attributes   : (SEARCHABLE, TEXTUAL DATA, CASE INS
               Access Rights: ----------------
     [1]       Name       : name
               Attributes   : (SEARCHABLE, TEXTUAL DATA, CASE INS
               Access Rights: ----------------
     [2]       Name       : addr
               Attributes   : (SEARCHABLE, TEXTUAL DATA, CASE INS
               Access Rights: ----------------
     [3]       Name       : comment
               Attributes   : (TEXTUAL DATA)
               Access Rights: ----------------
```

```
rootmaster# niscat -o [name=rootmaster],hosts.org_dir.Wiz.Com.
Object Name    : hosts
Owner          : rootmaster.Wiz.Com.
Group          : admin.Wiz.Com.
Domain         : org_dir.Wiz.Com.
Access Rights  : ----rmcdr---r---
Time to Live   : 12:0:0
Object Type    : ENTRY
       Entry data of type hosts_tbl
       Entry has 4 columns.
       .
       .
       .
#
```

nismatch, nisgrep

The `nismatch` and `nisgrep` commands search through NIS+ tables for entries that match a particular string or regular expression, respectively. They display either the entries themselves or a count of how many entries matched. The differences between the `nismatch` and `nisgrep` commands are highlighted in the table below.

Characteristics	`nismatch`	`nisgrep`
Search criteria	Accepts text only	Accepts regular expressions
Speed	Faster	Slower
Searches through	Searchable columns only	All columns, whether searchable or not
Syntax of search criteria	*column=string* ... *tablename* [*column=string*, ...] , *tablename*	*column=exp* ... *table-name*

The tasks and examples in this section describe the syntax for both commands.

To use either command, you must have Read access to the table you are searching through.

The examples in this section are based on the values in the following table, named races.Wiz.Com. Only the first two columns are searchable.

Name (S)	Year (S)	Winner
Derby	1992	LittleFeat
Derby	1991	Elvis
Derby	1990	LittleFeat
Stakes	1992	Dabulls
Stakes	1991	Dabulls
Stakes	1990	LittleFeat
AlmadenOpen	1992	LittleFeat
AlmadenOpen	1991	Buckaroo
AlmadenOpen	1990	Trigger

About Regular Expressions

Regular expressions are combinations of text and symbols that you can use to search for special configurations of column values. For example, the regular expression ^Hello searches for a value that begins with Hello. When using a regular expression in the command line, be sure to enclose it in quotes, since many of the regular expression symbols have special meaning to the Bourne and C shells. For example:

```
rootmaster% nisgrep -h greeting="^Hello" phrases.Wiz.Com.
```

The regular expression symbols are summarized in Table 25-1.

Table 25-1   Regular Expression Symbols

Symbol	Description
^*string*	Finds a value that begins with *string*.
string$	Finds a value that ends with *string*.
.	Finds a value that has a number characters equal to the number of periods.
[*chars*]	Finds a value that contains any of the characters in the brackets.
*expr	Finds a value that has zero or more matches of the *expr*.
+	Finds something that appears one or more times.
?	Finds any value.
\ '*s-char*'	Finds a special character, such as ? or $.
x | y	Finds a character that is either x or y.

Syntax

— *To search through the first column:*

```
nismatch  string table-name
nisgrep  reg-exp table-name
```

— *To search through a particular column:*

```
nismatch  column=string  table-name
nisgrep  column=reg-exp  table-name
```

— *To search through multiple columns:*

```
nismatch  column=string  ...  table-name
nismatch  [column=string,...],table-name
nisgrep   column=reg-exp  ...  table-name
```

— *Options:*

-c	Count. Instead of the entries themselves, display a count of the entries that matched the search criteria.
-h	Header. Display a header line above the entries, listing the name of each column.
-M	Master. Display only the entries of the table stored on the Master server. This option ensures the most up-to-date information and should be used only for debugging.

▼ How to Search Through the First Column

To search for a particular value in the first column of a table, simply enter the first column value and a *table-name*. In nismatch, the value must be a string. In nisgrep, the value must be a regular expression.

```
nismatch  [-h]  string table-name
nisgrep   [-h]  reg-expression table-name
```

This example searches through the Races table for all the entries whose first column has a value of derby:

```
rootmaster% nismatch  -h  derby  races.Wiz.Com.

--OR--

rootmaster% nisgrep  -h  derby  races.Wiz.Com.
Name**Year**Winner
Derby**1992**LittleFeat
Derby**1991**Elvis
Derby**1990**LittleFeat
```

▼ How to Search Through a Particular Column

To search through a particular column other than the first, use the following syntax:

```
nismatch  column=string  table-name
nisgrep   column=reg-expression  table-name
```

This example searches through the Races table for all the entries whose third column has a value of LittleFeat:

```
rootmaster% nismatch -h  Winner=LittleFeat  races.Wiz.Com.

--OR--

rootmaster% nisgrep  -h  Winner=LittleFeat \
                         races.org_dir.Wiz.Com.
Name**Year**Winner
Derby**1990**LittleFeat
Derby**1992**LittleFeat
Stakes**1990**LittleFeat
AlmadenOpen**1992**LittleFeat
```

▼ How to Search Through Multiple Columns

To search for entries with matches in two or more columns, use the following syntax:

```
nismatch  [-h]  column=string  ...  table-name  |
nismatch  [-h]  [column=string, ...] , table-name

nisgrep   [-h]  column=reg-exp  ...  table-name
```

This example searches for entries whose second column has a value of 1992 and whose third column has a value of LittleFeat:

```
rootmaster% nismatch -h [Year=1992,Winner=LittleFeat], \
                races.Wiz.Com.

--OR--

rootmaster% nisgrep -h Year=1992 Winner=LittleFeat \
                races.Wiz.Com.
Name**Year**Winner
Derby**1992**LittleFeat
AlmadenOpen**1992**LittleFeat
```

nisln

The nisln command creates symbolic links between NIS+ objects and table entries. You can use it to link objects to objects, entries to entries, or objects and entries to each other. All NIS+ administration commands accept the -L flag, which directs them to follow links between NIS+ objects.

To create a link to another object or entry, you must have Modify rights to the source object or entry; that is, the one that will point to the other object or entry.

Syntax

— *To create a link:*

> nisln *source target*

— *Options:*

-L	Follow Links. If *source* is itself a link, the new link will not be linked to it, but to that link's original source.
-D	Defaults. Specify a different set of defaults for the linked object.

▼ How to Create a Link

To create a link between objects, simply specify both object names, first the *source*, then the *target*. To create links between objects and entries or between entries, use indexed names.

```
nisln  source-object  target-object
nisln  source-object  [column=value, ...] , table-name
nisln  [column=value, ...] , table-name  target-object
nisln  [column=value, ...] , table-name  [column=value, ...] , table-name
```

nissetup

The nissetup command expands an existing NIS+ directory object into a domain by creating the org_dir and groups_dir directories and a full set of NIS+ tables. It does not, however, populate the tables with data. For that, you'll need the nisaddent command, described on page 375. Expanding a directory into a domain is part of the process of setting up a domain. For a complete description of the prerequisites and required operations, see Part 2.

The nissetup command can expand a directory into a domain that supports NIS clients as well.

To use nissetup, you must have Modify rights to the directory under which you'll store the tables.

Syntax

— *To expand a directory into an NIS+ domain:*

```
/usr/lib/nis/nissetup
/usr/lib/nis/nissetup  directory-name
```

— *To expand a directory into an NIS-compatible NIS+ domain:*

```
/usr/lib/nis/nissetup  -Y
/usr/lib/nis/nissetup  -Y  directory-name
```

▼ How to Expand a Directory into an NIS+ Domain

You can use the `nissetup` command with or without a directory name. If you don't supply the directory name, the command uses the default directory. Each object that is added is listed in the output.

```
rootmaster# /usr/lib/nis/nissetup Wiz.Com.
org_dir.Wiz.Com. created
groups_dir.Wiz.Com. created
auto_master.org_dir.Wiz.Com. created
auto_home.org_dir.Wiz.Com. created
bootparams.org_dir.Wiz.Com. created
cred.org_dir.Wiz.Com. created
ethers.org_dir.Wiz.Com. created
group.org_dir.Wiz.Com. created
hosts.org_dir.Wiz.Com. created
mail_aliases.org_dir.Wiz.Com. created
sendmailvars.org_dir.Wiz.Com. created
netmasks.org_dir.Wiz.Com. created
netgroup.org_dir.Wiz.Com. created
networks.org_dir.Wiz.Com. created
passwd.org_dir.Wiz.Com. created
protocols.org_dir.Wiz.Com. created
rpc.org_dir.Wiz.Com. created
services.org_dir.Wiz.Com. created
timezone.org_dir.Wiz.Com. created
```

▼ How to Expand a Directory into an NIS-compatible Domain

To expand a directory into a domain that supports NIS+ and NIS client requests, use the `-Y` flag. The tables are created with Read rights for the Nobody category so that NIS clients requests can access them.

```
rootmaster# /usr/lib/nis/nissetup -Y Test.Wiz.Com.
```

`nisaddent`

The `nisaddent` command loads information from text files or NIS maps into NIS+ tables. It can also dump the contents of NIS+ tables back into text files. If you are populating NIS+ tables for the first time, see the instructions in Chapter 16, "Setting Up NIS+ Tables." It describes all the prerequisites and related tasks.

You can use `nisaddent` to transfer information from one NIS+ table to another (for example, to the same type of table in another domain), but not directly. First you need to dump the contents of the table into a file, then load the file into the other table. Be sure, though, that the information in the file is formatted properly. Appendix A describes the format required for each table.

When you load information into a table, you can use any of three options: replace, append, or merge.

The append option simply adds the source entries to the NIS+ table.

With the replace option, NIS+ first deletes all existing entries in the table and then adds the entries from the source. In a large table, this procedure adds a large set of entries into the table's `.log` file (one set for removing the existing entries, another for adding the new ones), taking up space in `/var/nis` and making propagation to replicas time consuming.

The merge option produces the same result as the replace option, but uses a different process, one that can greatly reduce the number of operations that must be sent to the replicas. With the merge option, NIS+ handles three types of entries differently:

- Entries that exist only in the source are added to the table
- Entries that exist in both the source and the table are updated in the table
- Entries that exist only in the NIS+ table are deleted from the table

When updating a large table with a file or map whose contents are not vastly different from those of the table, the merge option can spare the server a great many operations. Because it deletes only the entries that are not duplicated in the source (the replace option deletes *all* entries, indiscriminately), it saves one delete and one add operation for every duplicate entry.

If you are loading information into the tables for the first time, you must have Create rights to the table object. If you are overwriting existing information in the tables, you must have Modify rights to the tables.

Syntax

— To load information from text files:

>   /usr/lib/nis/nisaddent -f *filename table-type* [*domain*]
>   /usr/lib/nis/nisaddent -f *filename* -t *table-name table-type* [*domain*]

— To load information from NIS maps:

>   /usr/lib/nis/nisaddent -y *NISdomain table-type* [*domain*]
>   /usr/lib/nis/nisaddent -y *NISdomain* -t *table-name table-type* [*domain*]
>   /usr/lib/nis/nisaddent -Y *map table-type* [*domain*]
>   /usr/lib/nis/nisaddent -Y *map* -t *table-name table-type* [*domain*]

— To dump information from an NIS+ table to a file:

>   /usr/lib/nis/nisaddent -d -t *table-name* > *filename*

— Options:

-a	Append. Add contents of the source to contents of the table.
-r	Replace. Substitute contents of the source for contents of the table.
-m	Merge. Merge contents of the source with contents of the table.
-d	Dump. Copy contents of the NIS+ table to stdout.
-v	Verbose. Prints verbose status messages.
-P	Follow path. If the command is unable to find a table, follow the search paths specified in the environment variable NIS_PATH.
-A	All data. Apply the operation to all the tables in the search path.
-M	Master server. Use the tables only in the Master server of the domain.
-D	Override defaults. For the new data being loaded into the tables, override existing defaults. For syntax, see "How to Override Defaults" on page 328.

▼ How to Load Information from a File

You can transfer the contents of a file into an NIS+ table in several different ways. One way is to use the -f option.

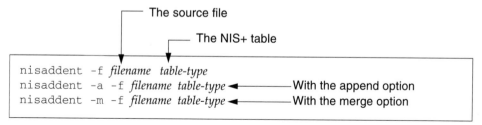

By default, -f *replaces* the contents of *table-type* in the local domain with the contents of *filename*. The -a option appends the contents of *filename* to *table-type*. The -m option merges the contents of *filename* into the contents of *table-type*. These two examples load the contents of a text file named /etc/passwd.xfr into the NIS+ Passwd table. The first transfer is into a table in the local domain, the second into a table in another domain.

```
rootmaster# /usr/lib/nisnisaddent -f /etc/passwd.xfr passwd

rootmaster# /usr/lib/nis/nisaddent -f /etc/passwd.xfr passwd \
            Sales.Wiz.Com.
```

Another way is to use stdin as the source. However, you cannot use the -m option with stdin. Here is an example:

The source file

The NIS+ table

```
cat filename > nisaddent  table-type
cat filename > nisaddent -a table-type ◄──────── With the append option
cat filename > nisaddent -a table-type NIS+domain ◄──── Into another domain
```

Here is the output of `cat` being piped into `nisaddent`:

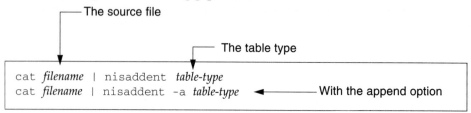

The source file

The table type

```
cat filename | nisaddent table-type
cat filename | nisaddent -a table-type          ◄──── With the append option
```

If the NIS+ table is one of the automounter tables or a nonstandard table, add the `-t` option and the complete name of the NIS+ table. To make them easier to find, they are highlighted in this example.

```
rootmaster# /usr/lib/nis/nisaddent -f /etc/auto_home.xfr \
            -t auto_home.org_dir.Wiz.Com. key-value

rootmaster# /usr/lib/nis/nisaddent -f /etc/auto_home.xfr \
            -t auto_home.org_dir.Sales.Wiz.Com. \
            key-value Sales.Wiz.Com.
```

▼ How to Load Data from an NIS Map

You can transfer information from an NIS map in two different ways, either by specifying the NIS domain or by specifying the actual NIS map. If you specify the domain, NIS+ will figure out which `dbm` file in `/var/yp/`*nisdomain*[1] to use as the source, based on the *table-type*.

NIS+ Table Type	NIS Map Name
Hosts	hosts.byaddr
Password	passwd.byname
Shadow	shadow.byname
Group	group.byaddr
Ethers	ethers.byname
Netmasks	netmasks.byaddr
Networks	networks.byname

---

1. `/var/yp/`*nisdomain* must be local files.

NIS+ Table Type	NIS Map Name
Protocols	`protocols.byname`
RPC	`rpc.bynumber`
Services	`services.byname`

To transfer by specifying the NIS domain, use the `-y` (lowercase) option and provide the NIS domain in addition to the NIS+ table type.

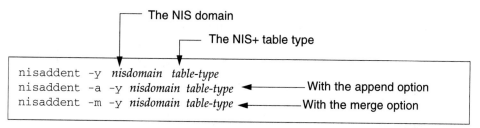

By default, `nisaddent` replaces the contents of the NIS+ table with the contents of the NIS map. Use the `-a` and `-m` options to append or merge. Here is an example that loads the NIS+ Passwd table from its corresponding NIS map (`passwd.byname`) in the OldWiz domain:

```
rootmaster# /usr/lib/nis/nisaddent -y OldWiz passwd

rootmaster# /usr/lib/nis/nisaddent -y OldWiz passwd \
            Sales.Wiz.Com.
```

The second example does the same thing, but for the Sales.Wiz.Com. domain instead of the local domain, Wiz.Com.

If the NIS+ table is one of the automounter tables or a nonstandard table, add the `-t` option and the complete name of the NIS table, just as you would if the source were a file. To make the option easier to find, it is highlighted in these examples.

```
rootmaster# /usr/lib/nis/nisaddent -y OldWiz \
            -t auto_home.org_dir.Wiz.Com. key-value

rootmaster# /usr/lib/nis/nisaddent -y OldWiz \
            -t auto_home.org_dir.Wiz.Com. key-value  Sales.Wiz.Com.
```

If, instead of using the dbm files for a domain, you prefer to specify a particular NIS map, use the -Y (uppercase) option and specify the map name. To make the option easier to find, it is highlighted in these examples.

```
rootmaster# /usr/lib/nis/nisaddent -Y hosts.byname hosts

rootmaster# /usr/lib/nis/nisaddent -Y hosts.byname hosts \
            Sales.Wiz.Com.
```

If the NIS map is one of the automounter maps or a nonstandard map, combine the -Y option with the -t option.

```
rootmaster# /usr/lib/nis/nisaddent -Y auto_home \
            -t auto_home.org_dir.Wiz.Com. key-value

rootmaster# /usr/lib/nis/nisaddent -Y auto_home \
            -t auto_home.org_dir.Wiz.Com. key-value Sales.Wiz.Com.
```

▼ How to Dump the Contents of an NIS+ Table to a File

To dump the contents of an NIS+ table into a file, use the -d and -t options. The -d option tells the command to dump, and the -t option specifies the NIS+ table.

```
/usr/lib/nis/nisaddent -d -t table-name > filename
```

Part 5—Appendices

Information in NIS+ Tables
This appendix summarizes the information contained in all the NIS+ tables except the Cred table, which is described in Chapter 4. It includes formatting guidelines.

Pre-setup Worksheets
This appendix contains several blank copies of the pre-planning worksheet described in Part 2 of this book. Use them to record planning information prior to setup.

NIS+ Scripts Error Messages
This appendix describes the error messages produced by the NIS+ scripts.

NIS+ API
This appendix provides an overview of the NIS+ API functions and includes code samples that demonstrate how to use them.

Information in NIS+ Tables

This appendix summarizes the information stored in the following NIS+ tables:

RPC Table	Page 394
Services Table	Page 395
Timezone Table	Page 395

The Cred table, because it contains only information related to NIS+ security, is described in Chapter 4, "Understanding NIS+ Security."

As explained in Chapter 1, without a network information service, the information in the NIS+ tables would be stored in /etc files. In fact, most NIS+ tables have corresponding /etc files. With the NIS service, you can combine the information in the NIS maps with the information in their corresponding /etc maps by using the +/- syntax. However, the Name Service Switch provides a better method.

The Name Service Switch allows you to specify one or more sources for different types of information. In addition to NIS+ tables, that source can be NIS maps, DNS maps, or /etc tables. The order in which you specify them determines how the information from different sources is combined. For more information, see Chapter 5, "Understanding the Name Service Switch."

Note – If you are creating input files for any of these tables, follow the two formatting requirements shared by most tables; that is, use one line per entry and separate the columns with one or more spaces or tabs. If a particular table has different or additional format requirements, they are described under a heading called "Input File Format."

Auto_Home Table

The Auto_Home table is an indirect automounter map that enables an NIS+ client to mount the home directory of any user in the domain. It does this by specifying a mount point for each user's home directory, the location of each home directory, and mount options, if any. Because it is an indirect map, the first part of the mount point is specified in the Auto_Master table, which is by default /home. The second part of the mount point (i.e., the subdirectory under /home) is specified by the entries in the Auto_Home map and is different for each user.

The Auto_Home Table has two columns:

Column	Description
Mount Point	The login name of every user in the domain.
Options and Location	The mount options for every user, if any, and the location of the user's home directory.

For example:

```
costas        barcelona:/export/partition2/costas
```

The home directory of the user `costas`, which is located on the server `barcelona` in the directory `/export/partition2/costas`, would be mounted under a client's `/home/costas` directory. No mount options were provided in the entry.

Auto_Master Table

The Auto_Master table lists all the automounter maps in a domain. For direct maps, the Auto_Master table simply provides a map name. For indirect maps, it provides both a map name and the top directory of its mount point. The Auto_Master table has two columns:

Column	Description
Mount Point	The top directory into which the map will be mounted. If the map is a direct map, this is a dummy directory, represented by /−.
Map Name	The name of the automounter map.

For example, assume these entries in the Auto_Master table:

```
/home       auto_home
/-           auto_man
/programs   auto_programs
```

The first entry names the `auto_home` map. It specifies the top directory of the mount point for all entries in the `auto_home` map: `/home`. (The `auto_home` map is an indirect map.) The second entry names the `auto_man` map. Because that map is a direct map, the entry provides only the map name. The `auto_man` map will itself provide the topmost directory, as well as the full pathname, of the mount points for each of its entries. The third entry names the `auto_programs` map and, since it provides the top directory of the mount point, the `auto_programs` map is an indirect map.

All automounter maps are stored as NIS+ tables. By default, Solaris 2.3 provides the `auto_master` map, which is mandatory, and the `auto_home` map, which is a great convenience. You can create more automounter maps for a domain, but be sure to store them as NIS+ tables and list them in the Auto_Master table. For more information about the automounter, consult books about the automounter or books that describe the NFS® filesystem.

Bootparams Table

The Bootparams table stores configuration information about every diskless workstation in a domain.   A diskless workstation is connected to a network but has no hard disk. Since it has no internal storage capacity, a diskless workstation stores its files and programs in the filesystem of a server on the network. It also stores its configuration information—or *boot parameters*—on a server.

Because of this arrangement, every diskless workstation has an initialization program that knows where the configuration information is stored. If the network has no network information service, the program looks for this information in the server's `/etc/bootparams` file. If the network uses the NIS+ name service, the program looks for the information in the Bootparams table.

The Bootparams table can store any configuration information about diskless workstations. It has two columns: one for the configuration key, another for its value. By default, it stores the location of each workstation's root, swap, and dump partitions. The default table has only two columns but uses them to provide the following four items of information:

Column	Description
Hostname	The diskless workstation's official hostname, as specified in the Hosts table.
Configuration	Root Partition: the location (server name and path) of the workstation's root partition.
	Swap Partition: the location (server name and path) of the workstation's swap partition.
	Dump Partition: the location (server name and path) of the workstation's dump partition.

Input File Format

The columns are separated with a tab character. Backslashes (\) are used to break a line within an entry. The entries for root, swap, and dump partitions have the following format:

client-name   root=*server*:*path* \
        swap=*server*:*path* \
        dump=*server*:*path*

Here is an example:

```
buckaroo  root=bigriver:/export/root1/buckaroo\
          swap=bigriver:/export/swap1/buckaroo\
          dump=bigriver:/export/dump/buckaroo
```

Ethers Table

The Ethers table stores information about the 48-bit Ethernet addresses of workstations on the Internet. It has two columns:

Column	Description
Ethernet Address	The 48-bit Ethernet address of the workstation.
Official Hostname	The name of the workstation, as specified in the Hosts table.

An Ethernet address has the form:

$n:n:n:n:n:n$ *hostname*

where n is a hexadecimal number between 0 and FF, representing one byte. The address bytes are always in network order.

Group Table

The Group table stores information about workstation user groups. Solaris 2.3 supports three kinds of groups: netgroups, NIS+ groups, and UNIX groups.

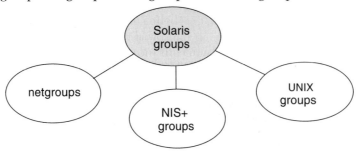

A netgroup is a group of workstations and users that have permission to perform remote operations on other workstations in the group. An NIS+ group is a set of NIS+ users that can be assigned access rights to an NIS+ object. They are described in Chapter 4, "Understanding NIS+ Security." A UNIX group is simply a collection of users who are given additional UNIX access permissions.

UNIX groups allow a set of users on the network to access a set of files on several workstations or servers without making those files available to everyone. For example, the engineering and marketing staff working on a particular project could form a workstation user group.

The Group table has four columns:

Field	Description
Name	The group's name.
Password	The group's password.
GID	The group's numerical ID.
Members	The names of the group members, separated by commas.

Previous releases of SunOS used a +/- syntax in local /etc/group files to incorporate or overwrite entries in the NIS group maps. Since Solaris 2.3 uses the Name Service Switch (described in Chapter 5) to specify a workstation's sources of information, this syntax is no longer necessary. All you have to do in Solaris 2.3 systems is edit a client's /etc/nsswitch.conf file to specify "files," followed by "nisplus" as the sources for the group information. This effectively adds the contents of the Group table to the contents of the client's /etc/group file.

Hosts Table

The Hosts table associates the names of all the workstations in a domain with their IP addresses. The workstations are usually also NIS+ clients, but they don't have to be. Other tables, such as Bootparams, Group, and Netgroup, rely on the network names stored in this table. They use them to assign other attributes, such as home directories and group memberships, to individual workstations. The Hosts table has four columns:

Column	Description
IP Address	The workstation's IP address (network number plus workstation ID number).
Hostname	The workstation's official name.
Nickname	An optional name used in place of the hostname to identify the workstation.
Comment	An optional comment about the record.

Mail Aliases Table

The Mail Aliases table lists the domain's mail aliases recognized by `sendmail`. It has two columns:

Column	Description
Alias Name	The name of the alias.
Members	A list containing the members that receive mail sent to this alias. Members can be users, workstations, or other aliases.

Input File Format

Each entry has the following format:

alias-name : *member* [, *member*] . . .

To extend an entry over several lines, use a backslash.

A

Netgroup Table

The Netgroup table defines network-wide groups used to check permissions for remote mounts, logins, and shells. The members of netgroups used for remote mounts are workstations; for remote logins and shells, they are users. The Netgroup table has two columns:

Column	Description
Group Name	The name of the network group.
List of Members	A list of the members in the group.

Input File Format

The input file consists of a group name and any number of members:

> *groupname   member-specification . . .*

A member specification can be the name of another netgroup or an ordered list with three fields:

> *member-spec* : : =*group-name* |
> (*hostname*, *username*, *domainname*)

The first field specifies the name of a workstation. The second field specifies the name of a user. The third field specifies the domain in which the member specification is valid.

A missing field indicates a wildcard. For example, this netgroup includes all workstations and users in all domains:

> `everybody (,,)`

A dash in a field is the opposite of a wildcard; it indicates that no workstations or users belong to the group. Here are two examples:

> `(host1,  -,Wiz.Com.)`
> `(-,joe,Wiz.Com.)`

The first specification includes one workstation, `host1`, in the Wiz.Com. domain but excludes all users. The second specification includes one user in the Wiz.Com. domain but excludes all workstations.

Netmasks Table

The Netmasks table contains the network masks used to implement standard Internet subnetting. The table has two columns:

Column	Description
Network Number	The IP number of the network.
Subnet Mask	The network mask to use on the network.

For network numbers, you can use the conventional IP dot notation used by workstation addresses, but leave zeroes in place of the workstation addresses. For example, this entry—

    128.32.0.0   255.255.255.0

—means that class B network 128.32.0.0 should have 16 bits in its network field, eight bits in its subnet field, and eight bits in its host field.

Networks Table

The Networks table lists the networks of the Internet. This table is normally created from the official network table maintained at the Network Information Control Center (NIC), though you may need to add your local networks to it. It has three columns:

Column	Description
Network Name	The official name of the network, supplied by the Internet.
Network Number	The official IP number of the network.
Aliases	An unofficial name for the network.

Passwd Table

The Passwd table contains information about the accounts of users in a domain. These users generally are, but do not have to be, NIS+ principals. Remember, though, that if they are NIS+ principals, their credentials are not stored here, but in the domain's Cred table. The Passwd table usually grants Read permission to the World (or to Nobody).

A

The information in the Passwd table is added when users' accounts are created. The Passwd table contains the following columns:

Column	Description
User Name	The user's login name, which is assigned when the user's account is created. The name can contain no uppercase characters and can have a maximum of eight characters.
Password	The user's encrypted password.
UID	The user's numerical ID, assigned when the user's account is created.
Group ID	The numerical ID of the user's group.
GCOS	The user's real name plus information that the user wishes to include in the "From:" field of a mail-message heading. An & in this column simply uses the user's login name.
Home Directory	The pathname of the user's home directory; that is, the directory the system summons after the user logs in.
Login Shell	The user's initial shell program. The default is the c-shell: `/usr/bin/csh`.

The Passwd table has an additional column: the Shadow column. It stores restricted information about user accounts. It includes the following information:

Item	Description
Lastchg	The number of days between January 1, 1970 and the date the password was last modified.
Min	The minimum number of days recommended between password changes.
Max	The maximum number of days that the password is valid.
Warn	The number of days' warning a user receives before being notified that his or her password has expired.
Inactive	The number of days of inactivity allowed for the user.
Expire	An absolute date past which the user's account is no longer valid.
Flag	Reserved for future use. Currently set to 0.

All About Administering NIS+

Previous releases of SunOS used a +/- syntax in local /etc/passwd files to incorporate or overwrite entries in the NIS password maps. Since Solaris 2.3 uses the Name Service Switch (described in Chapter 5) to specify a workstation's sources of information, this syntax is no longer necessary. All you have to do in Solaris 2.3 systems is edit a client's /etc/nsswitch.conf file to specify "files," followed by "nisplus" as the sources for the passwd information. This effectively adds the contents of the Password table to the contents of the /etc/passwd file.

However, if you still want to use the +/- method, edit the client's nsswitch.conf file to specify compat for the passwd source.

Protocols Table

The Protocols table lists the protocols used by the Internet. It has four columns:

Column	Description
Protocol Name	The protocol name.
Protocol Number	The number of the protocol.
Aliases	An unofficial alias used to identify the protocol.
Comments	Comments about the protocol.

Here is an example of an input file for the Protocols table:

```
#
# Internet (IP) Protocols
#
ip     0     IP    # internet protocol, pseudo protocol number
icmp   1     ICMP  # internet control message protocol
ggp    3     GGP   # gateway-gateway protocol
tcp    6     TCP   # transmission control protocol
pup    12    PUP   # PARC universal packet
udp    17    UDP   # user datagram protocol
#
```

RPC Table

The RPC table lists the names of RPC programs. It has four columns:

Column	Description
RPC Program Name	The name of the program.
RPC Program Number	The program number.
Aliases	Other names that can be used to invoke the program.
Comments	Comments about the RPC program.

Here is an example of an input file for the RPC table:

```
#
#  rpc file
#
rpcbind    100000    portmap    sunrpc    portmapper
rusersd    100002    rusers
nfs        100003    nfsprog
mountd     100005    mount      showmount
walld      100008    rwall      shutdown
sprayd     100012    spray
llockmgr   100020
nlockmgr   100021
status     100024
bootparam  100026
keyserv    100029    keyserver
#
```

Services Table

The Services table stores information about the Internet services available on the Internet. It has four columns:

Column	Description
Service Name	The official Internet name of the service.
Port/Protocol	The port number and protocol through which the service is provided (for instance, 512/tcp).
Aliases	The list of alternate names by which the service can be requested.
Comments	Comments about the service.

Timezone Table

The Timezone table lists the default time zone of every workstation in the domain. The default time zone is used during installation, but can be overridden by the installer. The table has three columns:

Field	Description
Timezone Name	The name of the time zone (e.g., US/Pacific).
Workstation or Domain Name	The name of the workstation or, if using only one line in the entire table, the name of the domain.
Comments	Comments about the time zone.

Pre-Setup Worksheets

B

Use the worksheets on the following pages to record planning information prior to setup. Chapter 6, "Planning and Transition Guidelines," provides a sample copy.

Domain: [   ]

Servers	Type	Name	Specifications
	Master		
	First Replica		
	Second Replica		

Credentials	Type of Principal	Type of Credential		
	Servers			
	Clients			
	Administrators			
	Users			

Rights	Types of Objects	Category & Rights				
	Directories	N	O	G	W	Use Defaults?
	Groups	N	O	G	W	Description

Domain: [   ] (*Continued*)

Rights
(*cont.*)

Types of Objects	Category & Rights				
Tables	**N**	**O**	**G**	**W**	**Notes**
Bootparams					
Hosts					
Passwd					
Cred					
Group					
Netgroup					
Aliases					
Timezone					
Networks					
Netmasks					
Ethers					
Services					
Protocols					
RPC					
Auto_Home					
Auto_Master					

B

Domain: [   ]

Servers	Type	Name	Specifications
	Master		
	First Replica		
	Second Replica		

Credentials	Type of Principal	Type of Credential
	Servers	
	Clients	
	Administrators	
	Users	

Rights	Types of Objects	Category & Rights				
	Directories	N	O	G	W	Use Defaults?
	Groups	N	O	G	W	Description

Domain: [   ] (*Continued*)

Rights
(*cont.*)

Types of Objects	Category & Rights				
Tables	**N**	**O**	**G**	**W**	**Notes**
Bootparams					
Hosts					
Passwd					
Cred					
Group					
Netgroup					
Aliases					
Timezone					
Networks					
Netmasks					
Ethers					
Services					
Protocols					
RPC					
Auto_Home					
Auto_Master					

Domain:

Servers	Type	Name	Specifications
	Master		
	First Replica		
	Second Replica		

Credentials	Type of Principal	Type of Credential
	Servers	
	Clients	
	Administrators	
	Users	

Rights	Types of Objects	Category & Rights				
	Directories	N	O	G	W	Use Defaults?
	Groups	N	O	G	W	Description

Domain: [   ]   (*Continued*)

Rights
(*cont.*)

Types of Objects	Category & Rights				
Tables	N	O	G	W	Notes
Bootparams					
Hosts					
Passwd					
Cred					
Group					
Netgroup					
Aliases					
Timezone					
Networks					
Netmasks					
Ethers					
Services					
Protocols					
RPC					
Auto_Home					
Auto_Master					

Domain:

Servers	Type	Name	Specifications
	Master		
	First Replica		
	Second Replica		

Credentials	Type of Principal	Type of Credential
	Servers	
	Clients	
	Administrators	
	Users	

Rights	Types of Objects	Category & Rights				
	Directories	N	O	G	W	Use Defaults?
	Groups	N	O	G	W	Description

Domain: [ ] *(Continued)*

Rights
(cont.)

Types of Objects	Category & Rights				
Tables	**N**	**O**	**G**	**W**	**Notes**
Bootparams					
Hosts					
Passwd					
Cred					
Group					
Netgroup					
Aliases					
Timezone					
Networks					
Netmasks					
Ethers					
Services					
Protocols					
RPC					
Auto_Home					
Auto_Master					

NIS+ Scripts Error Messages

C ≣

This appendix contains all the error messages produced by the NIS+ scripts along with explanations of why the messages appear and how to fix the problems they indicate. The error messages are ordered alphabetically by script.

The `nisclient`(1M) Script

This section lists the error messages you may see when you run the `nisclient`(1M) script.

```
**ERROR: chkey failed again.
Please contact your network administrator to verify your network
password.
```

This message indicates that you typed the wrong network password.

- If this is the first time you are initializing this machine, contact your network administrator to verify the network password.

- If this machine has been initialized before as an NIS+ client of the same domain, try typing the root login password at the Secure RPC password prompt.

- If this machine is currently an NIS+ client and you are trying to change it to a client of a different domain, rename the `/etc/.rootkey` file and then rerun the script, using the network password given to you by your network administrator.

```
**ERROR: conflicting -c option.
**ERROR: conflicting -i option.
**ERROR: conflicting -r option.
**ERROR: conflicting -u option.
```

These messages indicate that you typed some combination of the `-c`, `-i`, `-r`, or `-u` options. These options are mutually exclusive. Rerun the script with only one of these options.

```
**ERROR: could not restore file <filename>
```

This message indicates that NIS+ was unable to rename *<filename>*`.no_nisplus` to *<filename>*.

Check your system console for system error messages.

- If there is a system error message, fix the problem described in the error message and then rerun `nisclient -r`.

- If there aren't any system error messages, try renaming this file manually and then rerun `nisclient -r`.

```
**ERROR: Couldn't get the Server <NIS+_server>'s address.
```

The script was unable to retrieve the server's IP address for the specified domain. Manually add the IP address for the server *<NIS+_server>* into the `/etc/hosts` file. Then, rerun `nisclient -c`.

```
**ERROR: Don't know about the domain "<domainname>".
Please check your domainname.
```

This message indicates that you typed an unrecognized domain name. Rerun the script with the correct domain name.

```
**ERROR: invalid name "<client-name>"
It is neither an host nor a user name.
```

This message indicates that you typed an invalid *<client-name>*.

- If the *<client-name>* was spelled incorrectly, rerun `nisclient -c` with the correct *<client-name>*.

- If the *<client-name>* was spelled correctly but does not exist in the proper table, put *<client-name>* into the proper table and rerun `nisclient -c`. For example, a user client belongs in the Passwd table, and a host client belongs in the Hosts table.

`**ERROR: missing hostnames or usernames.`

This messages indicates that you did not type the client names on the command line. Rerun `nisclient -c` with the client names.

`**ERROR: nisinit failed.`

`nisinit` was unable to create the NIS+ coldstart file.

Check the following:

- Whether the NIS+ server that you specified with the –h option is running—use `ping(1)`

- Whether you typed the correct domain name with the –d option

- Whether `rpc.nisd`(1M) is running on the server

- Whether `nobody` has `read` permission for this domain

`**ERROR: this name "<client-name>" is in both the passwd and hosts tables.`
`You cannot have a username the same as the hostname.`

<client-name> appears in both the Passwd and Hosts tables. One name is not allowed to be in both of these tables. Manually remove the entry from either table. Then, rerun `nisclient -c`.

`**ERROR: You cannot use the -u option as a root user.`

This message indicates that the superuser tried to run `nisclient -u`. The –u option is for initializing ordinary users only. Superusers do not need to be initialized as NIS+ clients.

`**ERROR: you must specify one of these options: -c, -i, -u, -r.`

This message indicates that one of these options, `-c`, `-i`, `-u`, `-r`, was missing from the command line. Rerun the script with the correct option.

`**ERROR: You must be root to use -i option.`

This message indicates that an ordinary user tried to run `nisclient -i`. Only the superuser has permission to run `nisclient -i`.

**WARNING: *<alias-hostname>* is an alias name for host
<canonical_hostname>. "
You cannot create credential for host alias. "

> This message indicates that you have typed a host alias in the name list for
> nisclient -c. The script asks if you want to create the credential for the
> canonical host name, since you should not create credentials for host alias names.

The nispopulate (1M) Script

This section lists the error messages you may see when you run the nispopulate(1M)
script.

```
dumping passwd table...
loading credential table...
nisaddcred: no password entry for uid <userid>
nisaddcred: unable to create credential.
```

> The NIS+ command nisaddcred(1M) failed to add a LOCAL credential for user id
> *<userid>* on a remote domain. This only happens when you are trying to populate
> the Passwd table in a remote domain.

> To correct the problem, add a table path in the local Passwd table.

> # **nistbladm -u -p passwd.org_dir.***<remote-domain>* **passwd.org_dir**

> The *<remote-domain>* should be the same domain that you specified with the -d
> option when you ran nispopulate(1M). Then, rerun the script to populate the
> Passwd table.

```
**ERROR: conflicting -F option.
**ERROR: conflicting -Y option.
```

> Either message indicates that you typed both the -F and -Y options in the same
> command line. These options are mutually exclusive. Use -F to indicate files or -Y
> to indicate NIS maps as the source of data for this script.

```
**ERROR: directory <directory-path> does not exist.
```

> This message indicates that you typed an incorrect directory path. Type the correct
> directory path.

`**ERROR: failed dumping` *<tablename>* `table.`

The script was unable to populate the Cred table because the script did not succeed in dumping the named table.

- If `niscat` *<tablename>*`.org_dir` fails, make sure that all the servers are operating. Then, rerun the script to populate the *<tablename>* table.

- If `niscat` *<tablename>*`.org_dir` is working, the error may have been caused by the NIS+ server being temporarily busy. Rerun the script to populate the *<tablename>* table.

`**ERROR: NIS map transfer failed.`
<tablename> `table will not be loaded.`

NIS+ was unable to transfer the NIS map for this table to the NIS+ database.

- If the NIS server host is running, try running the script again. The error may have been due to a temporary failure.

- If all tables have this problem, try running the script again with a different NIS server.

`**ERROR(1): table` *<tablename>*`.org_dir.`*<domain>* `does not exist.`
<tablename> `table will not be loaded."`

The script did not find the NIS+ table *<tablename>*.

- If *<tablename>* is spelled incorrectly, rerun the script with the correct table name.

- If the *<tablename>* table does not exist, use `nissetup`(1M) to create the table if *<tablename>* is one of the standard NIS+ tables. Or, use `nistbladm`(1M) to create the private table *<tablename>*. Then, rerun the script to populate this table.

- If the *<tablename>* table exists, the error may have been caused by the NIS+ server being temporarily busy. Rerun the script to populate this *<tablename>* table.

`**ERROR: you must specify both the NIS domainname (-y) and the NIS`
`server hostname (-h).`

This message indicates that you did not type either the NIS domain name or the NIS server host name. Type the NIS domain name and the NIS server host name at the prompt or on the command line.

`**ERROR: you must specify one of these options: -Y or -F`

This message indicates that you did not type either the `-Y` or the `-F` option. Rerun the script with the correct option.

`**WARNING: failed to populate` *<tablename>* `table.`

The `nisaddent`(1M) command was unable to load the NIS+ *<tablename>* table. A more detailed error message usually appears before this warning message.

`**WARNING: file` *<directory-path>*`/`*<tablename>* `does not exist!` *<tablename>* `table will not be loaded.`

The script was unable to find the input file for *<tablename>*.

- If *<directory-path>*/*<tablename>* is spelled incorrectly, rerun the script with the correct table name.

- If the *<directory-path>*/*<tablename>* file does not exist, create and update this file with the proper data. Then, rerun the script to populate this table.

`**WARNING: NIS auto.master map conversion failed.` `auto.master table will not be loaded.`

The `auto.master` map conversion failed while trying to convert all the dots to underscores in the `auto_master` map. Rerun the script with a different NIS server.

`**WARNING: NIS netgroup map conversion failed.` `netgroup table will not be loaded.`

The `netgroup` map conversion failed while trying to convert the NIS domain name to the NIS+ domain name in the `netgroup` map. Rerun the script with a different NIS server.

`**WARNING: you must specify the NIS domainname.`

This message indicates that you did not type the NIS domain name at the prompt. Type the NIS server domain name at the prompt.

`**WARNING: you must specify the NIS server hostname.` `Please try again.`

This message indicates that you did not type the NIS server hostname at the prompt. Type the NIS server hostname at the prompt.

The `nisserver` (1M) Script

This section lists the error messages you may see when you run the `nisserver`(1M) script.

`**ERROR:` *`<domainname>`* `does not exist.`

This message indicates that you are trying to replicate a domain that does not exist.

- If *`<domainname>`* is spelled incorrectly, rerun the script with the correct domain name.

- If the *`<domainname>`* domain does not exist, create it and then you can replicate it.

`**ERROR:` *`<hostname>`* `is a master server for this domain. You cannot demote a master server to replica. If you really want to demote this master, you should promote a replica server to master using nisserver with the -M option.`

You cannot convert a master server to a replica server of the same domain. You can, however, change a replica to be the new master server of a domain by running `nisserver -M` with the replica hostname as the new master.

`**ERROR:` *`<parent-domain>`* `does not exist."`

This message indicates that the parent domain of the domain you typed on the command line does not exist. This message should only appear when you are setting up a nonroot master server.

- If the domain name is spelled incorrectly, rerun the script with the correct domain name.

- If the domain's parent domain does not exist, create the parent domain first; then you can create this domain.

`**ERROR: conflicting -M option.`
`**ERROR: conflicting -R option.`
`**ERROR: conflicting -r option.`

Any of these messages indicates that you typed some combination of the `-M`, `-R`, or `-r` options. These options are mutually exclusive. Rerun the script with only one of these options.

C

ERROR: host *<hostname>* is not a valid NIS+ principal in domain *<domainname>*. This host *<hostname>* must be defined in the credential table in domain *<domainname>*. Use nisclient -c to create the host credential

> A machine must be a valid NIS+ client with proper credentials before it can become an NIS+ server. To convert a machine to an NIS+ root replica server, the machine first must be an NIS+ client in the root domain. Follow the instructions on how to add a new client to a domain, then rerun nisserver -R.

> Before you can convert a machine to an NIS+ nonroot master or a replica server, the machine must be an NIS+ client in the parent domain of the domain that it plans to serve. Follow the instructions on how to add a new client to a domain, then rerun nisserver -M or nisserver -R.

> This problem should not occur when you are setting up a root master server.

ERROR: invalid group name.
It must be a group in the *<root-domain>* domain.

> This message indicates that you used an invalid group name while trying to configure a root master server. Rerun nisserver -r with a valid group name for *<root-domain>*.

ERROR: it failed to add the credential for root.

> The NIS+ command nisaddcred(1M) failed to create the root credential when trying to set up a root master server. Check your system console for system error messages.

> - If there is a system error message, fix the problem described in the error message and then rerun nisserver(1M).

> - If there aren't any system error messages, check to see if the rpc.nisd process is running. If it is not running, restart it and then rerun nisserver(1M).

ERROR: it failed to create the tables.

> The NIS+ command nissetup(1M) failed to create the directories and tables. Check your system console for system error messages.

> - If there is a system error message, fix the problem described in the error message and then rerun nisserver(1M).

> - If there aren't any system error messages, check to see if the rpc.nisd process is running. If it is not running, restart it and then rerun nisserver(1M).

All About Administering NIS+

**ERROR: it failed to initialize the root server.

The NIS+ command `nisinit -r` failed to initialize the root master server. Check your system console for system error messages. If there is a system error message, fix the problem described in the error message and then rerun `nisserver`(1M).

**ERROR: it failed to make the *<domainname>* directory.

The NIS+ command `nismkdir`(1M) failed to make the new directory *<domainname>*. The parent domain does not have Create permission to create this new domain.

- If you are not the owner of the domain or a group member of the parent domain, rerun the script as the owner or as a group member of the parent domain.

- If `rpc.nisd`(1M) is not running on the new master server of the domain that you are trying to create, restart rpc.nisd(1M).

**ERROR: it failed to promote new master for the *<domainname>* directory.

The NIS+ command `nismkdir`(1M) failed to promote the new directory *<domainname>*.

- If you do not have Modify permission in the parent domain of this domain, rerun the script as the owner or as a group member of the parent domain.

- If `rpc.nisd`(1M) is not running on the servers of the domain that you are trying to promote, restart rpc.nisd(1M) on these servers and rerun `nisserver`(1M).

**ERROR: it failed to replicate the *<directory-name>* directory.

The NIS+ command `nismkdir`(1M) failed to create the new replica for the directory *<directory-name>*.

- If `rpc.nisd`(1M) is not running on the master server of the domain that you are trying to replicate, restart `rpc.nisd`(1M) on the master server. Then, rerun `nisserver`(1M).

- If `rpc.nisd`(1M) is not running on the new replica server, restart it on the new replica. Then, rerun `nisserver`(1M).

**ERROR: NIS+ group name must end with a ".".

> This message indicates that you did not specify a fully qualified group name ending with a "dot." Rerun the script with a fully qualified group name.

**ERROR: NIS+ server is not running on <remote-host>. You must do the following before becoming a NIS+ server:
1. become a NIS+ client of the parent domain or any domain above the domain which you plan to serve. (nisclient)
2. start the NIS+ server. (rpc.nisd)

> This message indicates that rpc.nisd(1M) is not running on the remote machine that you are trying to convert to an NIS+ server. Use the nisclient(1M) script to become an NIS+ client of the parent domain or any domain above the domain you plan to serve. Then, start rpc.nisd(1M) on <remote-host>.

**ERROR: no permission to create directory <domainname>.

> The parent domain does not have Create permission to create this new domain. If you are not the owner of the domain or a group member of the parent domain, rerun the script as the owner or as a group member of the parent domain.

**ERROR: no permission to replicate directory <domainname>.

> This message indicates that you do not have permission to replicate the domain. Rerun the script as the owner or as a group member of the domain.

**ERROR: you must specify a fully qualified groupname.

> This message indicates that you did not specify a fully qualified group name ending with a "dot." Rerun the script with a fully qualified group name.

**ERROR: you must specify one of these options: -r, -M or -R.

> This message indicates that you did not type any of the -r, -M, or -R options. Rerun the script with the correct option.

**WARNING: <hostname> is already a server for this domain. If you choose to continue with the script, it will try to replicate the groups_dir and org_dir directories for this domain.

> This message warns you that <hostname> is already a replica server for the domain that you are trying to replicate.

> • If you are running the script to fix an earlier nisserver(1M) problem, continue running the script.

- If *<hostname>* was incorrectly spelled, rerun the script with the correct host name.

`**WARNING: domain` *<domainname>* `already exists.`

This message indicates that the domain you tried to create already exists.

- If you are trying to promote a new nonroot master server or are recovering from a previous `nisserver`(1M) problem, continue running the script.

- If *<domainname>* was spelled incorrectly, rerun the script with the correct domain name.

`**WARNING: failed to add new member` *<NIS+_principal>* `into the` *<groupname>* `group.`
`You will need to add this member manually:`
`1. /usr/sbin/nisgrpadm -a` *<groupname>* *<NIS+_principal>*

The NIS+ command `nisgrpadm`(1M) failed to add a new member into the NIS+ group *<groupname>*. As superuser, correct the situation as instructed in the warning.

`**WARNING: failed to create the` *<groupname>* `group. You will need to` `create this group manually:`
`1. /usr/sbin/nisgrpadm -c` *<groupname>*
`2. /usr/sbin/nisgrpadm -a` *<groupname>* *<NIS+_principal>*

The NIS+ command `nisgrpadm`(1M) failed to create the NIS+ group *<groupname>*. As superuser, correct the situation as instructed in the warning.

`**WARNING: hostname specified will not be used.`
`It will use the local hostname instead.`

This message indicates that you typed a remote hostname with the `-h` option. The `nisserver -r` script does not configure remote machines as root master servers.

- If the local machine is the one that you want to convert to an NIS+ root master server, no other action is needed. The `nisserver -r` script will ignore the hostname you typed.

- If you actually want to convert the remote host to an NIS+ root master server instead of the local machine, exit the script. Rerun the `nisserver -r` script on the remote host.

WARNING: nisupdkeys failed on directory *<directory-name>*
You will need to run nisupdkeys manually:
  1. /usr/lib/nis/nisupdkeys *<directory-name>*

> The NIS+ command nisupdkeys(1M) failed to update the keys in the listed directory object. As superuser, correct the situation as instructed in the warning.

**WARNING: nisupdkeys failed on directory *<domainname>*. This script will not be able to continue.
Please remove the *<domainname>* directory using 'nisrmdir'.

> The NIS+ command nisupdkeys(1M) failed to update the keys in the listed directory object. If rpc.nisd(1M) is not running on the new master server that is supposed to serve this new domain, restart rpc.nisd(1M). Then, remove the *<domainname>* directory using nisrmdir(1M). Afterwards, rerun nisserver(1M).

WARNING: this script removes directories and files related to NIS+ under /var/nis directory with the exception of the NIS_COLD_START and NIS_SHARED_DIRCACHE files which will be renamed to *<file>*.no_nisplus. If you want to save these files, you should abort from this script now to save these files first.

WARNING: once this script is executed, you will not be able to restore the existing NIS+ server environment. However, you can restore your NIS+ client environment using "nisclient -i" with the proper domainname and server information.
Use "nisclient -i" to restore your NIS+ client environment.

> These messages appear if you have already run the script at least once before to set up an NIS+ server. They indicate that all NIS+ related files will be removed if you decide to continue running this script.

- If it is all right for these NIS+ files to be removed, continue running the script.

- If you want to save these NIS+ files, exit the script by typing n at the Do you want to continue? prompt. Then, save the NIS+ files in a different directory and rerun the script.

NIS+ API

The NIS+ Application Programmer's Interface (API) is a group of functions that can be called by an application to access and modify NIS+ objects. The NIS+ API has 54 functions that fall into nine categories:

- Object manipulation functions (`nis_names`)
- Table access functions (`nis_tables`)
- Local name functions (`nis_local_names`)
- Group manipulation functions (`nis_groups`)
- Server-related functions (`nis_server`)
- Database access functions (`nis_db`)
- Error message display functions (`nis_error`)
- Transaction log functions (`nis_admin`)
- Miscellaneous functions (`nis_subr`)

The functions in each category are summarized in Table D-1. The category names match the names by which they are grouped in the NIS+ manpages.

D

Table D-1   NIS+ API Functions

Function	Description
nis_names	**Locate and Manipulate Objects**
nis_lookup()	Returns a copy of an NIS+ object. Can follow links. Though it cannot search for an entry object, if a link points to one, it can return an entry object.
nis_add()	Adds an NIS+ object to the namespace.
nis_remove()	Removes an NIS+ object in the namespace.
nis_modify()	Modifies an NIS+ object in the namespace.
nis_tables	**Search and Update Tables**
nis_list()	Searches a table in the NIS+ namespace and returns entry objects that match the search criteria. Can follow links and search paths from one table to another.
nis_add_entry()	Adds an entry object to an NIS+ table. Can be instructed to either fail or overwrite if the entry object already exists. Can return a copy of the resulting object if the operation was successful.
nis_freeresult()	Frees all memory associated with an **nis_result** structure.
nis_remove_entry()	Removes one or more entry objects from an NIS+ table. Can identify the object to be removed by using search criteria or by pointing to a cached copy of the object. If using search criteria, can remove all objects that match the search criteria; therefore, with the proper search criteria, can remove all entries in a table. Can return a copy of the resulting object if the operation was successful.
nis_modify_entry()	Modifies one or more entry objects in an NIS+ table. Can identify the object to be modified by using search criteria or by pointing to a cached copy of the object.
nis_first_entry()	Returns a copy of the first entry object in an NIS+ table.
nis_next_entry()	Returns a copy of the next entry object in an NIS+ table. Because a table can be updated and entries removed or modified between calls to this function, the order of entries returned may not match the actual order of entries in the table.

Table D-1   NIS+ API Functions (Continued)

Function	Description
nis_local_names	**Get Default Names for the Current Process**
nis_local_directory()	Returns the name of the workstation's NIS+ domain.
nis_local_host()	Returns the fully qualified name of the workstation. A fully qualified name has the form *<host-name>.<domain-name>*.
nis_local_group()	Returns the name of the current NIS+ group, which is specified by the environment variable NIS_GROUP.
nis_local_principal()	Returns the name of the NIS+ principal whose UID is associated with the calling process.
nis_getnames()	Returns a list of possible expansions to a particular name.
nis_freenames()	Frees the memory containing the list generated by nis_getnames.
nis_groups	**Group Manipulation and Authorization**
nis_ismember()	Tests whether a principal is a member of a group.
nis_addmember()	Adds a member to a group. The member can be a principal, a group, or a domain.
nis_removemember()	Deletes a member from a group.
nis_creategroup()	Creates a group object.
nis_destroygroup()	Deletes a group object.
nis_verifygroup()	Tests whether a group object exists.
nis_print_group_\ entry()	Lists the principals that are members of a group object.
nis_server	**Various Services for NIS+ Applications**
nis_mkdir()	Creates the databases to support service for a named directory on a specified host.
nis_rmdir()	Removes the directory from a host.
nis_servstate()	Sets and reads state variables of NIS+ servers and flushes internal caches.
nis_stats()	Retrieves statistics about a server's performance.
nis_getservlist()	Returns a list of servers that support a particular domain.
nis_freeservlist()	Frees the list of servers returned by nis_getservlist.

Table D-1   NIS+ API Functions (Continued)

Function	Description
nis_freetags()	Frees the memory associated with the results of nis_servstate and nis_stats.
nis_db	**Interface Between the NIS+ Server and the Database— Not To Be Used By an NIS+ Client**
db_first_entry()	Returns a copy of the first entry of the specified table.
db_next_entry()	Returns a copy of the entry succeeding the specified entry.
db_reset_next_entry()	Terminates a first/next entry sequence.
db_list_entries()	Returns copies of entries that meet specified attributes.
db_remove_entry()	Removes all entries that meet specified attributes.
db_add_entry()	Replaces an entry in a table identified by specified attributes with a copy of the specified object or adds the object to the table.
db_checkpoint()	Reorganizes the contents of a table to make access to the table more efficient.
db_standby()	Advises the database manager to release resources.
nis_error	**Functions that Supply Descriptive Strings Equivalent to NIS+ Status Values**
nis_sperrno()	Returns a pointer to the appropriate string constant.
nis_perror()	Displays the appropriate string constant on standard output.
nis_lerror()	Sends the appropriate string constant to syslog.
nis_sperror()	Returns a pointer to a statically allocated string to be used or to be copied with strdup().
nis_admin	**Transaction-Logging Functions Used by Servers**
nis_ping()	Timestamps the master server of a directory, forcing replicas of the directory to be updated.
nis_checkpoint()	Forces logged data to be stored in the table on disk.

Table D-1   NIS+ API Functions (Continued)

Function	Description
`nis_subr`	**Functions to Operate on NIS+ Names and Objects**
`nis_leaf_of()`	Returns the first label in an NIS+ name. The returned name does not have a trailing dot.
`nis_name_of()`	Removes all domain-related labels and returns only the unique object portion of the name. The name passed to the function must be either in the local domain or in one of its child domains, or the function returns NULL.
`nis_domain_of()`	Returns the name of the domain in which an object resides. The returned name ends in a dot.
`nis_dir_cmp()`	Compares any two NIS+ names. The comparison ignores case and states whether the names are the same, descendants of each other, or not related.
`nis_clone_object()`	Creates an exact duplicate of an NIS+ object.
`nis_destroy_object()`	Destroys an object created by `nis_clone_object`.
`nis_print_object()`	Prints the contents of an NIS+ object structure to `stdout`.

Sample Program

This program performs the following tasks:

- Determines the local principal and local domain.
- Looks up the local directory object.
- Creates a directory called `foo` under the local domain.
- Creates the `groups_dir` and `org_dir` directories under domain foo.
- Creates a group object `admins.foo`
- Adds the local principal to the admins group.
- Creates a table under `org_dir.foo`
- Adds two entries to the newly created table.
- Retrieves and display the new membership list of the admins group.
- Lists the namespace under the `foo` domain, using callbacks.
- Lists the contents of the table created, using callbacks.
- Cleans up all the objects that were created:
  - removes the local principal from the admins group

- removes the admins group
- removes the entries in the table followed by the table
- removes the `groups_dir` and `org_dir` directory objects
- removes the `foo` directory object

The example program is not a typical application. In a normal situation, the directories and tables would be created or removed through the command line interface, and applications would manipulate NIS+ entry objects.

Unsupported Macros

The sample program uses unsupported macros that are defined in the file `<rpcsvc/nis.h>`. These are not public APIs and can change or disappear in the future. They are used for illustration only; if you choose to use them, you do so at your own risk. The macros are:

- NIS_RES_OBJECT
- ENTRY_VAL
- DEFAULT_RIGHTS

Functions Used in the Example

The use of the following NIS+ C API functions is illustrated through this example:

```
nis_add()             nis_add_entry()        nis_addmember()
nis_creategroup()     nis_destroygroup()     nis_domain_of()
nis_freeresult()      nis_leaf_of ()         nis_list()
nis_local_directory() nis_local_principal()  nis_lookup()
nis_mkdir()           nis_perror()           nis_remove()
nis_remove_entry()    nis_removemember()
```

The Example

The program assumes that the NIS+ principal running this application has permission to create directory objects in the local domain. The program is compiled:

```
yourhost% cc -o example.c example -lnsl
```

It is invoked:

```
yourhost% example [dir]
```

where *dir* is the NIS+ directory in which the program creates all the NIS+ objects. Specifying no directory argument causes the objects to be created in the parent directory of the local domain. Note that for the call to `nis_lookup()`, a space and the name of the local domain are appended to the string that names the directory. The argument is the name of the NIS+ directory in which to create the NIS+ objects. The principal running this program should have Create permission in the directory.

```c
#include <stdio.h>
#include <string.h>
#include <stdlib.h>
#include <rpcsvc/nis.h>

#define    MAX_MESG_SIZE 512
#define    BUFFER_SIZE 64
#define    TABLE_TYPE "test_data"

main(argc, argv)
    int    argc;
    char   *argv[];
{
    char   *saved_grp, *saved_name, *saved_owner;
    char   dir_name[NIS_MAXNAMELEN];
    char   local_domain[NIS_MAXNAMELEN];
    char   local_princip [NIS_MAXNAMELEN];
    char   org_dir_name [NIS_MAXNAMELEN];
    char   grp_name [NIS_MAXNAMELEN];
    char   grp_dir_name [NIS_MAXNAMELEN];
    char   table_name [NIS_MAXNAMELEN];
    nis_object    *dirobj, entdata;
    nis_result    *pres;
    u_int  saved_num_servers;
    int    err;

    if (argc == 2)
        sprintf (local_domain, "%s.", argv[1]);
    else
        strcpy (local_domain, "");

    strcat (local_domain, (char *) nis_local_directory());
    strcpy (local_princip, (char *) nis_local_principal());
/*
    * Lookup the directory object for the local domain for two reasons:
    * 1.To get a template of a nis_object.
    * 2.To reuse some of the information contained in the directory
    * object returned. We could have declared a static nis_object, but
    * since we need to change very little, it is easier to make the
    * changes and not initiliaze the nis_object structure.
    */
```

```
pres = nis_lookup (local_domain, 0);
if (pres->status != NIS_SUCCESS) {
    nis_perror (pres->status, "unable to lookup local directory");
    exit (1);
}

/*
 * re-use most of the fields in the parent directory object - save
 * pointers to the fields that are being changed so that we can
 * free the original object and avoid dangling pointer references.
 */
dirobj = NIS_RES_OBJECT (pres);
saved_name = dirobj->DI_data.do_name;
saved_owner = dirobj->zo_owner;
saved_grp = dirobj->zo_group;

/*
 * set the new name, group, owner and new access rights for the
 * foo domain.
 */
sprintf (dir_name, "%s.%s", "foo", local_domain);
sprintf (grp_name, "%s.%s", "admins", dir_name);
dirobj->DI_data.do_name = dir_name;
dirobj->zo_group = grp_name;
dirobj->zo_owner = local_princip;

/*
 * Access rights in NIS+ are stored in a u_long with the highest
 * order bytes reserved for the "nobody" category, the next eight
 * bytes reserved for the owner, followed by group and world. In
 * this example we are giving access to the directory based on the
 * "----rmcdrmcd----" access right pattern.
 */
dirobj->zo_access = ((NIS_READ_ACC + NIS_MODIFY_ACC
                + NIS_CREATE_ACC + NIS_DESTROY_ACC) << 16)
                | ((NIS_READ_ACC + NIS_MODIFY_ACC
                + NIS_CREATE_ACC + NIS_DESTROY_ACC) << 8);

/*
 * Save the number of servers the parent directory object had so
 * that we can restore this value before calling nis_freeresult()
 * later and avoid memory leaks.
 */
saved_num_servers = dirobj->DI_data.do_servers.do_servers_len;

/* We want only one server to serve this directory */
```

```
dirobj->DI_data.do_servers.do_servers_len = 1;

dir_create (dir_name, dirobj);

/* create the groups_dir and org_dir directories under foo. */
sprintf (grp_dir_name, "groups_dir.%s", dir_name);
dirobj->DI_data.do_name = grp_dir_name;
dir_create (grp_dir_name, dirobj);

sprintf (org_dir_name, "org_dir.%s", dir_name);
dirobj->DI_data.do_name = org_dir_name;
dir_create (org_dir_name, dirobj);

grp_create (grp_name);

printf ("\nAdding principal %s to group %s ... \n",
          local_princip, grp_name);
err = nis_addmember (local_princip, grp_name);
if (err != NIS_SUCCESS) {
   nis_perror (err,
       "unable to add local principal to group.");
   exit (1);
}

sprintf (table_name, "test_table.org_dir.%s", dir_name);
tbl_create (dirobj, table_name);

/*
 * Now create NIS+ entry objects in the table that was just created
 */
stuff_table (table_name);

/* Display what we stuffed */
list_objs(dir_name, table_name, grp_name);

/* Clean out everything we created. */
cleanup (local_princip, grp_name, table_name, dir_name, dirobj);

/*
 * Restore the saved pointers from the orginal pres structure so that
 * we can free up the associated memory and have no memory leaks.
 */
dirobj->DI_data.do_name = saved_name;
dirobj->zo_group = saved_grp;
dirobj->zo_owner = saved_owner;
```

```
    dirobj->DI_data.do_servers.do_servers_len = saved_num_servers;
    (void) nis_freeresult (pres);
}
```

This routine is called by `main()` to create directory objects.

```
void
dir_create (dir_name, dirobj)
    nis_name  dir_name;
    nis_object*dirobj;
{
    nis_result *cres;
    nis_error err;

    printf ("\nAdding Directory %s to namespace ... \n", dir_name);
    cres = nis_add (dir_name, dirobj);
    if (cres->status != NIS_SUCCESS) {
        nis_perror (cres->status, "unable to add directory foo.");
        exit (1);
    }

    (void) nis_freeresult (cres);

    /*
     * NOTE: you need to do a nis_mkdir to create the table to store the
     * contents of the directory you are creating.
     */
    err = nis_mkdir (dir_name,
                    dirobj->DI_data.do_servers.do_servers_val);
    if (err != NIS_SUCCESS) {
        (void) nis_remove (dir_name, 0);
        nis_perror (err,
                "unable to create table for  directory object foo.");
        exit (1);
    }
}
```

This routine is called by `main()` to create the group object. Since `nis_creategroup()` works only on group objects, the "groups_dir" literal is not needed in the group name.

```
void
grp_create (grp_name)
    nis_name  grp_name;
{
    nis_error err;

    printf ("\nAdding %s group to namespace ... \n", grp_name);
```

```
    err = nis_creategroup (grp_name, 0);
    if (err != NIS_SUCCESS) {
        nis_perror (err, "unable to create group.");
        exit (1);
    }
}
```

This routine is called by `main()` to create a table object laid out as follows:

	Column1	Column2
Name:	ID	Name
Attributes:	Searchable, Text	Searchable, Text
Access Rights	----rmcdr---r---	----rmcdr---r---

The `TA_SEARCHABLE` constant indicates to the service that the column is searchable. Only text (the default) columns are searchable. `TA_CASE` indicates to the service that the column value is to be treated in a case-insensitive manner during searches.

```
#define    TABLE_MAXCOLS 2
#define    TABLE_COLSEP ':'
#define    TABLE_PATH 0

void
tbl_create (dirobj, table_name)
    nis_object *dirobj; /* need to use some of the fields */
    nis_name   table_name;
{
    nis_result    *cres;
    static nis_objecttblobj;
    static table_col tbl_cols[TABLE_MAXCOLS] = {
        {"Id", TA_SEARCHABLE | TA_CASE, DEFAULT_RIGHTS},
        {"Name", TA_SEARCHABLE | TA_CASE, DEFAULT_RIGHTS}
    };

    tblobj.zo_owner = dirobj->zo_owner;
    tblobj.zo_group = dirobj->zo_group;
    tblobj.zo_access = DEFAULT_RIGHTS;       /* macro defined in nis.h  */
    tblobj.zo_data.zo_type = TABLE_OBJ;      /* enumerated type in nis.h */
    tblobj.TA_data.ta_type = TABLE_TYPE;
    tblobj.TA_data.ta_maxcol = TABLE_MAXCOLS;
    tblobj.TA_data.ta_sep = TABLE_COLSEP;
    tblobj.TA_data.ta_path = TABLE_PATH;
    tblobj.TA_data.ta_cols.ta_cols_len =
        tblobj.TA_data.ta_maxcol;      /* ALWAYS ! */
```

```
    tblobj.TA_data.ta_cols.ta_cols_val = tbl_cols;

/*
 * Use a fully qualified table name i.e. the "org_dir" literal should
 * be embedded in the table name.  This is necessary because nis_add
 * operates on all types of NIS+ objects and needs the full path name
 * if a table is created.
 */
    printf ("\nCreating table %s ... \n", table_name);
    cres = nis_add (table_name, &tblobj);
    if (cres->status != NIS_SUCCESS) {
        nis_perror (cres->status, "unable to add table.");
        exit (1);
    }
    (void) nis_freeresult (cres);
}
```

This routine is called by `main()` to add entry objects to the table object. Two entries are added to the table object. Note that the column width in both entries is set to include the NULL character for a string terminator.

```
#define    MAXENTRIES 2
void
stuff_table(table_name)
    nis_name table_name;
{
    int        i;
    nis_objectentdata;
    nis_result*cres;
    static entry_col ent_col_data[MAXENTRIES][TABLE_MAXCOLS] = {
            {0, 2, "1", 0, 5, "John"},
            {0, 2, "2", 0, 5, "Mary"}
    };

    printf ("\nAdding entries to table ... \n");

    /*
     * Look up the table object first since the entries being added
     * should have the same owner, group owner and access rights as
     * the table they go in.
     */
    cres = nis_lookup (table_name, 0);
    if (cres->status != NIS_SUCCESS) {
        nis_perror (cres->status, "Unable to lookup table");
        exit(1);
    }
    entdata.zo_owner = NIS_RES_OBJECT (cres)->zo_owner;
```

```
    entdata.zo_group = NIS_RES_OBJECT (cres)->zo_group;
    entdata.zo_access = NIS_RES_OBJECT (cres)->zo_access;

    /* Free cres, so that it can be reused. */
    (void) nis_freeresult (cres);

    entdata.zo_data.zo_type = ENTRY_OBJ; /* enumerated type in nis.h */
    entdata.EN_data.en_type = TABLE_TYPE;
    entdata.EN_data.en_cols.en_cols_len = TABLE_MAXCOLS;
    for (i = 0; i < MAXENTRIES; ++i) {
        entdata.EN_data.en_cols.en_cols_val = &ent_col_data[i][0];
        cres = nis_add_entry (table_name, &entdata, 0);
        if (cres->status != NIS_SUCCESS) {
            nis_perror (cres->status, "unable to add entry.");
            exit (1);
        }
        (void) nis_freeresult (cres);
    }
}
```

This routine is the print function for the `nis_list()` call. When `list_objs()` calls `nis_list()`, a pointer to `print_info()` is one of the calling arguments. Each time the service calls this function, it prints the contents of the entry object. The return value indicates to the library to call with the next entry from the table.

```
int
print_info (name, entry, cbdata)
    nis_name  name;       /* Unused */
    nis_object*entry;     /* The NIS+ entry object */
    void      *cbdata;    /* Unused */
{
    static u_int firsttime = 1;
    entry_col    *tmp;  /* only to make source more readable */
    u_int        i, terminal;

    if (firsttime) {
        printf ("\tId.\t\t\tName\n");
        printf ("\t---\t\t\t----\n");
        firsttime = 0;
    }
    for (i = 0; i < entry->EN_data.en_cols.en_cols_len; ++i) {
        tmp = &entry->EN_data.en_cols.en_cols_val[i];
        terminal = tmp->ec_value.ec_value_len;
        tmp->ec_value.ec_value_val[terminal] = '\0';
    }

    /*
```

```
 * ENTRY_VAL is a macro that returns the value of a specific
 * column value of a specified entry.
 */
printf("\t%s\t\t\t%s\n", ENTRY_VAL (entry, 0),
                          ENTRY_VAL (entry, 1));
return (0); /* always ask for more */
}
```

This routine is called by `main()` to list the contents of the group, table, and directory objects. It also demonstrates the use of callbacks. It retrieves and displays the membership of the group. The group membership list is not stored as the contents of the object, so it is queried through the `nis_lookup()` instead of the `nis_list()` call. We must use the "groups_dir" form of the group name since `nis_lookup()` works on all types of NIS+ objects.

```
void
list_objs(dir_name, table_name, grp_name)
        nis_name   dir_name, table_name, grp_name;
{
    group_obj *tmp; /* only to make source more readable */
    u_int    i;
    char     grp_obj_name [NIS_MAXNAMELEN];
    nis_result*cres;
    char     index_name [BUFFER_SIZE];

    sprintf (grp_obj_name, "%s.groups_dir.%s",
            nis_leaf_of (grp_name), nis_domain_of (grp_name));
    printf ("\nGroup %s membership is: \n", grp_name);

    cres = nis_lookup(grp_obj_name, 0);
    if (cres->status != NIS_SUCCESS) {
        nis_perror (cres->status, "Unable to lookup group object.");
        exit(1);
    }
    tmp = &(NIS_RES_OBJECT(cres)->GR_data);
    for (i = 0; i < tmp->gr_members.gr_members_len; ++i)
        printf ("\t %s\n", tmp->gr_members.gr_members_val[i]);
    (void) nis_freeresult (cres);

    /*
     * Display the contents of the foo domain without using callbacks.
     */
    printf ("\nContents of Directory %s are: \n", dir_name);
    cres = nis_list (dir_name, 0, 0, 0);
    if (cres->status != NIS_SUCCESS) {
        nis_perror (cres->status,
```

```
                              "Unable to list Contents of Directory foo.");
     exit(1);
  }
  for (i = 0; i < NIS_RES_NUMOBJ(cres); ++i)
     printf("\t%s\n", NIS_RES_OBJECT(cres)[i].zo_name);
  (void) nis_freeresult (cres);

  /*
   * List the contents of the table we created using the callback form
   * of nis_list().
   */
  printf ("\nContents of Table %s are: \n", table_name);
  cres = nis_list (table_name, 0, print_info, 0);
  if(cres->status != NIS_CBRESULTS && cres->status != NIS_NOTFOUND){
     nis_perror (cres->status,
        "Listing entries using callback failed");
     exit(1);
  }
  (void) nis_freeresult (cres);

  /*
   * List only one entry from the table we created. We will
   * use indexed names to do this retrieval.
   */

  printf ("\nEntry corresponding to id 1 is:\n");
  /*
   * The name of the column is usually extracted from the table
   * object, which would have to be retrieved first.
   */
  sprintf (index_name, "[Id=1],%s", table_name);
  cres = nis_list (index_name, 0, print_info, 0);
  if(cres->status != NIS_CBRESULTS && cres->status != NIS_NOTFOUND){
     nis_perror (cres->status,
     "Listing entry using indexed names and callback failed");
     exit(1);
  }
  (void) nis_freeresult (cres);
}
```

This routine is called by cleanup() to remove a directory object from the namespace. It also informs the servers serving the directory about this deletion. Notice that the memory-containing result structure, pointed to by cres, must be freed after the result has been tested.

```
void
dir_remove(dir_name, srv_list, numservers)
    nis_name  dir_name;
    nis_server*srv_list;
    u_int     numservers;
{
    nis_result*cres;
    nis_error err;
    u_int     i;

    printf ("\nRemoving %s directory object from namespace ... \n",
                         dir_name);
    cres = nis_remove (dir_name, 0);
    if (cres->status != NIS_SUCCESS) {
        nis_perror (cres->status, "unable to remove directory");
        exit (1);
    }
    (void) nis_freeresult (cres);

    for (i = 0; i < numservers; ++i) {
        err = nis_rmdir (dir_name, &srv_list[i]);
        if (err != NIS_SUCCESS) {
            nis_perror (err,
            "unable to remove server from directory");
            exit (1);
        }
    }
}
```

This routine is called by `main()` to delete all the objects that were created in this example. Note the use of the `REM_MULTIPLE` flag in the call to `nis_remove_entry()`. All entries must be deleted from a table before the table itself can be deleted.

```
void
cleanup(local_princip, grp_name, table_name, dir_name, dirobj)
    nis_name  local_princip, grp_name, table_name, dir_name;
    nis_object*dirobj;
{
    char   grp_dir_name [NIS_MAXNAMELEN];
    char   org_dir_name [NIS_MAXNAMELEN];
    nis_error err;
    nis_result*cres;

    sprintf (grp_dir_name, "%s.%s", "groups_dir", dir_name);
    sprintf (org_dir_name, "%s.%s", "org_dir", dir_name);

    printf ("\n\n\nStarting to Clean up ... \n");
```

```
printf ("\n\nRemoving principal %s from group %s \n",
                local_princip, grp_name);
err = nis_removemember (local_princip, grp_name);
if (err != NIS_SUCCESS) {
   nis_perror (err,
   "unable to delete local principal from group.");
   exit (1);
}

/*
 * Delete the admins group. We do not use the "groups_dir" form
 * of the group name since this API is applicable to groups only.
 * It automatically embeds the groups_dir literal in the name of
 * the group.
 */
printf ("\nRemoving %s group from namespace ... \n", grp_name);
err = nis_destroygroup (grp_name);
if (err != NIS_SUCCESS) {
   nis_perror (err, "unable to delete group.");
   exit (1);
}

printf ("\nDeleting all entries from table %s ... \n", table_name);
cres = nis_remove_entry(table_name, 0, REM_MULTIPLE);
switch (cres->status) {
   case NIS_SUCCESS:
   case NIS_NOTFOUND:
      break;
   default:
      nis_perror(cres->status, "Could not delete entries from
                          table");
      exit(1);
}
(void) nis_freeresult (cres);

printf ("\nDeleting table %s itself ... \n", table_name);
cres = nis_remove(table_name, 0);
if (cres->status != NIS_SUCCESS) {
   nis_perror(cres->status, "Could not delete table.");
exit(1);
}
(void) nis_freeresult (cres);

/* delete the groups_dir, org_dir and foo  directory objects. */
dir_remove (grp_dir_name,
               dirobj->DI_data.do_servers.do_servers_val,
```

```
                    dirobj->DI_data.do_servers.do_servers_len);
      dir_remove (org_dir_name,
                       dirobj->DI_data.do_servers.do_servers_val,
                       dirobj->DI_data.do_servers.do_servers_len);
      dir_remove (dir_name, dirobj->DI_data.do_servers.do_servers_val,
                       dirobj->DI_data.do_servers.do_servers_len);
}
```

Running the program displays the following on the screen:

```
myhost% domainname
sun.com
myhost% ./sample
Adding Directory foo.sun.com. to namespace ...
Adding Directory groups_dir.foo.sun.com. to namespace ...
Adding Directory org_dir.foo.sun.com. to namespace ...
Adding admins.foo.sun.com. group to namespace ...
Adding principal myhost.sun.com. to group admins.foo.sun.com. ...
Creating table test_table.org_dir.foo.sun.com. ...
Adding entries to table ...
Group admins.foo.sun.com. membership is:
        myhost.sun.com.
Contents of Directory foo.sun.com. are:
        groups_dir
        org_dir

Contents of Table test_table.org_dir.foo.sun.com. are:
        Id.                   Name
        ---                   ----
        1                     John
        2                     Mary

Entry corresponding to id 1 is:
        1                     John

Starting to Clean up ...

Removing principal myhost.sun.com. from group admins.foo.sun.com.
Removing admins.foo.sun.com. group from namespace ...
Deleting all entries from table test_table.org_dir.foo.sun.com. ...
Deleting table test_table.org_dir.foo.sun.com. itself ...
Removing groups_dir.foo.sun.com. directory object from namespace ...
Removing org_dir.foo.sun.com. directory object from namespace ...
Removing foo.sun.com. directory object from namespace ...
myhost%
```

As a debugging aid, the same operations are performed by the following command sequence. The first command—

```
% niscat -o 'domainname'
```

—displays the name of the master server. Substitute the master server name where the variable *master* appears below.

```
% nismkdir -m master foo.'domainname'.

# Create the org_dir.foo subdirectory with the specified master
% nismkdir -m master org_dir.foo.'domainname'.
# Create the groups_dir.foo subdirectory with the specified master
% nismkdir -m master groups_dir.foo.'domainname'.
# Create the "admins" group
% nisgrpadm -c admins.foo.'domainname'.

# Add yourself as a member of this group
% nisgrpadm -a admins.foo.'domainname'. 'nisdefaults -p'

# Create a test_table with two columns : Id and Name
% nistbladm -c test_data id=SI Name=SI \
test_table.org_dir.foo.'domainname'

# Add one entry to that table.
% nistbladm -a id=1 Name=John test_table.org_dir.foo.'domainname'.
# Add another entry to that table.
% nistbladm -a id=2 Name=Mary test_table.org_dir.foo.'domainname'.

# List the members of the group admins
% nisgrpadm -l admins.foo.'domainname'.
# List the contents of the foo directory
% nisls foo.'domainname'.
# List the contents of the test_table along with its header
% niscat -h test_table.org_dir.foo.'domainname'.

# Get the entry from the test_table where id = 1
% nismatch id=1 test_table.org_dir.foo.'domainname'.

# Delete all we created.
# First, delete yourself from the admins group
% nisgrpadm -r admins.foo.'domainname'. 'nisdefaults -p'
# Delete the admins group
% nisgrpadm -d admins.foo.'domainname'.
# Delete all the entries from the test_table
% nistbladm -r "[],test_table.org_dir.foo.'domainname'."
# Delete the test_table itself.
```

```
% nistbladm -d test_table.org_dir.foo.'domainname'.
# Delete all three directories that we created
% nisrmdir groups_dir.foo.'domainname'.
% nisrmdir org_dir.foo.'domainname'.
% nisrmdir foo.'domainname'.
```

Index

Index

All About Administering NIS+